TIME FOR K

ALMANAC
2015

Produced by

DOWNTOWN
BOOKWORKS INC.

PRESIDENT: Julie Merberg
EDITORIAL DIRECTOR: Sarah Parvis
EDITORIAL ASSISTANT: Sara DiSalvo
SENIOR CONTRIBUTORS: Beth Adelman, Susan Perry, Margaret Smith
SERIES CONTRIBUTORS: Kerry Acker, Thea Feldman, Marge Kennedy, Jeanette Leardi, Lori Stein
SI KIDS PHOTO RESEARCH: Marguerite Schropp Lucarelli
SPECIAL THANKS: Julie Merberg, Lorin Driggs, Krissy Roleke, Barbara Collier, Mary Gower, Patty Brown, Stephen Callahan, Morris Katz, Nathanael Katz, Kal Katz, Maccabee Katz, Janice and Jeff Wilcoxson, Taylor Ballantyne, the book cover focus group at P.S. 234

Designed by
Brian Michael Thomas/Our Hero Productions

TIME For Kids
PUBLISHER: Bob Der
MANAGING EDITOR, TIME For Kids MAGAZINE: Nellie Gonzalez Cutler

Time
HOME ENTERTAINMENT

PUBLISHER: Jim Childs
VICE PRESIDENT, BRAND & DIGITAL STRATEGY: Steven Sandonato
EXECUTIVE DIRECTOR, MARKETING SERVICES: Carol Pittard
EXECUTIVE DIRECTOR, RETAIL & SPECIAL SALES: Tom Mifsud
EXECUTIVE PUBLISHING DIRECTOR: Joy Bomba
DIRECTOR, BOOKAZINE DEVELOPMENT & MARKETING: Laura Adam
VICE PRESIDENT, FINANCE: Vandana Patel
PUBLISHING DIRECTOR: Megan Pearlman
ASSOCIATE GENERAL COUNSEL: Helen Wan
ASSISTANT DIRECTOR, SPECIAL SALES: Ilene Schreider
BRAND MANAGER: Jonathan White
ASSOCIATE PREPRESS MANAGER: Alex Voznesenskiy
ASSOCIATE PRODUCTION MANAGER: Kimberly Marshall
ASSOCIATE PROJECT MANAGER: Stephanie Braga

EDITORIAL DIRECTOR: Stephen Koepp
SENIOR EDITOR: Roe D'Angelo
COPY CHIEF: Rina Bander
DESIGN MANAGER: Anne-Michelle Gallero
EDITORIAL OPERATIONS: Gina Scauzillo

Special Thanks
Keith Aurelio, Katherine Barnet, Brad Beatson, Jeremy Biloon, Dana Campolattaro, Susan Chodakiewicz, Rose Cirrincione, Natalie Ebel, Assu Etsubneh, Mariana Evans, Christine Font, Susan Hettleman, Hillary Hirsch, David Kahn, Amy Mangus, Nina Mistry, Dave Rozzelle, Ricardo Santiago, Adriana Tierno, Time Inc. Premedia

For information on TIME For Kids magazine for the classroom or home, go to TIMEFORKIDS.COM or call 1-800-777-8600.

For subscriptions to SI Kids, go to SIKIDS.COM or call 1-800-889-6007.

Published by TIME For Kids Books,
an imprint of Time Home Entertainment Inc.
135 West 50th Street
New York, New York 10020

ISBN 10: 1-60320-987-5
ISBN 13: 978-1-60320-987-8

TIME For Kids is a trademark of Time Inc.

We welcome your comments and suggestions about TIME For Kids Books. Please write to us at:

TIME For Kids BOOKS
ATTENTION: BOOK EDITORS
P.O. BOX 11016
DES MOINES, IA 50336-1016

If you would like to order any of our TIME For Kids or SI Kids hardcover Collector's Edition books, please call us at 1-800-327-6388 (Monday through Friday, 7:00 a.m.–8:00 p.m. or Saturday, 7:00 a.m.–6:00 p.m. Central Time).

1 QGT 14

CONTENTS

Boston Dy

5

WHAT'S IN THE NEWS?

Twins in Illinois are shooting for a record. **Page 15**

NAMES IN THE NEWS

POP-UMENTARY STARS

The boys of One Direction have made headlines worldwide for their award-winning songs, new album releases, and sold-out concerts. And in August 2013, a documentary film about the pop stars (from left) Niall Horan, Harry Styles, Liam Payne, Zayn Malik, and Louis Tomlinson hit theaters. The movie, *This Is Us,* shares the story of the singers' rise to fame and includes concert footage, backstage scenes, and more.

One Direction

SUPER SPELLER

Arvind Mahankali, a 13-year-old boy from Bayside Hills, New York, won the 86th Scripps National Spelling Bee, on May 30, 2013. He beat 280 other great spellers and won by spelling the word *knaidel* correctly. A *knaidel* is a dumpling, made of matzo meal, eggs, and salt, often served in soup. Arvind has competed in the Bee before, but words of German origin, like *knaidel,* have always stumped him. Not this time, though! "The German curse has turned into a German blessing," said Arvind.

Arvind Mahankali is the first boy since 2008 to win the Scripps National Spelling Bee.

A ROYAL INFANT

Britain's Prince William, Duke of Cambridge, and his wife, Kate, Duchess of Cambridge, had a baby boy on July 22, 2013. The royal baby, George Alexander Louis, is now third in line for the throne.

Meet His Royal Highness Prince George of Cambridge.

At the start of 2014, there were 47,000 U.S. troops serving in Afghanistan alone.

THE PERSON OF THE YEAR IS . . .

In December, TIME FOR KIDS magazine asked its readers to choose the most important newsmaker of 2013. More than 11,000 votes were cast, and for the fifth year in a row, TFK readers chose the 1.4 million men and women serving in the U.S. Armed Forces. Members of the U.S. Armed Forces received more than 3,000 votes in the TFK poll.

Actress and singer Ariana Grande received the second-highest number of votes in TFK's 2013 Person of the Year poll. Grande stars as Cat on Nickelodeon's *Sam & Cat*. Her popular debut album, *Yours Truly*, featured the song "The Way," which became a Top 10 hit on the *Billboard* Hot 100 list.

TFK readers also recognized 16-year-old Malala Yousafzai. As a student, she fought for the right for women and girls to go to school in Pakistan. Her activism angered members of the Taliban, a group that follows a strict version of Islam and believes that girls should not go to school. In 2012, Yousafzai was shot by members of the Taliban in a remote and dangerous area of Pakistan. She recovered and continues to fight for women and girls around the world. Yousafzai's 2013 memoir, *I Am Malala,* tells the story of her life before and after the attack.

In 2013, Malala Yousafzai became the youngest person ever to be nominated for a Nobel Peace Prize.

Ariana Grande was named New Artist of the Year at the 2013 American Music Awards.

9

FRONT-PAGE ANIMALS

NAME THAT PANDA

On July 15, 2013, Lun Lun, a 15-year-old giant panda from China, gave birth to two babies at Zoo Atlanta. The black-and-white cubs became the first giant pandas born in the United States since 1987. In keeping with a Chinese custom, the zoo waited 100 days before naming the pandas. During those 100 days, zookeepers organized a vote so the public could weigh in on the pandas' names.

In 13 days, more than 51,000 people voted for their favorite of the following pairs of names:

😳 Mei Lun and Mei Hua, meaning "Lun Lun's twin cubs born in the United States"

😳 Mei Lun and Mei Huan, which come from a Chinese saying that also means "something indescribably beautiful and magnificent".

😳 Lan Tian and Bi Shui, meaning "blue sky and clear water"

😳 Tian Lun and Tian Le, a version of another Chinese saying meaning "joy of family life" or "family happiness"

😳 Da Lan and Xiao Lan, meaning "bigger one and smaller one of the twins born in Atlanta."

And the winning names are . . . Mei Lun and Mei Huan. Which names would you have picked?

Panda fans can learn more about Mei Lun and Mei Huan by visiting *zooatlanta.org* and clicking on Panda Cam.

GUESS WHAT? The National Zoo, in Washington D.C., also held a vote to name its new panda cub. In December 2013, the zoo announced the winning name: Bao Bao, meaning "precious" or "treasure" in Chinese.

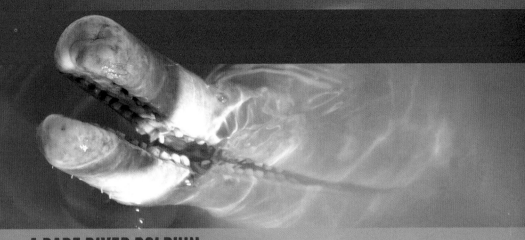

A RARE RIVER DOLPHIN

Most dolphins live in salt water in the ocean, but some can be found in freshwater. River dolphins are some of the rarest and most endangered dolphins in the world. They resemble marine dolphins but have long snouts. Scientists have recently discovered what they believe is a new species of river dolphin, in the Araguaia River in central Brazil. This is the first new type of river dolphin found since 1918.

TOP DOG!

A wire fox terrier named Sky won the award for Best in Show at the 138th annual Westminster Kennel Club Dog Show. Held in New York City in February 2014, the show honors dogs who most perfectly match the standards of their breed.

Sky, the dog show champ

GUESS WHAT? The rat terrier, Portuguese podengo pequeno, and Chinook are three breeds that were allowed to compete in the Westminster Kennel Club Dog Show for the first time in 2014.

BIG DISCOVERY

Even though big cats have roamed the Earth for millions of years, scientists are still learning new things about them. A recent study proves that the skull of an ancient cat found in Tibet is about 4.4 million years old. It's the oldest big-cat fossil ever found.

The skull belongs to an ancestor of the snow leopard. Scientists have named the species *Panthera blytheae.* Before this important find, the oldest known big-cat fossil was 3.6 million years old and had been found in Africa. The *Panthera blytheae* skull helps support the theory that cats first evolved in Central Asia and then spread around the world.

A drawing of *Panthera blytheae*

WHAT'S IN THE NEWS?

SUPER SMOG IN CHINA

One of the terrible effects of pollution is smog, a mixture of smoke and fog that turns air into a thick haze. And the smog situation in China is out of control. In October 2013, officials had to close some highways and schools and recommend that residents stay inside because of the smoggy conditions. Cyclists and drivers could not see far in front of themselves, making travel dangerous.

Breathing polluted air can make people very sick. China's environmental protection agency takes readings of the amount of harmful particles in the air. In the city of Harbin, they found these numbers to be 40 times as high as the levels considered safe by the World Health Organization.

The air pollution in northern China is terrible year-round because of emissions from factories, the huge numbers of cars and trucks, and the burning of coal to heat buildings. The Chinese government is beginning to take action to decrease air pollution in the future.

Many people in China, especially in the industrial areas in the north, wear masks to protect themselves while breathing polluted air.

A TERRIBLE TYPHOON

Damage from Typhoon Haiyan

Typhoon Haiyan slammed into the Philippines in November 2013, destroying the coastal city of Tacloban. The storm, called Typhoon Yolanda in the Philippines, was one of the strongest to ever hit land. Winds gusted up to 190 miles (306 km) per hour, damaging or destroying more than 1.1 million homes and leaving more than 6,000 people dead.

CIVIL WAR IN SYRIA

Major antigovernment protests in Syria began in 2011 and eventually led to a countrywide civil war. Millions of people fled their homes in search of safety from the fighting. Millions more have left the country and become refugees. By September 2013, more than 120,000 people had died in the conflict, and the United Nations (U.N.) confirmed that chemical weapons had been used. Leaders around the world demanded that Syrian officials give up their stockpiles of chemical weapons. U.N. workers began destroying the chemicals in October 2013. But the civil war continues.

A young protester in Syria

A NEW POPE

Catholics around the world were shocked when Pope Benedict XVI announced he would step down. Because of health concerns and his advancing age, the pope felt he was no longer suited for the job of running the Catholic Church. It was the first time in 600 years that a pope had resigned. In March 2013, a large group of Cardinals met in Rome to choose the next pope: Jorge Mario Bergoglio, of Argentina. After his election, the new pope picked the name Francis.

Pope Francis is the first non-European pope in about 1,300 years.

WHAT'S IN THE NEWS?

"I do not want to live in a world where everything I do and say is recorded," said Snowden.

TOP SECRET?

In 2013, the *Guardian,* a British newspaper, revealed that the U.S. government had been spying on its own citizens. The government ordered Verizon, a major phone-service provider, to give the phone records of millions of Americans to the National Security Agency (NSA). These records showed the dates and times of phone calls, as well as the length of each call. They did not include any information about what was said on the calls.

Later, the *Washington Post* reported that the NSA and the Federal Bureau of Investigation (FBI) had been secretly collecting e-mails and Internet data from the servers of major U.S. Internet companies.

The 2001 Patriot Act gives the government the power to take records from companies as long as the records are related to a national security investigation. But many people believe the NSA and the FBI are invading people's privacy.

THE WHISTLE-BLOWER

At first no one knew how the newspapers found out about these top-secret security programs. But then it was revealed that a young man named Edward Snowden had shared the information. Snowden had worked at the Central Intelligence Agency (CIA) and the NSA, and he felt the public had a right to know and to decide if these programs were legal and acceptable.

A BANKRUPT CITY

On July 18, 2013, Detroit filed for bankruptcy. That means the city government did not have enough money to pay its bills and repay its debts. By declaring bankruptcy, the city was able to propose a plan to reduce its debt. With less debt, the city will have more money available to pay policemen, firemen, and other workers, and to afford city improvements. Detroit is the largest U.S. city to take this step to solve its financial troubles. Residents of the city hope the move will offer them a fresh start and a better future.

GOVERNMENT SHUTDOWN

The U.S. Constitution gives Congress the power to approve government spending. It costs money to run government programs. If members of Congress cannot agree about how to fund these programs and pass a budget, the government must shut down. In October 2013, members of Congress disagreed about providing funding for the Affordable Care Act, also referred to as Obamacare, a law that passed in 2010.

Congress's failure to pass a budget led to a 16-day partial shutdown of the government. It was the first time in 17 years that the government had been shut down. Visitors to museums and national parks were turned away, and most government employees were told to stay home. Mail carriers continued to deliver mail, and members of the Armed Forces stayed on the job.

NOTICE
The Bureau of Land Management is
CLOSED
because of the government shutdown.

Trespass onto or damage to federal facilities is prohibited by State and Federal law.

TWINS FOR THE RECORD

Luke and Ryan Novosel, a pair of twins in Illinois, set out to win a world record. They tried a few activities before settling on a subject that was near to their hearts: twins. They counted up their classmates and found that their fifth-grade class had a possibly record-setting number. The current Guinness World Record is 16 pairs of twins in a single grade. At Highcrest Middle School, in Wilmette, Illinois, where Luke and Ryan go to school, there are 24 pairs of twins. Three pairs are boys. Eleven pairs are girls. And 10 sets of twins are boy-girl.

Out of the 24 pairs of twins in the same class, only two pairs are identical.

WHAT'S IN THE NEWS?

SCIENCE MAKING HEADLINES

THE PLANE OF THE FUTURE?

Swiss pilots Bertrand Piccard and André Borschberg made history when they completed a cross-country journey in an aircraft powered only by solar energy. The plane, called *Solar Impulse,* flew across the United States in 2013 without using a single drop of fuel. The trip was a major feat for aviation and the development of renewable energy. The 3,511-mile (5,650 km) trip lasted a total of 105 hours and 41 minutes.

Using 11,628 solar cells across its wings, the plane collected enough sunlight during the day to fly itself throughout the night. This eliminated the need to use fossil fuels, which pollute the air and hurt the environment.

Swiss pilots Bertrand Piccard (right) and André Borschberg

8-26 B5

A MEDIEVAL KING UNEARTHED

Workers in Leicester, England, recently stumbled upon a skeleton while digging under a parking lot. Scientists have confirmed that the bones belong to Britain's King Richard III, who ruled from 1483 to 1485. Richard III died in the Battle of Bosworth Field in 1485. The bones show evidence of the same wounds Richard had. The skeleton has a severely curved spine, just as Richard did. And scientists matched DNA from the skeleton to DNA from a living relative of the king's.

In William Shakespeare's play *Richard III*, the king is portrayed as a cruel hunchback who schemes, plots, and murders his family members to take the throne of England. Some historians do not believe this description is accurate. Now that this ancient king is back in the news, they hope researchers will re-examine Richard's life and revise his image.

Richard III

AN ENORMOUS UNDERWATER VOLCANO

In September 2013, scientists discovered the biggest volcano ever recorded on Earth. But nearby residents don't have to worry about its becoming active and spewing out lava anytime soon. That's because the volcano is underwater. Known as Tamu Massif, and located about 1,000 miles (1,600 km) east of Japan in the Pacific Ocean, the volcano has been inactive for about 140 million years. It is not nearly as tall as the world's tallest volcano, Mauna Loa in Hawaii, but it takes up an enormous amount of space on the seafloor. Tamu Massif is a whopping 400 miles (644 km) wide.

A 3D image of Tamu Massif

GUESS WHAT? Tamu Massif is about the size of New Mexico!

SALTY WATER FROM EARTH'S PAST

Scientists have found water in a mine in Ontario, Canada, that is 1.5 miles (2.4 km) below the surface of the Earth. They tested it and discovered that the water is 2.6 billion years old.

If you found a rare and ancient water sample, would you taste it? A lead researcher on the project did just that. She tried the water and reported that it tastes terrible. It is saltier than the seawater we find today, and it is thicker—like maple syrup.

ancient seawater

Russia hosted the 2014 Winter Olympics in Sochi, a town on the coast of the Black Sea. Here are just a few of the amazing stories that came out of the historic competition.

Meryl Davis and Charlie White

SOLID GOLD ICE DANCING

Meryl Davis and Charlie White won America's first ice dancing gold medal with world-record scores in both the short dance and the free dance. At the Olympics four years before in Vancouver, they won silver medals behind Canada's Tessa Virtue and Scott Moir. This time, the positions were reversed, and the Canadians took the silver.

GUESS WHAT? Meryl Davis and Charlie White have been skating together for 17 years.

A FIRST FOR SKI JUMPING

Women's ski jumping made its Olympic debut in Sochi. Germany's Carina Vogt captured the gold, Austria's Daniela Iraschko-Stolz the silver, and France's Coline Mattel the bronze. "I cannot find the right words," Vogt said. "It's amazing. I'm the first woman Olympic champion in ski jumping."

SOMETHING NEW

Women's ski jumping wasn't the only new event showcased in Sochi. There were 12 new Olympic events, including team figure skating, luge team relay, and women's and men's ski slopestyle and halfpipe. The first Olympic men's slopestyle ski competition was swept by Americans: Joss Christensen won gold, Gus Kenworthy took silver, and Nick Goepper won bronze.

OLYMPIC GAMES

HOCKEY POWER PLAYS

Canada's powerhouse hockey team won the gold medals in both men's and women's hockey. But the bronze-medal games were especially exciting.

On the women's side, Switzerland beat the heavy favorite, Sweden. It was Switzerland's first Olympic hockey medal since 1948, when the men won bronze.

On the men's side, Finland took home the bronze thanks to the outstanding play of 43-year-old Teemu Selanne, a forward who played for the Anaheim Ducks in the NHL. It was his fourth medal in his sixth Olympics, and Selanne was named MVP of the men's hockey tournament.

SHOOTOUT STAR

A highlight for the American men's hockey team came when they defeated Russia 3–2 in the preliminary round. The game ended in a tie and went to an eight-round shootout. First-time Olympian T.J. Oshie squared off against Russian goalie Sergei Bobrovsky six times. Oshie made four of his shots, and lifted his team to an emotional win. The 27-year-old plays right wing for the St. Louis Blues and is a Native American—a member of the Ojibwe people.

T.J. Oshie prepares to shoot.

A YEAR-ROUND OLYMPIC CHAMP

Lauryn Williams, from the silver-medal bobsledding team, became just the third woman (the first from the United States) to medal in both the Winter and Summer Games. A sprinter, Williams was part of the gold-medal foursome in the women's 100-meter relay in London in 2012 and won a silver medal in the 100-meter sprint at the 2004 Athens Games. She became a bobsledder only seven months before the Sochi Olympics.

Lauryn Williams (right) with her bobsled partner, Elana Meyers

ANIMALS

This sea lion was removed from the threatened species list! **Page 31**

Solved: A Mammal Mystery BY BRYAN WALSH FOR TIME MAGAZINE

Each year, as many as 100,000 species go extinct. That's why it's considered a big deal whenever a new creature—especially a mammal—is discovered. On August 15, 2013, scientists at the Smithsonian National Museum of Natural History, in Washington, D.C., announced such a discovery. This mammal, called the olinguito, lives in the cloud forests of Ecuador and Colombia.

A new species of carnivorous mammal hasn't been found since 2010. And no mammals have been discovered in the Western Hemisphere since 1978. "The discovery of the olinguito shows us that the world is not yet completely explored, its most basic secrets not yet revealed," Smithsonian zoologist Kristofer M. Helgen told *Smithsonian* magazine. Helgen has uncovered dozens of mammal species, and he led the effort to identify the olinguito.

ON THE HUNT

In 2003, Helgen was at Chicago's Field Museum studying olingos, another South American species. He found specimens that had long, reddish-brown fur. He was puzzled because known species of olingos have short, gray fur. He visited nearly 20 museums and uncovered dozens of other specimens that didn't match what he knew about olingos.

Helgen then traveled to the forests of Ecuador with other scientists to find living specimens. They managed to capture one. Tests showed that the animal was not an olingo. Instead, it was a smaller relative of the olingo, which they called an olinguito.

The solving of this mammal mystery gives hope that other species may be discovered in the dusty archives of museums around the world.

GUESS WHAT? Olinguitos are about the size of kittens. They have small, curved claws that help them climb trees.

FROM TIME FOR KIDS MAGAZINE

THE ANIMAL KINGDOM

There are three important ways in which animals differ from other living things.

Animals are made up of many cells with complex structures. That makes them different from single-cell organisms, like bacteria.

Animals can move about from place to place. That makes them different from plants. But not all animals are mobile. Certain sea animals—like corals and sea squirts—remain in the same place for most, if not all, of their lives. But they still catch, eat, and digest food.

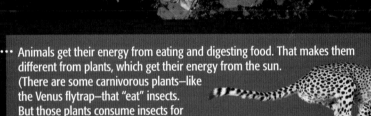

Animals get their energy from eating and digesting food. That makes them different from plants, which get their energy from the sun. (There are some carnivorous plants—like the Venus flytrap—that "eat" insects. But those plants consume insects for nutrients rather than for energy.)

GUESS WHAT? The cheetah is the world's fastest land animal.

TOP 5 LONGEST SNAKES

Talk about long! Reticulated pythons grow to be an average of 35 feet (10.7 m) long. That's as long as a school bus. Here are the world's longest snakes.

1. **RETICULATED PYTHON** 35 feet (10.7 m)

2. **GREEN ANACONDA** 28 feet (8.5 m)

3. **INDIAN PYTHON** 25 feet (7.6 m)

4. **DIAMOND PYTHON** 21 feet (6.4 m)

5. **KING COBRA** 19 feet (5.8 m)

SOURCE: *TOP 10 OF EVERYTHING,*
OCTOPUS PUBLISHING GROUP LTD.

ANIMAL FACT FILES

SLOW-MOVING SEAHORSES

Seahorses are the slowest fish in the ocean. The top speed of a dwarf seahorse is 0.001 miles (0.0016 km) per hour. That means the seahorse takes an hour to swim only 5.2 feet (1.6 m)!

Unlike most other fish, seahorses do not have scales. The bony plates that protect their bodies are covered instead with a thin layer of skin.

A seahorse can look backward and forward at the same time! That's because its two eyes are able to move independently of each other.

Seahorses change color quickly when they are stressed. They do this to camouflage themselves and hide from danger.

Male seahorses get pregnant, not females! The female deposits her eggs into a pouch in the male's stomach. The male then carries the eggs around until they hatch.

BIG-EYED TARSIERS

Tarsiers are the only completely carnivorous (meat-eating) primates in the world. They don't eat any plants. Most of their diet consists of insects, but they also catch and eat frogs, lizards, and even small birds and snakes.

Tarsiers have the largest eyes relative to their body size of any mammal. The huge eyes help them hunt in the dark. Each eye weighs more than a tarsier's brain!

Tarsiers are able to turn their head 180 degrees—and in both directions. They can see behind themselves without moving their body!

Tarsiers live mostly in trees. They even sleep in trees.

Ancient relatives of the tarsier were once found throughout North America, Europe, Africa, and mainland Asia. But today tarsiers live only on densely forested islands in Southeast Asia.

Tarsiers like to sing with their high-pitched voices. Males and females often sing duets together.

GUESS WHAT? The tarsier's unusually long anklebone enables it to jump distances that are more than 40 times its own body length.

HIGH-FLYING BATS

Bats are the only mammals that can fly. Some bats have incredible flying skills. The Mexican free-tailed bat, for example, can fly as high as 10,000 feet (3,048 m).

There are more than 1,000 different species of bats. One-fourth of all mammal species in the world are bats!

Most bats eat insects, but some eat fruit, fish, frogs, and even blood!

The three species of bats that feed on blood are nicknamed vampire bats. They are found in certain areas of Mexico and South America. Their sharp teeth can pierce the skin of an animal, like a cow, without the animal even noticing it has been bitten. Vampire bats don't suck blood, though. They lick the blood off their prey's skin.

Bats hunt for their food at night. Almost all bats find their way around in the dark by using a sophisticated type of hearing called echolocation. As a bat flies, it makes a high-pitched sound (too high to be heard by humans) from its mouth. The sound bounces off every object it hits, creating an echo. The bat uses those echoes to figure out where everything is in the dark—including insects and other food.

GUESS WHAT? Flying foxes, the largest bats in the world, use sight rather than echolocation to navigate in the dark. Some of these megabats have wingspans of 5 feet (1.5 m)!

COLOR-CHANGING CHAMELEONS

Chameleons can rotate each eye in a different direction. That means they enjoy a full 360-degree view of their surroundings. They can also keep their eyes on two different things at the same time!

A chameleon changes its color to match its mood and body temperature. The warmer or angrier a chameleon is, the brighter its color becomes.

The tongues of these lizards have sticky tips, which are used to catch insects.

A chameleon can shoot its tongue at speeds that accelerate from of 0 to 20 feet per second (0 to 6 m per second) in about 20 milliseconds. That's five times faster than the acceleration of most fighter jets!

There are more than 160 species of chameleons. More than half of them are found on a single island—Madagascar, which is off the east coast of Africa.

DIFFERENT-COLORED EYES FOR DIFFERENT SEASONS

Forget about Rudolph and his red nose! Real reindeer (also called caribou) have a facial feature that's equally colorful: their eyes. During summer, the reindeer's eyes are a golden yellow. But when winter rolls around, their eyes turn a deep blue.

The reindeer need their changeable eye color because of the extreme seasonal differences in lighting in the Arctic tundra, where they live. Summer includes weeks of total sunlight, and winter includes weeks of total darkness. When the reindeer's eyes are dark blue, they capture much more light than when they are yellow. That makes it easier for the reindeer to see during winter. Without that color change, the reindeer would have a very difficult time finding food and avoiding predators, especially wolves.

Scientists announced this incredible fact about Arctic reindeer just recently, in 2013.

GUESS WHAT? The hooves of the Arctic reindeer also change from season to season. They get bigger in the summer when the ground is soft and smaller in the winter when the ground is hard.

ELEPHANTS GET THE POINT!

Elephants can understand the human gesture of pointing without being trained to do so, reported a team of researchers in 2013. That finding surprised many zoologists (scientists who study animals). It's long been known that domesticated animals, such as dogs, cats, horses, and even goats, can understand pointing and other human cues. But nondomesticated species of animals—including humans' closest relatives, great apes and chimps—have always failed the pointing test.

For this latest study, researchers tested 11 African elephants that regularly gave rides to tourists in the African country of Zimbabwe. None of the elephants had previously been trained to understand human gestures.

For the test, the researchers hid a snack in one of two containers. Then, in full view of each elephant, they silently pointed to the container with the food in it. The elephants went to the correct container more than two-thirds of the time. That's almost as often as 1-year-old human babies do when given a similar test!

Why do African elephants understand human pointing? The researchers think it's because the elephants already use pointing to communicate among themselves. When a wild elephant smells the odor of a nearby lion, for example, it will lift its trunk and point the tip in the direction of the smell to warn other elephants of the danger.

GUESS WHAT? The hyrax is the animal most closely related to the elephant. But the hyrax and the elephant do not look anything alike. Hyraxes are small and furry.

MIND-BLOWING ANIMALS

Chatty dolphins, speedy sand crabs, and snowball-making monkeys are just a few of the amazing animals found around the world.

An **elephant's** trunk contains about 100,000 muscles and can lift up to 600 pounds (272 kg). But the trunk is not all about strength. Elephants also have fingerlike structures at the tip of their trunk that they can use to grab small objects—a branch, for example, or even blades of grass. African elephants have two of these useful structures on their trunk. Asian elephants have only one.

Sheep can recognize the faces of up to 50 other members of their flock—and they can remember them for up to two years. Scientists have discovered that sheep, like humans, have specialized areas in their brain for remembering faces.

Bottlenose dolphins (which are actually small whales) give themselves individual "whistle names." The animals use these whistles to meet and greet other dolphins. It's a way of saying, "Hi. I'm so-and-so, and I'm friendly." The dolphins seem to decide on their personal whistle names when they are very young.

Male **king penguins** can store undigested food in their stomach for up to three weeks. Scientists believe the penguins produce a chemical that kills off any bacteria in their digestive system. That keeps the food (mostly fish and squid) from going bad. The male penguin can then regurgitate (bring back up) the food at any time to feed its chicks.

The tongue of a **giraffe** is almost 20 inches (51 cm) long. It's covered with horny bumps and has a blue-black color. The length and toughness of the giraffe's tongue make it easier for the animal to safely get at its favorite food: the leaves of the thorn-covered acacia tree. Scientists think the tongue's dark color protects it from getting sunburned while the giraffe is eating.

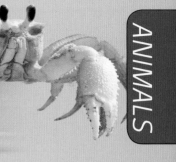

Ghost crabs, which live in burrows on sandy beaches, are very fast runners. They can cover more than 6 feet (2 m) in just one second. Not many animals could beat them in a land race.

When it's hot, **crocodiles** sleep with their mouth open. That's because they do not sweat. So when they get overheated, they must release heat through their mouth.

Some animals will break off a body part to escape an attacker. For example, a **lizard** will quickly shed part of its tail if it is caught by a predator. A **crab** will detach one of its claws. And a **stick insect** will give up a leg. The injured animals then scurry away to safety—and start growing a new tail or claw or leg.

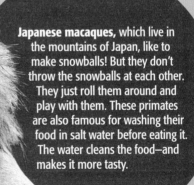

Japanese macaques, which live in the mountains of Japan, like to make snowballs! But they don't throw the snowballs at each other. They just roll them around and play with them. These primates are also famous for washing their food in salt water before eating it. The water cleans the food—and makes it more tasty.

AMAZING INSECTS

There are more types of insects than any other animal on Earth. And each species of insect has its own habits, behaviors, and abilities.

If insects were to have a beauty contest, one of the top contenders would be the **orchid mantis.** This type of praying mantis has lobes on its four legs that resemble the petals of an orchid flower. Most orchid mantises are white, but some are pink. They live in the tropical rain forests of Southeast Asia.

The insect with the fastest-beating wings is the tiny **midge.** It can flap its wings more than 62,000 times per minute. The insect with the slowest wingbeat is the **swallowtail butterfly.** It flaps its wings about 300 times per minute.

A **cockroach** can live for weeks without its head. That's because a headless cockroach can continue to breathe through spiracles, or little holes, in its body. But it can't eat, so eventually it dies.

Some **termites** build mounds to live in. They create the tallest homes of any insect. Some of these mounds, found in Africa, can be as tall as a four-story building!

The loudest animal in the world for its size is a tiny European insect known as the **water boatman.** Although less than ½ inch (1.3 cm) long, its singing can reach volumes of up to 99.2 decibels. That's about the same sound volume as a diesel truck. But because the insect lives in water, 99% of the sound is not heard by people.

SENSATIONAL SEA CREATURES

Meet three amazing animals that live in the water.

The deep-sea **anglerfish** lives deep in the ocean, where there is no light. Female anglerfish have a spine that sticks out from their head. The tip of the spine glows, attracting prey. When a fish swims toward the light, it is gobbled up by the anglerfish. It's like having a built-in fishing rod.

The **Pompeii worm** may have the hottest home on Earth. It lives in the deep volcanic vents at the bottom of the Pacific Ocean, where temperatures climb to 176°F (80°C). Scientists don't know how the hairy, 4-inch-long (10 cm) worms survive the scalding water or the toxic chemicals that spew out of the vents.

Sharks are among the longest-living animals on Earth. Most live for 20 to 30 years, but some live much, much longer. Scientists believe large, slow-moving **whale sharks** can live for up to 150 years.

TIME FOR KIDS

GAME

ODD OCTOPUS

One of these octopuses is not like the others. Can you spot the odd one out?

Answer on page 276

ANIMALS IN DANGER

VANISHED: EXTINCT ANIMALS

Earth has been home to living things for billions of years. During that time, millions of animal species have come and gone. In fact, some 99.9% of all the animal species that once lived on Earth no longer exist. They have become extinct. Dinosaurs are the most famous of all extinct animals. They disappeared about 65 million years ago.

Pterodactyl

ON THE BRINK: ENDANGERED AND THREATENED ANIMALS

Since 1973, the United States has had a law—the Endangered Species Act—that protects animals and plants that are at risk of becoming extinct. Animals needing protection are put into one of two categories. **Endangered animals** are those that may become extinct within a few years if nothing is done to help them. **Threatened animals** are those that are likely to become endangered soon.

When an animal species gets put on the endangered or threatened list, steps are taken to keep it from disappearing. Hunting the animal may be banned, for example. Some animals in the United States that are on the list today are the piping plover, Kemp's ridley sea turtle, gray wolf, Florida panther, northern spotted owl, grizzly bear, black-footed ferret, Miami blue butterfly, wood stork, and blue-tailed mole skink.

Black-footed ferret

Blue-tailed mole skink

Threats to Animals

LOSS OF HABITAT

Every year, animals lose large areas of their natural habitat—the places they live—because they are used for new buildings and roads. When trees are cut down for timber or to clear farmland, more animals lose their homes.

OVERHUNTING

Many animals are overhunted or overfished because people want to eat or use their meat, fur, feathers, shells, horns, or other body parts.

POLLUTION

Toxic chemicals and other substances can poison the water, air, or soil in an animal's habitat. The chemicals may kill an animal, or they may kill off other living things that the animal needs for food or shelter.

Super News for Sea Lions BY STEPHANIE KRAUS WITH AP REPORTING

Steller sea lions have a reason to celebrate. The eastern population has been taken off the threatened species list. The National Oceanic and Atmospheric Administration (NOAA) decided that the population no longer meets the criteria to be considered endangered. In 30 years, the population has grown by more than 50,000 animals.

The Steller sea lion, also known as the northern sea lion, is the largest member of the otariid (eared seal) family. The eastern population's habitat ranges from the coast of Alaska to California. It is the first animal to be delisted by NOAA since the eastern North Pacific gray whale. That creature was taken off the list nearly 20 years ago, NOAA spokeswoman Julie Speegle said.

Experts at NOAA recommended delisting the Steller sea lions in 2013. "We're delighted to see the recovery of the eastern population of Steller sea lions," Jim Balsiger said in a statement. He is the administrator of NOAA Fisheries' Alaska region. "We'll be working with the states and other partners to monitor this population to ensure its continued health."

TO PROTECT AND PRESERVE

The delisting of the eastern population does not affect the Steller sea lions' western population. That group's habitat ranges from Cape Suckling, Alaska, to Russia. The western population remains on the endangered list.

NOAA estimated there were 18,000 sea lions in the eastern population in 1979. The group was listed as threatened in 1990. The decline was blamed on fishermen and other people killing the animals because sea lions eat fish and are considered a nuisance. In 2010, the most recent year a count was available, the agency estimated there were just over 70,000 sea lions.

Although the species is being removed from the list, it will still receive protection under the Marine Mammal Protection Act. When an animal is delisted, the Endangered Species Act requires a monitoring plan that covers five years. NOAA has decided to double that length of time and to monitor the sea lions over a 10-year period. "We are just proceeding carefully and cautiously to ensure that this species can be maintained in the recovered status," Speegle said.

Steller sea lions raise up their heads and bark in the Oregon Islands National Wildlife Refuge.

Steller sea lions relax in Kenai Fjords National Park, Alaska.

FROM
TIME
FOR KIDS
MAGAZINE

MOST POPULAR DOG BREEDS

1. Labrador retriever
2. German shepherd
3. Golden retriever
4. Beagle
5. English bulldog
6. Yorkshire terrier
7. Boxer
8. Poodle
9. Rottweiler
10. Dachshund

SOURCE: AMERICAN KENNEL CLUB

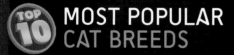

MOST POPULAR CAT BREEDS

1. Persian
2. Exotic
3. Maine coon
4. Ragdoll
5. British shorthair
6. Abyssinian
7. American shorthair
8. Sphynx
9. Cornish rex
10. Devon rex

SOURCE: CAT FANCIERS' ASSOCIATION

MOST POPULAR NAMES FOR DOGS AND CATS

DOG NAMES

1. Bella
2. Max
3. Bailey
4. Lucy
5. Molly
6. Daisy
7. Charlie
8. Buddy
9. Maggie
10. Sophie

CAT NAMES

1. Bella
2. Max
3. Chloe
4. Oliver
5. Lucy
6. Charlie
7. Sophie
8. Lily
9. Shadow
10. Tiger

SOURCE: VETERINARY PET INSURANCE

GUESS WHAT?
Dalmatian puppies are born white. They get their spots as they grow.

TOP NAMES FOR OTHER PETS

Not every pet owner opts for a cat or a dog. Some choose birds, fish, hamsters, and other animals. Coco is tops for birds and other pets. The next most common options for other pets are Max, Buddy, and Bella, followed by Charlie, Baby, Sunny, Angel, Gizmo, and Rocky. If you had a bird, what would you name it? How about a pet iguana? Or a ferret?

PARTNERS FOR LIFE

When two living things depend on each other, the relationship is called symbiosis (sim-bee-*o*-sis). Check out these examples.

A **cleaner shrimp** uses its claws to pick tiny animals from a **tomato grouper's** body. The shrimp gets an easy meal, and the fish gets a cleaning.

Some animals have symbiotic relationships with plants. A **fruit bat** loves figs. But it never eats fruit while near the **fig tree**. As the bat eats, seeds fall and sprout some distance away. The parent tree will not have to compete with a new tree for nutrients.

Aphids are tiny, wingless insects that live on plants. They suck the sap that runs through plant stems. After they've digested the sap, the aphids release it back onto the plants. This new sugary fluid is called honeydew. Certain types of **ants** like to munch on the honeydew released by the aphids. So they take care of the aphids. Sometimes, the ants gently pick up the aphids in their mouths and move them to places where there is more plant sap for the aphids to eat. Ants will also attack other insects, like ladybugs, that feed on aphids. They chase the ladybugs away to keep the aphids safe.

An **oxpecker** bird picks insects from an **impala's** fur. The insects could cause disease. The bird helps the impala stay healthy in exchange for a tasty meal.

CRITTERS ACROSS. . . AND DOWN

Use the clues below to fill in the crossword puzzle.
If you are stumped, check the word list.

WORD LIST

cheetah	llama
doe	octopus
dolphin	orangutan
eel	ostrich
hyena	ram
jellyfish	shrimp
kangaroo	skunk
leech	stork

ACROSS

2. A tall bird that cannot fly but has strong legs that are great for running and kicking

4. A tall white bird that "goes fishing" by putting its open bill underwater and snapping it shut when a fish swims in

6. A baby of this Australian species is carried around in its mother's pouch

9. A male sheep

10. A clever mammal that lives in the water and makes sounds like clicks, squeaks, and whistles

12. A boneless, often see-through creature that floats around in the ocean current

13. The fastest runner on land

15. A tall South American mammal that looks like a camel without a hump

DOWN

1. A large reddish-brown ape found on the islands of Borneo and Sumatra, in Asia

3. A female deer

4. A small, bottom-dwelling crustacean that often ends up as a meal for crabs, sea stars, whales, seabirds, or humans

5. A black-and-white creature you don't want to startle or you might get sprayed—*pee-yoo!*

7. A sea creature with eight strong arms that are covered with suckers

8. An African animal that hunts in packs or eats dead animals and is known for the wails, howls, and screeches that it makes (some say they sound like laughter)

11. A worm that latches onto its victims and sucks their blood

14. A snakelike fish

Answers on page 276

35

ART

Go behind the scenes at the famous Christie's art auction house. **Page 40**

COLORS ARE AMAZING!

The three **PRIMARY COLORS** are red, blue, and yellow. Painters mix different amounts of these three colors to achieve a wide range of shades in their works of art. Mixing nonprimary colors together will never create a primary color.

The **SECONDARY COLORS**—violet, green, and orange—are made by combining equal amounts of two primary colors. Blue and red mixed together make violet. Blue and yellow make green. Red and yellow make orange.

TERTIARY COLORS (*tur*-she-air-ee) are all the shades that can be made by mixing a primary and secondary color. They are usually referred to using two words, such as yellow-orange, red-orange, red-purple, and blue-green.

MYSTERY PERSON

I was born in 1928 in Brooklyn, New York. During my career as a writer and an artist, I illustrated more than 80 children's books. In 1964, I won a Caldecott Medal for my book *Where the Wild Things Are.*

WHO AM I?

Answer on page 276

THE COLOR WHEEL

By arranging colors on a color wheel, we can see how they relate to one another. Colors that are opposite from each other on the wheel are called complementary colors. Complementary colors contrast with each other and appear more vivid when placed side by side.

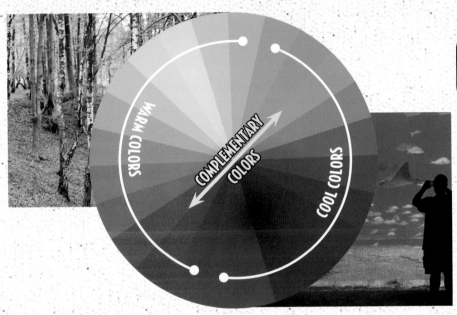

On one side of the color wheel are the warm colors. These include orange, yellow, many shades of red, and some yellowish greens. Think about the sun, fire, and other warm things—each has a warm color sense. Cool colors are on the opposite side of the wheel. They include blue, purple, some purplish reds, and some shades of blue-green.

PLAYING TRICKS

Colors look different to us depending on their surroundings. For example, notice how the color red on the left looks bright and vibrant against a black background. The red circle looks duller on a brown background or an orange background.

Look at the circles below. Do they look like the same color to you? They are! Both are the same shade of orange.

Which of the two stripes is the same as the stripe in the box?

A
B

The green stripe may look like it fades, but it doesn't. The green is the same throughout the stripe, just like **A**.

PAINTING STYLES

Art has always been a form of communication and expression for people. The world's oldest paintings date back 40,000 years. Found on the walls of caves, these paintings often feature large animals. Finger flutings are another type of cave art. They are impressions in the walls of caves made by people's fingers.

Over the years and centuries, there have been many different styles of painting. Here are just a few examples. Check out a museum near you to see more!

ITALIAN RENAISSANCE PAINTING

Renaissance means "rebirth," and the Renaissance in Europe, which lasted from the 14th century to the 17th century, was a time of great growth for all kinds of learning, culture, and art, including painting. The city of Florence, Italy, was considered the birthplace and center of the Renaissance art movement. Many Renaissance paintings were commissioned by the Catholic Church and feature religious themes. One of the most famous of these paintings is Leonardo da Vinci's *Last Supper*, painted on a church wall. Wealthy families commissioned portraits of themselves and family members. Some paintings, like *Birth of Venus*, by Sandro Botticelli, captured themes from classical literature. Even when showing fictional characters, Renaissance paintings portrayed people and other subjects as realistically as possible.

DUTCH GOLDEN AGE

In the 17th century, the Dutch Republic (which is now the Netherlands) was the richest country in Europe. During this time, Dutch painters were known for several different styles of painting. Many paintings depicted scenes of middle-class and peasant life, such as *The Milkmaid*, by Johannes Vermeer. Other themes included landscapes, townscapes, still lifes, and seascapes. Wealthy families posed for many portraits. Rembrandt van Rijn painted individual as well as group portraits, like *The Night Watch*. Painters from this period often emphasized light and shadow.

GUESS WHAT? Vermeer painted on very small canvases. *Girl with a Pearl Earring* is 17.5 inches (44.5 cm) tall and 15.35 inches (39 cm) wide.

Girl with a Pearl Earring is one of the most beloved paintings by Johannes Vermeer.

IMPRESSIONISM

Paris, France, was the center of the art world in the late 1800s, when a new painting style called Impressionism became popular. These paintings featured ordinary people, scenes of everyday life, landscapes, and still lifes. Impressionist artists painted with a brighter range of colors than many previous artists. This is evident in many paintings, including Claude Monet's *Water Lilies* series. Painters also used shorter brushstrokes that are visible to the viewer, such as in Vincent van Gogh's *The Starry Night* and in portraits by Auguste Renoir, including *Madame Georges Charpentier and Her Children*. Impressionist works were often less realistic looking than those of painters who had come before them.

GUESS WHAT? The term *Impressionism* came from a critic's response to an art show featuring the Monet painting *Impression, Sunrise*. The critic thought the paintings in the exhibit looked sketchy and unfinished. When he referred to the paintings looking like "impressions," he meant it as an insult.

Madame Georges Charpentier and Her Children, by Auguste Renoir, hangs in the Metropolitan Museum of Art, in New York City.

MODERNISM

Modernism is less a style of art than an entire movement. Modern art is all about an artist's individual experimentation with paint and materials and his or her interpretation of objects and emotions. That explains why these works of art are incredibly varied and inventive. Modern artists include the early-20th-century painters Henri Matisse and Pablo Picasso, as well as Piet Mondrian, who worked mostly in the 1930s, and Jackson Pollock, who painted mainly in the 1940s. Some modern artists who became well known in the 1950s and 1960s are Andy Warhol, Roy Lichtenstein, Mark Rothko, Frank Stella, Jasper Johns, and Helen Frankenthaler.

Kids' Day at Christie's BY TFK KID REPORTER ADRIANA PALMIERI

Can you imagine having sheep in your living room—as furniture? Or having a huge painting of candy hanging on your bedroom wall? These were just some of the art items that were on display at the postwar and contemporary art show at Christie's art auction house in New York City in 2012.

Christie's Auction House hosted a special Kids' Day. Dozens of kids came to create art and to learn about famous artists. Natasha Schlesinger led a tour for all the event attendees. Schlesinger is the founder of a program called ArtMuse that creates educational art tours especially for kids. She taught us all about some of America's greatest artists, including Andy Warhol. "He was one of the art superstars," Schlesinger said. "He truly loved America." Warhol painted things that he loved about our country, including the Statue of Liberty, American movie stars, and even Campbell's soup cans. He also loved to take photographs. He could be called a pop star of art!

EXPLORING ART

The tour taught us about Roy Lichtenstein, who used an art method called *frottage. Frottage* is a method of making a work of art using dots of color. You can make your own artwork with *frottage* by taking a grater and putting it under a paper. As you start to color on the paper, little dots form. Lichtenstein used that technique to make his artwork look like an ad in a newspaper.

We also saw a series of sculptures by Alexander Calder, works that hang in the air. His artwork inspired mobiles, the spinning design that you find hanging over baby cradles. He was very interested in stars and created his sculptures after them. A candy painting by Barbara Kruger, who is famous for being an advocate of human and women's rights, caught my eye. As did François-Xavier Lalanne's sheep sculptures.

Christie's gets its pieces from owners and estates—from people who are looking to sell artwork, jewelry, or even houses. The auction house maintains these famous works of art so people can enjoy them for many years to come.

Andy Warhol's silkscreen of the Statue of Liberty was one of the day's main attractions.

FROM
TIME
FOR KIDS
MAGAZINE

THE FORECAST IS... RADIANT

Have you ever noticed that every year the colors of clothing available in stores are a little bit different? Sometimes, there are more pastel colors. Other times, every sweater and T-shirt is bold and bright.

A company called Pantone has created a system to assign numbers to colors. This system, called the Pantone Matching System (PMS), is used by graphic designers, paint manufacturers, and others as a way of ensuring that colors can be named and re-created. When a client in London wants a banner made in the orange color known as PMS 1665, a fabric maker halfway across the world will be able to use the correct shade every time.

Pantone follows the trends, and every year, it announces a color of the year. The color for 2014 is PMS 18-3224, known as Radiant Orchid. It's a cheerful pinkish purple. You'll probably spot Radiant Orchid in clothing, makeup, and design trends throughout the year.

TIME FOR KIDS GAME

MASTERPIECE MATCHUP

Match the number of each painting or sculpture to the art terms below.

Answers on page 276

○ **WATERCOLORS** are usually mixed with water and used on paper.

○ A **RELIEF** is a type of sculpture that looks like it is raised from its background.

○ A **FRESCO** is a painting created quickly on wet plaster.

○ A **STILL LIFE** shows groups of inanimate objects.

○ A **PORTRAIT** features an image of a person or group of people.

○ **COLLAGES** are made by cutting up materials and pasting them together.

So Long, Sweets! BY CAMERON KEADY

Since March 1, 1980, the NPD Group has been surveying households across the United States about how they eat. The study includes 5,000 people in 2,000 households. Families taking part in the survey keep a journal of their daily diets for two weeks. During that time, each individual keeps a tally on how many sweets and sugary treats he or she consumes.

The study shows that a large percentage of Americans still satisfy their sweet tooth but in smaller amounts. Nearly 98% of the adults and children surveyed still have at least one sweet every week or two. "It's not a question of whether or not you're going to have a sweet," said NPD vice president Harry Balzer. "It's a matter of how frequently you're going to have a sweet." While there is no formal definition for what classifies a "sweet," NPD selected 20 products to conduct the study. The list is expansive, ranging from cookies and brownies to fruit juice and yogurt. Kids today are eating cookies 8 times less than they did in 1998, and drinking fruit juice 16 times less.

DOWNWARD TREND

According to the Centers for Disease Control and Prevention (CDC), the percentage of obese kids ages 6 to 19 tripled in the U.S. between 1980 and 2000. About 9 million children were excessively overweight in 2000. Today, obesity rates are not falling, but they aren't growing either. "There are three points to every trend," said Balzer. "There's the movement upward, the leveling off, and the decline. Right now, we're [at the leveling off point]."

Schools nationwide are doing their part to put childhood obesity on a downward trend. Fried food has disappeared from many cafeteria menus. Whole-wheat bread has replaced white bread. Water and low-fat milk have replaced sugary beverages, such as fruit punch, sports drinks, and soda. Many schools have also banned junk food and now require healthier snack options in their vending machines. These efforts, both at home and in school, are slowly putting kids on the right track for healthy eating.

41

...ay, on average, kids are ...ting and drinking sugary ...mes less than they did in 1998.

FROM
TIME
FOR KIDS
MAGAZINE

THE AMAZING HUMAN BODY

An adult's brain
usually weighs about 3 pounds [1.4 kg].

The smallest bone in the body is the **stapes** [*stay*-peez], which is the innermost of three tiny bones in the middle ear. It is only about 0.12 inches [3 mm] long.

The average person **eats** about **50 tons** of food in a lifetime.

Most people have 24 ribs [12 pairs]. These bones protect the soft internal organs, such as the heart and liver.

The "funny bone" is not really a bone. It is a nerve that passes through your elbow.

Once you reach adulthood, your stomach will remain the same size, whether you eat a **lot** or a little.

There are 27 BONES in each HAND [and 26 in each foot].

The **longest bone** in your body is the FEMUR, or thighbone.

10 TIPS TO KEEP YOU

1 **WEAR SUNSCREEN,** even in the snow. Be sure to apply it to all your exposed skin. People often forget to cover the backs of the knees, the ears, the area around the eyes, and the neck. And don't forget to reapply at least every two hours.

2 **DRINK PLENTY OF WATER** on hot days and when you're playing sports.

3 **TELL A TEACHER** or other trusted adult if you are being **BULLIED** or see someone else being harassed or hurt.

4 **BE ACTIVE.** Get some form of exercise for an hour every day. Find a workout that is fun for you. Jumping rope, playing soccer or basketball, doing jumping jacks, taking a dance class, swimming, playing tag, or practicing yoga are just a few great workout ideas.

5 Limit the amount of sugar in your diet, and beware of hidden sugars. **EAT MORE FRUITS, VEGETABLES, AND WHOLE GRAINS,** and cut down on eating packaged, processed foods.

SAFE AND HEALTHY

6 **WASH YOUR HANDS** frequently to keep from getting a cold. Germs pass quickly from person to person.

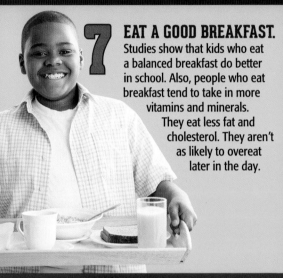

7 **EAT A GOOD BREAKFAST.** Studies show that kids who eat a balanced breakfast do better in school. Also, people who eat breakfast tend to take in more vitamins and minerals. They eat less fat and cholesterol. They aren't as likely to overeat later in the day.

8 **ALWAYS WEAR A HELMET** and pads when riding a bike or skateboarding, and make sure your bike has reflectors and a horn or bell. If you ride at night, ride with others and wear reflective clothing.

BODY AND HEALTH

9 **STAY IN TOUCH.** Always let your parents or guardians know where you'll be and when you plan to return home. Don't rely on your cell phone for your contact numbers. Memorize your parents' work and cell phone numbers, as well as your home phone number.

10 **GET PLENTY OF SLEEP EACH NIGHT.** Sleep is important for your growth and health. One way to sleep better is to avoid staring at a screen in bed. Turn off all electronics before bedtime, and try to get to bed at the same time every night.

CURIOUS QUESTIONS
ABOUT THE HUMAN BODY

Do Humans Shed?

Yes! Your body sheds about 40,000 skin cells every hour—or about 1 million cells each day. In fact, every five weeks or so, the surface of your skin is entirely new.

Here's how it happens. Your skin has several layers. The top layer, called the **epidermis,** is made up almost completely of cells known as **keratinocytes.** They form a barrier that protects your body from infections, parasites, heat, water loss, and many other potential dangers.

New keratinocytes are created at the bottom of the epidermis, just above the skin's second layer, the **dermis.** Once they form, the keratinocytes push their way up through the epidermis to the skin's surface. It takes the cells about five weeks to get to the top.

When they reach the surface, the keratinocytes die. The dead cells create a thin "coating" to the epidermis that is called the **stratum corneum.** Those cells eventually fall off the skin. Other keratinocytes then quickly move up to take their place—like items on a conveyor belt!

This regeneration of the skin goes on nonstop, even while you're sleeping. That means you shed a lot of skin—about 8 pounds (3.6 kg) each year!

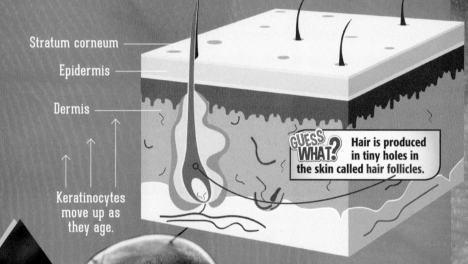

Stratum corneum

Epidermis

Dermis

Keratinocytes
move up as
they age.

GUESS WHAT? Hair is produced in tiny holes in the skin called hair follicles.

E e e e ewWW!
Dust mites, which are invisible without a microscope, feed on all the dead skin cells lying around your house.

GUESS WHAT? Skin cells aren't the only ones that are constantly replaced. The cells that line the inside of your stomach completely replace themselves every three to five days. New cells are needed to keep the lining from being "eaten away" by the acids that your stomach produces to break down the food you eat.

What Causes Goosebumps?

Cold temperatures can give you goosebumps. So can any kind of strong emotion, such as fear or excitement. The cold or the emotion causes your body to release a stress hormone called adrenaline. That hormone then makes the tiny muscles around your skin's individual hair follicles contract, creating a bumpy appearance. The contractions also make the hair in the follicles stand up straight.

Goosebumps are an involuntary reflex. In other words, you can't control when you get them. Goosebumps are also an ancient reflex, left over from when our human ancestors had a lot of body hair. By making hair stand upright, goosebumps may have helped our ancestors keep warm in cold weather—and look bigger and more menacing to their predators.

GUESS WHAT? Goosebumps got their name because they resemble a goose's skin after its feathers have been plucked.

Why Does Your Mouth Water?

The main reason your mouth waters is to help with the digestion of your food. The saliva, or spit, in your mouth makes food wet and easier to swallow. It also contains chemicals that help break down food as soon as you begin munching on it.

Saliva is produced in several salivary glands located inside your cheeks and at the bottom of your mouth. Your mouth creates about 3 pints (1.4 L) of saliva daily—enough to fill 3 bathtubs each year!

BODY AND HEALTH

Why Do Feet Stink?

Your feet are one of the sweatiest parts of your body. You have about 250,000 sweat glands in each foot—about as many as are in your armpits. Sweat, which is made up of salt and water, doesn't smell on its own. It needs tiny organisms called bacteria for that.

Bacteria (which can be seen only with a microscope) are everywhere around us, including on our skin. Some bacteria eat sweat. The waste they excrete after digesting the sweat has a bad odor.

When you're wearing socks and shoes, sweat gets trapped on your feet. Sweat-eating bacteria then have a feast! The result: stinking feet (and socks and shoes).

Find the perfect book on black holes, volcanoes, or sea creatures. **Page 52**

Kenn Nesbitt's New Role BY ANDREA SACHS FOR TIME

Kenn Nesbitt loves his job. As a poet for kids, he travels the country to visit schools and give interactive workshops and assemblies about poetry. "It's a blast!" Nesbitt told TIME over the phone, as he was on his way to visit another elementary school. "There's nothing more fun than actually getting to perform my work and write with a couple hundred third graders."

That passion is one reason that Nesbitt was named the children's poet laureate of the United States by the Poetry Foundation, an organization based in Chicago, Illinois. So what exactly does a children's poet laureate do? Nesbitt laughs when presented with the frequently asked question. His primary duty, he explains, is to crisscross the United States as the top cheerleader for poetry among youth. He will give several public readings for his young readers and their families, as well as advise the Poetry Foundation about children's literature. He will serve in the role for a two-year term.

"Poetry does have a tremendous impact on kids," says Nesbitt, a true believer in the potential of rollicking rhymes. "It has a power with kids that other kinds of writing might not. A poem can pack a lot of emotional punch in just a few lines," he says. "Children's poetry is typically not more than one page or two pages long. And yet, within that one or two pages, kids can get a really strong positive emotional response that encourages them to want to read another poem."

A POET'S LIFE

Nesbitt wasn't always a professional poet. He began his full-time writing career after 20 years in the computer industry. He says he "loved poetry as a kid, but we didn't study it in school. I don't remember ever reading a poem in school, and I certainly didn't write one." So Nesbitt pursued another passion. "When I was in high school, I absolutely fell in love with computers," he says. "I taught myself how to program."

The multitalented programmer started writing humorous children's poetry as a hobby, after hearing a recording of Shel Silverstein reciting his poem "Sarah Cynthia Sylvia Stout." After his first book of children's poetry was published, poetry grew into a second career.

The playful poet's work now includes numerous books of poetry for kids, including *The Tighty-Whitey Spider, My Hippo Has the Hiccups,* and *Revenge of the Lunch Ladies.* Nesbitt's poetry can also be found in hundreds of magazines, textbooks, and anthologies internationally and on his website, *poetry4kids.com.*

Kenn Nesbitt

FROM
TIME
FOR KIDS
MAGAZINE

AWARD-WINNING BOOKS AND AUTHORS

2014 NEWBERY MEDAL (for best children's book) *Flora & Ulysses: The Illuminated Adventures,* by Kate DiCamillo, illustrated by K.G. Campbell

2014 CALDECOTT MEDAL (for best picture book) *Locomotive,* by Brian Floca

2014 CORETTA SCOTT KING AUTHOR AWARD (for African American authors and illustrators) Rita Williams-Garcia, author of *P.S. Be Eleven*

2014 ROBERT F. SIBERT INFORMATIONAL BOOK MEDAL *Parrots over Puerto Rico,* by Susan L. Roth and Cindy Trumbore, illustrated by Susan L. Roth

2014 PURA BELPRE ILLUSTRATOR AWARD (for Latino/Latina illustrators whose work celebrates the Latino experience) *Niño Wrestles the World,* by Yuyi Morales

2014 SCOTT O'DELL AWARD FOR HISTORICAL FICTION *Bo at Ballard Creek,* by Kirkpatrick Hill, illustrated by LeUyen Pham

2014 YALSA AWARD FOR EXCELLENCE IN NONFICTION FOR YOUNG ADULTS *The Nazi Hunters: How a Team of Spies and Survivors Captured the World's Most Notorious Nazi,* by Neal Bascomb

2014 MARGARET A. EDWARDS AWARD (for a significant and lasting contribution to young adult literature) Markus Zusak, author of *The Book Thief*

2013 NATIONAL BOOK AWARD FOR YOUNG PEOPLE'S LITERATURE *The Thing About Luck,* by Cynthia Kadohata

2013 EDGAR ALLAN POE AWARD, BEST JUVENILE (for mystery and crime writers) *The Quick Fix,* by Jack D. Ferraiolo

BOOKS

FALL FOR FICTION

There's nothing like the feeling of picking up a book and getting swept away by its story. And there are countless great books to choose from. Here are some recommendations from librarians.

A TANGLE OF KNOTS
by Lisa Graff

This story is set in a world where everyone has a particular talent, like making origami, whistling, levitating, or spitting really far. Eleven-year-old Cady is an incredible baker with the ability to guess every person's ideal cake. She's also an orphan who finds herself allied with a strange group of people living above a lost-luggage store. Their journey together sets them up against a talent thief, who steals people's special abilities—and who holds the secret to Cady's past.

TRUE BLUE SCOUTS OF SUGAR MAN SWAMP
by Kathi Appelt

Raccoon brothers Bingo and J'miah get more than they bargained for when they join the Official Sugar Man Swamp Scouts. When a pack of wild hogs and an insane alligator wrestler (among others) threaten their beloved swamp, the brothers set out on a quest to awaken the Sugar Man. This folksy story has tons of charm and an ecological message.

RUMP: THE TRUE STORY OF RUMPELSTILTSKIN
by Liesl Shurtliff

In the magic kingdom of Rump's birth, a person's name affects everything in his or her life. Rump is certain that his name is incomplete and sets off on a quest to discover his real name and his destiny.

THE MIGHTY MISS MALONE
by Christopher Paul Curtis

Deza Malone and her older brother Jimmie endure tough times in Gary, Indiana, and Flint, Michigan, during the Great Depression. Together with their parents, they find ways to survive. This remarkable story is about love, determination, and following your dreams.

DON'T FORGET THE POETRY!

There are countless wonderful fiction and nonfiction books to be read, but there are also wonderful collections of poetry to enjoy. Poetry fans and curious readers should check out *Technically, It's Not My Fault: Concrete Poems,* by John Grandits. This playful collection of poems comes from the point of view of 11-year-old Robert. He tells tales of science experiments gone wrong, battles with his annoying older sister, and missteps on the basketball court. He even invents the ultimate roller coaster, the Spew Machine. The poems are creative, interesting, and often hilarious.

NAVIGATING EARLY
by Clare Vanderpool

In post-World War II Maine, Jack Baker and his rather odd friend Early Auden set out on the Appalachian Trail to find the truth about a legendary black bear, timber rattlesnakes, and a missing school hero, the Fish. It is a story of friendship and buried secrets.

WONDER
by R.J. Palacio

Ten-year-old August Pullman was born with a facial deformity. For the first time, he will be starting mainstream school. All he wants to do is blend in, but it seems that he was born to stand out.

GHOST HAWK
by Susan Cooper

Little Hawk, a Wampanoag, and John Wakely, a colonial settler, become friends. But, as the relationship between the colonists and the Native Americans in the area turns sour, the friendship between the boys becomes complicated and dangerous. The boys' stories offer an unsettling look at early U.S. history.

ESCAPE FROM MR. LEMONCELLO'S LIBRARY
by Chris Grabenstein

Kyle is one of 12 seventh graders to win a spot in an overnight lock-in at the new library (which was designed by a renowned game maker). When the students attempt to leave in the morning, they find themselves really locked in. They must find a hidden way out using only library resources. Part mystery, part survival show, and part online game, this story is a fabulous library adventure.

FORTUNATELY, THE MILK
by Neil Gaiman, illustrated by Skottie Young

In this tale by master storyteller Neil Gaiman, Dad takes care of the children while Mom is away. The adventures in this book involve everything from time travel and pirates to aliens and breakfast cereal.

BOOKS

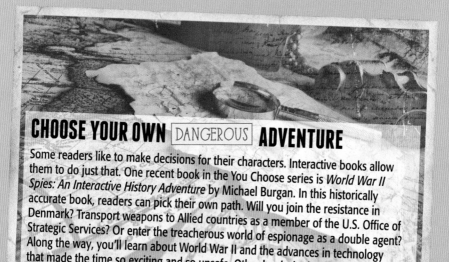

CHOOSE YOUR OWN DANGEROUS ADVENTURE

Some readers like to make decisions for their characters. Interactive books allow them to do just that. One recent book in the You Choose series is *World War II Spies: An Interactive History Adventure* by Michael Burgan. In this historically accurate book, readers can pick their own path. Will you join the resistance in Denmark? Transport weapons to Allied countries as a member of the U.S. Office of Strategic Services? Or enter the treacherous world of espionage as a double agent? Along the way, you'll learn about World War II and the advances in technology that made the time so exciting and so unsafe. Other books in the series delve into different historical periods and events.

LEARN SOMETHING NEW!

Become an expert on black holes, bone up on the American Revolution, or make cool crafts from recyclable materials. Here are some librarians' picks for awesome nonfiction titles.

SEA-SATIONAL
by Allyson Kulavis

Have you ever heard of nudibranchs (*new*-dih-bronks)? They're some of the most colorful animals on Earth. Did you know that the octopus has a beak like a parrot? Or that a sea star can regrow its entire body from a single limb? In this book, readers will discover that male seahorses carry their babies, phytoplankton produce about a third of the oxygen on Earth today, and frogfish use their fins as legs to walk on the seafloor. And the book comes with a dried sea star and a sand dollar!

GUESS WHAT? *Sea-sational* is part of a book series called Science with Stuff. Every book in the series comes with an object. *Insect-O-Mania* comes with a preserved beetle. *Fossil-icious,* includes a real fossil for the reader to identify. And *Bird-acious* has an owl pellet for the reader to break open.

A BLACK HOLE IS NOT A HOLE
by Carolyn Cinami DeCristofano, illustrated by Michael Carroll

Explaining what a black hole is can be difficult for nearly anyone, but not for Carolyn Cinami DeCristofano. In a lively and helpful way, DeCristofano takes on a complex subject and uses paintings, telescopic photographs, and more to make it clear and understandable. By the end, readers will have gone on a fun romp through the galaxy and will know a lot more about space, stars, gravity, and black holes.

ERUPTION! VOLCANOES AND THE SCIENCE OF SAVING LIVES
by Elizabeth Rusch

More than 1 billion people live in areas around volcanoes known as danger zones. And that's why the work of an international volcano crisis team is so important. Author Elizabeth Rusch offers an incredible insider's look at the life-saving work of these volcano experts. The book also includes spectacular images of volcanoes from everywhere from Chile to the Philippines.

SCIENTISTS AT WORK

Eruption! is part of a series called Scientists in the Field. Other titles in this awesome series include:
Digging for Bird Dinosaurs, by Nic Bishop
The Polar Bear Scientists, by Peter Lourie
Project Seahorse, by Pamela S. Turner
Saving the Ghost of the Mountain, by Sy Montgomery
Science Warriors, by Sneed B. Collard III
The Tarantula Scientist, by Sy Montgomery
The Wildlife Detectives by Donna M. Jackson

REMAKE IT! RECYCLING PROJECTS FROM THE STUFF YOU USUALLY SCRAP
by Tiffany Threadgould

This handy title includes step-by-step instructions for 95 eco-friendly projects. Readers can use old T-shirts, empty tissue boxes, broken umbrellas, and their parents' dusty old albums (with their permission, of course) to build new treasures.

MOONBIRD: A YEAR ON THE WIND WITH THE GREAT SURVIVOR B95
by Phillip Hoose

Moonbird is a type of shorebird called a red knot. Scientists have been tracking this bird's movements since 1995. Every February, Moonbird leaves Tierra del Fuego (the southernmost tip of South America) and flies 9,000 miles (14,484 km) to its breeding ground in the Canadian Arctic. At the end of the summer, the bird makes the return journey. This 4-ounce (113 g) athlete can fly for days without stopping and has already flown the distance from Earth to the moon and halfway back. Read how scientists are trying to ensure the survival of this amazing species.

KING GEORGE: WHAT WAS HIS PROBLEM? THE WHOLE HILARIOUS STORY OF THE AMERICAN REVOLUTION
by Steve Sheinkin

Push your school textbooks aside, and crack open this book to get an insider's look at soldiers, spies, and salmon sandwiches during the American Revolution. The little-known details in the book are entirely true.

THE BOY ON THE WOODEN BOX: HOW THE IMPOSSIBLE BECAME POSSIBLE . . . ON SCHINDLER'S LIST
by Leon Leyson

During the Holocaust, a man named Oskar Schindler saved more than 1,000 Jews by employing them in a factory and bribing officials to leave them alone. *The Boy on the Wooden Box* is the story of Leon Leyson, who was Number 289 on Schindler's list. The youngest person on the list, Leon had to stand on a box to work on the machines in Schindler's factory. This touching memoir allows readers to witness the Holocaust through the eyes of an innocent child.

HOW TO BE A WORLD EXPLORER
by Joel Levy

Have you ever wanted to explore the world? Are you curious about how to wrestle an alligator, ride an elephant, tame a camel, or remove a leech from your skin? Can you find food and water in the wild? Do you know how to build an igloo or use clues from nature to predict storms? In this book, from Lonely Planet's Not-for-Parents series, you will learn some amazing tricks from explorers who have seen and done it all.

MYSTERY PERSON

I was born on April 3, 1783. I was an author who sometimes used the pen name Diedrich Knickerbocker. *The Legend of Sleepy Hollow*, a tale about a headless horseman, is one of my stories.

WHO AM I?

Answer on page 276

BOOKS

BUILDINGS AND ARCHITECTURE

Check out some of the coolest architecture from across the globe! **Page 58**

Up on the Roof BY ELIZABETH WINCHESTER

What's growing on the roof? In the spring, grass, wildflowers, shrubs, and vines grow on the roof of Chicago's City Hall, 12 stories above the street. In New York City, herbs, salad greens, tomatoes, and other crops grow at Brooklyn Grange, a 2.5-acre (10,117 sq m) farm that is on two roofs. Since 2010, the farm has sold more than 120,000 pounds (54,431 kg) of produce.

Green roofs are roofs that are partly or completely covered with plant growth. They can be found atop homes, hospitals, schools, museums, and other buildings across the country. Soil scientist Mary Lusk says that as city populations continue to rise, the use of green roofs will too. "Green roofs are catching on now as we look for more and more ways to ensure that cities protect the environment," she told TFK.

These types of roofs have been used for hundreds of years. Before electricity was invented, people in northern Europe used sod roofs as insulation. In the 1800s, people in North Dakota, New York City, and other parts of the United States used green roofs. Sod roofs helped keep homes cool in the summer and warm in the winter.

Landscape architect Bruce Dvorak, who helped design Chicago City Hall's green roof, says that some early green roofs had problems with leaking and getting plants to grow. But those problems have, for the most part, been fixed.

DIGGING IN

In the 1970s, scientists in Germany worked to improve green-roof technology. Today, engineers, architects, and soil scientists collaborate to build green roofs that function well.

"Engineers and architects make sure that the roof can support the weight, and they keep the roof watertight," Dvorak says. "Landscape architects select plants, soil, and drainage systems." Because rooftops can be windy, hot, and sunny, plants need to be hardy to grow there. Soil scientists are sometimes brought to a project to help builders choose plants.

Green roofs cost more to build than regular roofs, but fans say the benefits outweigh the costs. "Green roofs can reduce flooding, cool buildings, clean the air and water, and provide habitat for wildlife," says Dvorak. Rooftop gardens also give people in cities a place to grow crops and feel connected to nature. With a green roof, the sky's the limit!

Things are looking up for the environment, as green roofs become more popular in cities across the country.

FROM TIME FOR KIDS MAGAZINE

WHoOOOSH!

The Bahrain World Trade Center, in the city of Manama, stands 50 stories tall. It is made of two towers that are shaped like the sails of a sailboat, and it has another very special feature. It generates some of its own clean energy, using three giant wind turbines that connect the two structures.

The shape of the towers helps funnel air through the space between them. It also makes the wind speed up as it rushes between the two structures. The energy generated by the building's wind turbines can fill only 11 to 15% of the building's electricity needs, but it is a step in the right direction.

Other environmentally friendly features include solar-powered outdoor lights, windows that can be opened to cool the building on warm days, and a sink-water recycling system.

SKYSCR

Supremely tall buildings present architects and engineers with special challenges. How will the building stay upright? What will keep it from sinking into the ground? Can a strong wind blow it over?

TECHNOLOGY THAT CHANGED CONSTRUCTION FOREVER

Before the late 1800s, the tallest buildings were rarely higher than 10 stories. The solid brick walls at the bottom needed to be very heavy and thick (which takes up a lot of space) to support the weight of the upper floors. Once advances were made in the iron and steel industries, architects were able to plan for taller buildings. Builders could use long beams of solid iron and, later, beams of solid steel (which is actually stronger and lighter than iron).

The development of fire-resistant building materials and the invention of the passenger elevator also changed the future of skyscraper architecture.

GUESS WHAT?

It took workers only one year and 45 days to build the Empire State Building.

Many years ago, workers walked freely around the highest parts of skyscraper sites. Without any safety gear to prevent them from falling, they bolted together the steel beams that would form the structure of a building. Today, workers still perform these tasks, but they are strapped to safety equipment.

MOVING AND SWAYING

All buildings sway a little bit in the wind, but this motion can make the people inside feel uncomfortable. Builders create structures that move together as a single piece. This prevents one floor from moving separately from the floors above or below it and keeps the building from twisting, which might weaken the structure. It also means that swaying is felt more on the upper floors of tall buildings. Some skyscrapers have enormous weights at the top that shift depending on the wind outside. The movement of the weights keeps the structure from swaying too much and making people inside feel queasy.

This enormous round weight hangs between the 88th and 92nd floors of Taipei 101, one of the world's tallest buildings. This weight can shift position to keep the building balanced against the force of the wind.

Taipei 101

THE FOUNDATION

Builders must know a lot about the land that will support a building. In New York City, much of the ground below skyscrapers is bedrock, the solid, sturdy rock that makes up the Earth's crust. This makes laying a foundation simpler. In Chicago, the ground is clay, which is softer. It is more difficult and expensive to create a solid foundation on soft ground.

The vertical beams of a structure are attached to an underground plate made of cast iron. This plate sits atop groupings of heavy horizontal steel beams, called girders, that form grillage. Each layer of beams in the grillage is wider than the one above it, making a hefty underground pyramid. The grillage rests on an even wider concrete pad.

Steel beams are often used to construct the strong "skeleton" of a skyscraper. The horizontal beams are called girders.

COOL CONSTRUCTION

When it was built, the **Space Needle**, in Seattle, Washington, was the tallest U.S. building west of the Mississippi River. High-speed elevators go from the ground to the 520-foot-high (158 m) observation deck in 43 seconds. The Needle is built to withstand winds of 200 miles (322 km) per hour.

Located in Sydney Harbour, the **Sydney Opera House** is the best-known building in Australia. Danish architect Jorn Utzon won a design competition for his idea, which featured a unique roof made from interlocking "shells." The Sydney Opera House opened its doors in 1973.

Built in Agra, India, around 1648, the **Taj Mahal** was the tomb of Mumtaz Mahal, the wife of the Muslim emperor Shah Jahan, who was later buried there as well. The Taj Mahal is noted for its detailed stone carvings, its colorful tiles, and the four tall minarets, or towers, that flank its corners. The Taj Mahal's majestic surroundings consist of a reflecting pool and a garden lined with trees and fountains.

Known throughout England as the Gherkin (a gherkin is a small pickled cucumber), the **Swiss Re Tower** is a commercial office building. It is said to be London's first environmentally sustainable skyscraper. Designed by Foster and Partners, the building was the winner of the 2004 RIBA Stirling Prize for Architecture.

GUESS WHAT? The Seattle Space Needle is fastened to its foundation with 72 bolts, each 30 feet (9 m) in length.

Sweet Architecture! BY CAMERON KEADY

Each year, with the help of her mother, Peggy, and her daughter, Sofia, Jennifer Roth creates a gingerbread house that is anything but ordinary. Using only edible materials, the trio built a towering gingerbread model of Paris's Notre Dame Cathedral in 2012.

When Sofia was just 3 years old, she told her mother she should make a gingerbread carousel. Roth agreed it would be a fun project, so she took Sofia's idea and created her first unusual gingerbread structure. Using candy canes, colorful frosting, and carefully molded gingerbread, Roth brought the carousel to life. After completing this magical merry-go-round, she went on to create the Eiffel Tower and the Taj Mahal. Roth's love of both architecture and baking inspired her to bring these wonders of the world to life for the holiday season.

Artist Jennifer Roth stands with her mother, Peggy Roth, in front of her prize-winning gingerbread model of Notre Dame.

MIXING AND MEASURING

Before starting construction, Roth spends hours researching and planning. As a lover of historic architecture, Roth insists on building each project exactly as it appears in real life. "We go to the library, and we take out lots of books about our subject," Roth told TFK. "We look at pictures and create drawings based on the pictures. Then I take the drawings and use them to make a cardboard model of the gingerbread house."

Each piece is measured, calculated, and cut to scale. All original details are given attention, from the arched doorways to the stained-glass windows, made from crushed candy cookies. For Notre Dame, 150 pieces of gingerbread were required. Roth bakes the gingerbread herself and uses icing to keep all the pieces together.

While Roth is the primary architect for each project, building is a joint effort. TFK asked Roth if as a kid she spent as much time building gingerbread houses as she does now. "When I was little, we built chocolate houses instead," she said. "They were considerably smaller than this gingerbread Notre Dame, and we always ate them!"

Notre Dame, in Paris

FROM TIME FOR KIDS MAGAZINE

Learn about the Muslim holy festival Eid al-Fitr. **Page 67**

2015

January

S	M	T	W	T	F	S
				1	2	3
4	5	6	7	8	9	10
11	12	13	14	15	16	17
18	19	20	21	22	23	24
25	26	27	28	29	30	31

February

S	M	T	W	T	F	S
1	2	3	4	5	6	7
8	9	10	11	12	13	14
15	16	17	18	19	20	21
22	23	24	25	26	27	28

March

S	M	T	W	T	F	S
1	2	3	4	5	6	7
8	9	10	11	12	13	14
15	16	17	18	19	20	21
22	23	24	25	26	27	28
29	30	31				

April

S	M	T	W	T	F	S
			1	2	3	4
5	6	7	8	9	10	11
12	13	14	15	16	17	18
19	20	21	22	23	24	25
26	27	28	29	30		

GUESS WHAT? The solstice happens twice a year: when the sun is the farthest north and the farthest south of the equator. The summer solstice is the longest day of the year, and the winter solstice is the shortest day of the year. In the Northern Hemisphere, the 2015 summer solstice will fall on June 21 and the winter solstice will fall on December 22. In the Southern Hemisphere, the 2015 winter solstice will be June 21 and the summer solstice will be December 22.

May

S	M	T	W	T	F	S
					1	2
3	4	5	6	7	8	9
10	11	12	13	14	15	16
17	18	19	20	21	22	23
24	25	26	27	28	29	30
31						

June

S	M	T	W	T	F	S
	1	2	3	4	5	6
7	8	9	10	11	12	13
14	15	16	17	18	19	20
21	22	23	24	25	26	27
28	29	30				

July

S	M	T	W	T	F	S
			1	2	3	4
5	6	7	8	9	10	11
12	13	14	15	16	17	18
19	20	21	22	23	24	25
26	27	28	29	30	31	

August

S	M	T	W	T	F	S
						1
2	3	4	5	6	7	8
9	10	11	12	13	14	15
16	17	18	19	20	21	22
23	24	25	26	27	28	29
30	31					

September

S	M	T	W	T	F	S
		1	2	3	4	5
6	7	8	9	10	11	12
13	14	15	16	17	18	19
20	21	22	23	24	25	26
27	28	29	30			

October

S	M	T	W	T	F	S
				1	2	3
4	5	6	7	8	9	10
11	12	13	14	15	16	17
18	19	20	21	22	23	24
25	26	27	28	29	30	31

November

S	M	T	W	T	F	S
1	2	3	4	5	6	7
8	9	10	11	12	13	14
15	16	17	18	19	20	21
22	23	24	25	26	27	28
29	30					

December

S	M	T	W	T	F	S
		1	2	3	4	5
6	7	8	9	10	11	12
13	14	15	16	17	18	19
20	21	22	23	24	25	26
27	28	29	30	31		

TIME TO CELEBRATE 2015!

January 1: New Year's Day

January 19: Martin Luther King Jr. Day

February 2: Groundhog Day

February 14: Valentine's Day

February 16: Presidents' Day

February 17: Mardi Gras

February 19: Chinese New Year

March 8: Daylight saving time begins

March 17: St. Patrick's Day

April 1: April Fools' Day

April 4-11: Passover*

April 5: Easter

April 22: Earth Day

May 5: Cinco de Mayo

May 10: Mother's Day

May 25: Memorial Day

June 21: Father's Day

July 4: Independence Day

September 7: Labor Day

September 14-15: Rosh Hashanah*

September 23: Yom Kippur*

October 12: Columbus Day

October 31: Halloween

November 1: Daylight saving time ends

November 11: Veterans Day

November 26: Thanksgiving

December 7-14: Hanukkah*

December 25: Christmas

December 26-January 1: Kwanzaa

*All Jewish holidays begin at sundown the evening before.

Mother's Day was created by Anna Jarvis, who wanted it to be a day of prayer where each person gave thanks to his or her mother. Jarvis later filed a lawsuit to try to stop a Mother's Day festival in New York. She did not want the holiday to become about spending money and buying things. She lost. Today, in the United States, Mother's Day is celebrated on the second Sunday in May.

TIME FOR KIDS GAME

PICK THE RIGHT PUMPKIN!

Molly's ring slipped off while she was carving Halloween jack-o'-lanterns. Use the hints below to figure out which pumpkin her ring is in.

1. The pumpkin is not crying.

2. There is not a bat on the pumpkin.

3. The pumpkin does not have three teeth.

4. The curled vine on the pumpkin's stem is on the left.

5. The pumpkin is smiling.

Answer on page 276

RING IN THE NEW YEAR!

Families in different countries around the world have different new year celebration traditions.

In the Netherlands, people eat a deep-fried, donutlike treat called an *oliebol* around the new year. They also set off lots of fireworks and light bonfires, often burning up their Christmas trees.

At the stroke of midnight, many Kenyans howl at the top of their lungs. They cheer, sing, dance, and honk car horns.

Spanish people **pop 12 grapes into their mouths** at midnight. It is considered good luck.

In Peru, some people play a game with potatoes. A peeled potato (symbolizing having no money), a partially peeled potato (symbolizing having an average amount of money), and a potato with its skin on (representing having lots of money) are placed under a chair. Without looking, party guests choose a potato. The potato they pick predicts what kind of financial success they'll have that year.

Greeks bake a cake for their new year's festivities. It is called a *vasilopita*. A coin is hidden inside. The diner who finds the coin in his or her piece of cake will be extra lucky all year long.

Many Japanese people clean their houses and forgive any grudges they may be holding in order to start off the year in a good place. At midnight, **Buddhist monks strike gongs** 108 times to chase away 108 kinds of human weakness. Decorations called *shimekazari,* which are made of twisted rice-straw rope, are hung in doorways. They are often adorned with *shide,* which are paper strips cut in zigzag patterns. These decorations keep bad spirits away. Other good luck items, such as ferns and oranges, may be included in a *shimekazari.*

Kadomatsu **are Japanese decorations made of bamboo, pine tree branches, and flowers. They are placed in pairs at the entrance to homes and buildings to attract good spirits.**

WELCOME TO THE **YEAR OF THE SHEEP**

The Chinese calendar is based on the lunar calendar, and the Chinese New Year is on the first day of the lunar calendar. In 2015, the Chinese New Year will be on February 19. People celebrate by wearing red, setting off fireworks, and sharing meals with their families. They enjoy oranges, which are considered good luck for finding wealth in the new year, and eat noodles, which symbolize living a long life.

Each year on the Chinese calendar corresponds to one of 12 animals in the Chinese zodiac. 2015 is the Year of the Sheep (or goat). Other Years of the Sheep include 2003, 1991, 1979, 1967, 1955, 1943, 1931, and 1919. People who are born under this sign are thought to be kind, gentle, polite, calm, clever, and artistic. In what year were you born? How about your brothers, sisters, and friends? See the boxes below to find out where your birth year falls on the Chinese zodiac.

SHEEP
2027, 2015, 2003, 1991, 1979, 1967, 1955, 1943

MONKEY
2028, 2016, 2004, 1992, 1980, 1968, 1956, 1944

ROOSTER
2029, 2017, 2005, 1993, 1981, 1969, 1957, 1945

DOG
2030, 2018, 2006, 1994, 1982, 1970, 1958, 1946

PIG
2031, 2019, 2007, 1995, 1983, 1971, 1959, 1947

RAT
2032, 2020, 2008, 1996, 1984, 1972, 1960, 1948

OX
2033, 2021, 2009, 1997, 1985, 1973, 1961, 1949

TIGER
2034, 2022, 2010, 1998, 1986, 1974, 1962, 1950

RABBIT
2035, 2023, 2011, 1999, 1987, 1975, 1963, 1951

DRAGON
2036, 2024, 2012, 2000, 1988, 1976, 1964, 1952

SNAKE
2037, 2025, 2013, 2001, 1989, 1977, 1965, 1953

HORSE
2038, 2026, 2014, 2002, 1990, 1978, 1966, 1954

MYSTERY PERSON

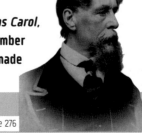

I was born in 1812 in Portsmouth, England. *A Christmas Carol*, one of my most famous books, was published in December 1843. The tale of stingy Ebenezer Scrooge has been made into dozens of films.

WHO AM I?

Answer on page 276

Dyngus Day
(Monday after Easter)

Some Christians take part in Lent, which is a period of 40 days before Easter, during which they fast—give up something they enjoy—and reflect on their sins. Celebrated in Poland, Dyngus Day is a day of fun and silliness that follows Lent. Boys chase girls and try to drench them with buckets of water or squirt guns. Girls have a chance to do the same on the following day.

Basler Fasnacht
(Monday through Thursday after Ash Wednesday)

The largest popular festival in Switzerland is Basler Fasnacht, or the Carnival of Basel. Starting at 4 a.m. on Monday, people in huge, cartoonish masks and colorful costumes begin to march through the streets. They carry lanterns, play instruments, sing songs, and act out scenes from the year before.

GUESS WHAT? About 15,000 to 20,000 masked people take part in the Basler Fasnacht festivities every year. Only members of local organizations are allowed to dress up and participate in the activities. Tourists and other locals may watch.

AROUND THE WORLD

Eid al-Fitr
(End of Ramadan; usually in late
July, August, or early September)

Ramadan is the holiest month of the year
for Muslims. During Ramadan, Muslims
pray, perform acts of charity, and refrain
from eating or drinking during the day.
Eid al-Fitr (*eed* al-fit-tuhr) is the festival
at the end of the month. It's celebrated with
prayers, gifts, charity, new
clothing, and big family
meals that include lots of
sweet dishes.

Many children
wear costumes
with headdresses
featuring colorful
drawings of a
cow head.

Gai Jatra
(A day in August or September)

A popular celebration in Nepal is Gai Jatra,
which means "festival of the cows." Any
person who has lost a family member in the
year leading up to the festival leads a cow in
a parade. If a person does not have a cow
handy, he or she will lead a young child
dressed as a cow. The kids may be fed milk
or given money or gifts. Cows are sacred to
members of the Hindu religion. According
to the tradition, the cows in the parade help
usher people's ancestors into heaven. Even
though the festival commemorates the dead,
it is not a somber event. After the parade,
people dress up, wear masks, make jokes,
and have a great time.

Looking for a few good games? **Page 72**

Get to Know Shigeru Miyamoto BY TFK KID REPORTER YUSUF HALABI

Shigeru Miyamoto is the artist and designer behind video game titles including *Donkey Kong, Super Mario Bros.*, and *Legend of Zelda*. Miyamoto has been creating video games for more than 30 years.

Miyamoto grew up and works in Kyoto, Japan, but he has always been a big fan of American culture. TFK Kid Reporter Yusuf Halabi interviewed Miyamoto, with the help of a translator, at Nintendo of America's offices in New York City.

TFK: What inspired you to become a video game engineer?

SHIGERU MIYAMOTO: Actually, I am not an engineer. I started off as an artist, drawing with brushes and things like that. When I was younger, I used to draw comics. I wasn't very suited to working in digital media so I went to school and studied industrial design. After I went to school, I was able to join Nintendo and was hoping to help create fun and interesting toys. Shortly after I joined [Nintendo], video games started to become popular. I helped out with the video games by drawing

Shigeru Miyamoto

the artwork and characters of the games. I quickly realized that drawing for video games was a lot like creating comics and toys. Even though I wasn't initially interested in digital art, I decided to study and learn more about it so I could create things in video games. I started talking to the technical people and engineers at Nintendo and they were very excited to teach an artist like me how video games are created.

TFK: What was the inspiration behind the first *Super Mario Bros.* game?

MIYAMOTO: Before the original *Super Mario Bros.*, I had created games called *Donkey Kong* and *Excitebike*. After we created *Donkey Kong*, where Mario was very small, we wanted to create a game with a bigger character that you could move around. The problem was that if you had a bigger character, there was less space to move around. In *Excitebike*, the screen scrolled so that there was more room to play. We used this screen-scrolling technology to create a bigger Mario, allowing him more room to move. So we made Mario bigger and had him running across the screen, which turned out to be fun. However, we made Mario smaller so that the space in the game seemed bigger. We enjoyed the big and small Mario, so we thought it would be more fun if Mario could change sizes during the game and that is when we introduced the Super Mushroom to allow Mario to change size. That is how Mario became Super Mario.

TFK Kid Reporter Yusuf Halabi and Shigeru Miyamoto

TFK: What was your favorite game to work on?

MIYAMOTO: I've enjoyed making every game that I was a part of. When we started creating the hardware and games for the Nintendo 64, we were transitioning from 2D games to 3D worlds. This was the first time people were using 3D technology in an interactive way. There was nobody to tell us how to create these types of 3D games. We were essentially creating our own rules of how 3D games should be designed. It was very exciting and fun for us. These rules and designs led to many patents. While others may have found it difficult and challenging with the new technology and game designs, I had fun.

TFK: What would you say to children who are interested in video game design?

MIYAMOTO: Today, a single video game is typically created by teams of 50 to 100 people. Even though there are many people working on the video game, there is typically one person who is directing the project. For kids who are interested in creating video games, obviously you need to be able to play video games. However, what's even more important is to have many other experiences outside of video games so you can imagine different possibilities in the games you are creating. Things like playing sports or communicating with friends. Talking to them and sharing ideas are all important activities that will help you become a great video game designer. So my advice is to go out and experience lots of different things.

TFK: What do you hope kids gain from playing your games?

MIYAMOTO: The most important thing about interactive entertainment like video games is the way the players think about what they can do with the game. What's important to players is to think creatively, then try out what they're thinking, and then see it [come to life] in the game. For example, when playing a game like *Super Mario Bros.*, the players hit blocks to find different items. I want those players to think about all of the possibilities of what they might find or new worlds that they might uncover. My hope is that kids will test their creativity and think of different fun and silly ways to interact with the game.

FROM
TIME
FOR KIDS
MAGAZINE

The Webby Awards

Winners of the 17th Annual Webby Awards were announced May 21, 2013. Check them out online and on your handheld devices.

OUTSTANDING COMEDIC PERFORMANCE
Jerry Seinfeld

MEDIA STREAMING
netflix.com

LIFETIME ACHIEVEMENT
Steve Wilhite, inventor of the GIF file format

PERSON OF THE YEAR
Frank Ocean

BREAKOUT OF THE YEAR
Obama for America 2012
barackobama.com

ATHLETE OF THE YEAR
Chris Kluwe

ACTIVISM
Change.org

ART
The Creators Project
thecreatorsproject.vice.com

BEST NAVIGATION/STRUCTURE
cloudsovercuba.com

BEST USE OF PHOTOGRAPHY
humansofnewyork.com

CHARITABLE ORGANIZATIONS/ NONPROFIT
DoSomething.org

EDUCATION
TED-Ed
ed.ted.com

EDUCATION & REFERENCE
(HANDHELD DEVICES)
MoMA Art Lab

ENTERTAINMENT
(HANDHELD DEVICES)
Lego Super Heroes Movie Maker

SCIENCE
The First Men on the Moon:
The *Apollo 11* Lunar Landing
firstmenonthemoon.com

EDUCATION &
REFERENCE
(TABLET & ALL
OTHER DEVICES)
Leonardo da Vinci: Anatomy

FAMILY/PARENTING
Nick Jr. Playtime
nickjr.com/kids

GAMES
(HANDHELD DEVICES)
Draw a Stickman Epic

HEALTH
webmd.com

MOVIE & FILM
The Hunger Games: Capitol Tour
thecapitol.pn

MUSIC
vevo.com

SOCIAL
(TABLET & ALL OTHER DEVICES)
Skype

SOCIAL GAMING
(TABLET & ALL OTHER DEVICES)
The Hunger Games Adventures

SPORTS
(IPAD)
NBA Digital's NBA Game Time for iPad

TELEVISION
Hulu.com

WEB SERVICES &
APPLICATIONS
dropbox.com

WEIRD
onetinyhand.com

YOUTH
pbskids.org

READY, SET, GAME!

Meet monsters, help strangers, fling birds, and race cars while playing games on your computer, PlayStation, Wii U, or other device.

F1 RACE STARS

A racing game, *F1 Race Stars* features Formula One cars and teams. Players can test their skills on many different circuits. There are time trial events and online multiplayer races too. *F1 Race Stars* is available on most game platforms.

MOSHI MONSTERS: MOSHLINGS THEME PARK

Cute pet monsters known as Moshlings have arrived at Gee Whizz Island to visit Buster Bumblechops. But there has been a storm, and Buster is missing. Players (on Nintendo 3DS/DS) explore and fix up the theme park and play games as they search for their friends.

ANGRY BIRDS: STAR WARS II

The Angry Birds are back! And this time, each Angry Bird is dressed up as a *Star Wars* character, such as Luke Skywalker or Chewbacca. In this game, Darth Vader and the Stormtroopers are pigs. There are more than 20 levels. The game is available on most game platforms.

SCRIBBLENAUTS UNLIMITED

This creative puzzle game (on Nintendo 3DS, Wii U, and PC) allows players to take on the role of Maxwell, who travels around helping people. As he encounters problems or people who need things, Maxwell uses his magical notepad to fix the situation. For example, when a player sees a cat stuck in a tree, he or she can type in "ladder," and the object will appear. With *Scribblenauts Unlimited,* players can let their imaginations go wild.

SCORE
510
BATTERY
10
GOALS

PAUSE

Click the Birdie

THERE'S AN APP FOR THAT!

CLICK THE BIRDIE

Travel around the country finding birds in their native habitats. Test your speed and knowledge by snapping photos of featured birds and spotting birds that have popped up in the wrong places. Players earn points and learn cool bird facts.

COLORBOOK

With the artsy ColorBook app, you can put your own spin on family photos. Get rid of the color, leaving new images that can be filled in like the pages of a coloring book.

THE ULTIMATE DINOPEDIA

Chock-full of prehistoric paintings, cool videos, and interesting facts, the Ultimate Dinopedia is the perfect app for anyone who wants to know more about dinosaurs.

SCRIBBLE PRESS

This app lets kids write and illustrate their own books on the iPad.

CHICKTIONARY

Seven googly-eyed hens, each with a different letter on her chest, cluck at you while you try to unscramble the letters and spell as many words of three or more letters as possible. You have to hurry, though—the clock is ticking.

MONSTER PHYSICS

Users can combine parts, such as wheels, propellers, ropes, rockets, and wings, to build robots and machines. With their new inventions, kids can complete fun missions.

Monster Physics

COUNTRIES

See Stonehenge and other amazing places! **Page 108**

A Tale of Two Koreas BY STEPHANIE KRAUS AND VICKIE AN

North Korea and South Korea share a history, a language, and a peninsula. But for more than 60 years, conflict and distrust have separated the nations.

Korea was a colony of Japan from 1910 to 1945. After Japan's defeat in World War II, Korea was divided into two countries. The split became permanent in 1948. North Korea established a communist government. South Korea became a republic. Each wanted to reunify Korea under its own government.

On June 25, 1950, the North Korean military invaded South Korea, starting the Korean War. A cease-fire agreement was signed in July 1953. A demilitarized zone (DMZ) was created along the border dividing North and South. Soldiers patrol each side of the DMZ. Millions of families are separated. Tension between the two nations runs high.

While South Korea has become an industrial giant, North Korea is a secretive communist country with many economic problems. In years past, South Korea tried to improve relations by giving aid to North Korea. But the North has not let down its guard, continuing to grow its army and nuclear-weapons program. Because of this, South Korea and the United States stopped food aid to North Korea.

Kim Jong Un is the leader of North Korea. His father, Kim Jong Il, led the country from 1994 until 2011. Both leaders have used military threats to display their power and control. North Korea has one of the world's largest armies, with access to destructive nuclear weapons.

Pyongyang, North Korea

Seoul, South Korea

Kim Jong Un

NATIONS
FROM A TO Z

This sample entry for Egypt explains the kinds of information you will find in this section.

This tells the main language(s) and the official language(s) (if any) spoken in a nation.

This is the type of currency, or money, used in the nation.

Life expectancy is the number of years a person can expect to live. It's affected by heredity, a person's health and nutrition, the health care and wealth of a nation, and a person's occupation.

This tells the percentage of people who can read and write.

This is an interesting fact about the country.

EGYPT

LOCATION: Africa
CAPITAL: Cairo
AREA: 386,660 sq mi (1,001,450 sq km)
POPULATION ESTIMATE (2013): 85,294,388
GOVERNMENT: Republic
LANGUAGE: Arabic
MONEY: Egyptian pound
LIFE EXPECTANCY: 73
LITERACY RATE: 74%

GUESS WHAT? *Ancient Egyptians worshipped cats as sacred. They believed that the animals protected households.*

AFGHANISTAN

LOCATION: Asia
CAPITAL: Kabul
AREA: 251,737 sq mi (652,230 sq km)
POPULATION ESTIMATE (2013): 31,108,077
GOVERNMENT: Islamic republic
LANGUAGES: Afghan Persian (Dari) and Pashto (both official), Uzbek, Turkmen
MONEY: Afghani
LIFE EXPECTANCY: 50
LITERACY RATE: 28%

GUESS WHAT? *The national sport of Afghanistan is buzkashi, or goat grabbing. During the game, riders on horseback compete to grab a goat or a calf carcass and drop it off in a goal area.*

ALBANIA

LOCATION: Europe
CAPITAL: Tirana
AREA: 11,100 sq mi (28,748 sq km)
POPULATION ESTIMATE (2013): 3,011,405
GOVERNMENT: Parliamentary democracy
LANGUAGES: Albanian (Tosk is the official dialect), Greek, others
MONEY: Lek
LIFE EXPECTANCY: 78
LITERACY RATE: 97%

GUESS WHAT? *Traditionally, in Albania, if you nod your head up and down, it means no. And if you shake your head side to side, it means yes.*

ALGERIA

LOCATION: Africa
CAPITAL: Algiers
AREA: 919,590 sq mi (2,381,741 sq km)
POPULATION ESTIMATE (2013): 38,087,812
GOVERNMENT: Republic
LANGUAGES: Arabic (official), French, Berber dialects
MONEY: Dinar
LIFE EXPECTANCY: 76
LITERACY RATE: 73%

GUESS WHAT? *Because much of Algeria is dry and desertlike, most people live along the coast of the Mediterranean Sea. More than 90% of people living in Algeria live in only 12% of the country.*

ANDORRA

LOCATION: Europe
CAPITAL: Andorra la Vella
AREA: 181 sq mi (468 sq km)
POPULATION ESTIMATE (2013): 85,293
GOVERNMENT: Parliamentary democracy
LANGUAGES: Catalan (official), French, Castilian, Portuguese
MONEY: Euro (formerly French franc and Spanish peseta)
LIFE EXPECTANCY: 83
LITERACY RATE: 100%

GUESS WHAT? *There are no airports or train stations in Andorra.*

COUNTRIES

ANGOLA

LOCATION: Africa
CAPITAL: Luanda
AREA: 481,350 sq mi (1,246,700 sq km)
POPULATION ESTIMATE (2013): 18,565,269
GOVERNMENT: Republic
LANGUAGES: Portuguese (official), Bantu, other African languages
MONEY: Kwanza
LIFE EXPECTANCY: 55
LITERACY RATE: 70%

GUESS WHAT? *After many years of civil war, Angola's countryside has many dangerous land mines.*

ANTIGUA AND BARBUDA

LOCATION: Caribbean
CAPITAL: Saint John's
AREA: 171 sq mi (443 sq km)
POPULATION ESTIMATE (2013): 90,156
GOVERNMENT: Constitutional monarchy with a parliamentary system of government
LANGUAGES: English (official), local dialects
MONEY: East Caribbean dollar
LIFE EXPECTANCY: 76
LITERACY RATE: 99%

GUESS WHAT? *Every year, Antiguans celebrate Carnival, a 10-day festival commemorating the end of slavery in Antigua. Slavery ended in 1834, the earliest of any colony in the British Caribbean.*

ARGENTINA

LOCATION: South America
CAPITAL: Buenos Aires
AREA: 1,073,518 sq mi (2,780,400 sq km)
POPULATION ESTIMATE (2013): 42,610,981
GOVERNMENT: Republic
LANGUAGES: Spanish (official), Italian, English, German, French, native languages
MONEY: Argentine peso
LIFE EXPECTANCY: 77
LITERACY RATE: 98%

GUESS WHAT? *The tango is a dance that began in poor districts of Buenos Aires. Eventually, it became a popular and fashionable dance worldwide.*

ARMENIA

LOCATION: Asia
CAPITAL: Yerevan
AREA: 11,484 sq mi (29,743 sq km)
POPULATION ESTIMATE (2013): 3,064,267
GOVERNMENT: Republic
LANGUAGES: Armenian (official), others
MONEY: Dram
LIFE EXPECTANCY: 74
LITERACY RATE: 100%

GUESS WHAT? *Armenia is slightly smaller than the state of Maryland.*

AUSTRALIA

LOCATION: Oceania, between the Pacific Ocean and Indian Ocean
CAPITAL: Canberra
AREA: 2,988,902 sq mi (7,741,220 sq km)
POPULATION ESTIMATE (2013): 22,262,501
GOVERNMENT: Federal parliamentary democracy
LANGUAGES: English, others
MONEY: Australian dollar
LIFE EXPECTANCY: 82
LITERACY RATE: 99%

GUESS WHAT? *From 1838 to 1902, it was illegal to swim during the day at public beaches in Australia. Authorities considered it immoral.*

AUSTRIA

LOCATION: Europe
CAPITAL: Vienna
AREA: 32,382 sq mi (83,871 sq km)
POPULATION ESTIMATE (2013): 8,221,646
GOVERNMENT: Federal republic
LANGUAGES: German (official), Croatian (official in Burgenland), Turkish, Serbian, others
MONEY: Euro (formerly schilling)
LIFE EXPECTANCY: 80
LITERACY RATE: 98%

GUESS WHAT? *Austria is made up of nine federal provinces, each with its own government. On May 15, 1955, the country declared its permanent neutrality in future wars.*

AZERBAIJAN

LOCATION: Asia
CAPITAL: Baku
AREA: 33,400 sq mi (86,600 sq km)
POPULATION ESTIMATE (2013): 9,590,159
GOVERNMENT: Republic
LANGUAGES: Azerbaijani (official), Lezgi, Russian, Armenian, others
MONEY: Azerbaijani manat
LIFE EXPECTANCY: 72
LITERACY RATE: 100%

GUESS WHAT? *Azerbaijan is home to more than a third of the world's mud volcanoes, which spew mud and gases instead of magma and water.*

THE BAHAMAS

LOCATION: Caribbean
CAPITAL: Nassau
AREA: 5,359 sq mi (13,880 sq km)
POPULATION ESTIMATE (2013): 319,031
GOVERNMENT: Constitutional parliamentary democracy
LANGUAGES: English (official), Creole
MONEY: Bahamian dollar
LIFE EXPECTANCY: 72
LITERACY RATE: 96%

GUESS WHAT? *The Bahamas is made up of approximately 700 islands. Only 30 of the islands are inhabited.*

BAHRAIN

LOCATION: Middle East
CAPITAL: Manama
AREA: 293 sq mi (760 sq km)
POPULATION ESTIMATE (2013): 1,281,332
GOVERNMENT: Constitutional monarchy
LANGUAGES: Arabic (official), English, Farsi, Urdu
MONEY: Bahraini dinar
LIFE EXPECTANCY: 78
LITERACY RATE: 95%

GUESS WHAT? *Women in Bahrain were granted the right to vote in 2002.*

BANGLADESH

LOCATION: Asia
CAPITAL: Dhaka
AREA: 55,598 sq mi (143,998 sq km)
POPULATION ESTIMATE (2013): 163,654,860
GOVERNMENT: Parliamentary democracy
LANGUAGES: Bangla (official), English
MONEY: Taka
LIFE EXPECTANCY: 70
LITERACY RATE: 58%

GUESS WHAT? *Plastic bags have clogged drains and been a major cause of flooding in Bangladesh. In 2002, Bangladesh became the first country to ban plastic bags.*

BARBADOS

LOCATION: Caribbean
CAPITAL: Bridgetown
AREA: 166 sq mi (430 sq km)
POPULATION ESTIMATE (2013): 288,725
GOVERNMENT: Parliamentary democracy
LANGUAGE: English
MONEY: Barbadian dollar
LIFE EXPECTANCY: 75
LITERACY RATE: 100%

GUESS WHAT? *The town of St. Andrew in Barbados was once believed to have healing properties. Many people traveled there and covered themselves in the sands of Cattlewash Beach in hopes of curing their health problems.*

BELARUS

LOCATION: Europe
CAPITAL: Minsk
AREA: 80,154 sq mi (207,600 sq km)
POPULATION ESTIMATE (2013): 9,625,888
GOVERNMENT: Republic in name but actually a dictatorship
LANGUAGES: Belarusian and Russian (both official), others
MONEY: Belarusian ruble
LIFE EXPECTANCY: 72
LITERACY RATE: 100%

GUESS WHAT? *The movement of glaciers in Belarus has helped create many bodies of water. There are about 11,000 lakes and 20,000 rivers and creeks in the country.*

COUNTRIES

BELGIUM

LOCATION: Europe
CAPITAL: Brussels
AREA: 11,787 sq mi (30,528 sq km)
POPULATION ESTIMATE (2013): 10,444,268
GOVERNMENT: Federal parliamentary democracy under a constitutional monarchy
LANGUAGES: Dutch, French, and German (all official)
MONEY: Euro (formerly Belgian franc)
LIFE EXPECTANCY: 80
LITERACY RATE: 99%

GUESS WHAT? *Belgium has more castles per square mile than any other country in the world.*

BELIZE

LOCATION: Central America
CAPITAL: Belmopan
AREA: 8,867 sq mi (22,966 sq km)
POPULATION ESTIMATE (2013): 334,297
GOVERNMENT: Parliamentary democracy
LANGUAGES: English (official), Spanish, Creole, Mayan dialects, others
MONEY: Belizean dollar
LIFE EXPECTANCY: 68
LITERACY RATE: 77%

GUESS WHAT? *Altun Ha, an area filled with Mayan ruins built from 200 to 900 A.D., is one of the most visited sites in Belize.*

BENIN

LOCATION: Africa
CAPITAL: Porto-Novo
AREA: 43,483 sq mi (112,622 sq km)
POPULATION ESTIMATE (2013): 9,877,292
GOVERNMENT: Republic
LANGUAGES: French (official), Fon, Yoruba, tribal languages
MONEY: CFA franc
LIFE EXPECTANCY: 61
LITERACY RATE: 42%

GUESS WHAT? *Benin is made up of about 42 African ethnic groups, with the majority living in the south.*

BHUTAN

LOCATION: Asia
CAPITAL: Thimphu
AREA: 14,824 sq mi (38,394 sq km)
POPULATION ESTIMATE (2013): 725,296
GOVERNMENT: Constitutional monarchy
LANGUAGES: Dzongkha (official), Sharchhopka, Lhotshamkha, others
MONEY: Ngultrum
LIFE EXPECTANCY: 68
LITERACY RATE: 53%

GUESS WHAT? *In 2004, Bhutan became the first country in the world to ban the sale of tobacco.*

BOLIVIA

LOCATION: South America
CAPITALS: La Paz (seat of government), Sucre (legislative capital)
AREA: 424,162 sq mi (1,098,581 sq km)
POPULATION ESTIMATE (2013): 10,461,053
GOVERNMENT: Republic
LANGUAGES: Spanish, Quechua, and Aymara (all official), others
MONEY: Boliviano
LIFE EXPECTANCY: 68
LITERACY RATE: 91%

GUESS WHAT? *Bolivia and Paraguay are the only two landlocked countries in South America.*

BOSNIA AND HERZEGOVINA

LOCATION: Europe
CAPITAL: Sarajevo
AREA: 19,767 sq mi (51,197 sq km)
POPULATION ESTIMATE (2013): 3,875,723
GOVERNMENT: Emerging federal democratic republic
LANGUAGES: Bosnian, Croatian, Serbian (all official)
MONEY: Convertible mark
LIFE EXPECTANCY: 76
LITERACY RATE: 98%

GUESS WHAT? *Bosnia and Herzegovina declared independence from Yugoslavia in 1991. The Bosnian War broke out between different ethnic groups in 1992, lasting until 1995.*

BOTSWANA

LOCATION: Africa
CAPITAL: Gaborone
AREA: 224,607 sq mi
(581,730 sq km)
POPULATION ESTIMATE (2013):
2,127,825
GOVERNMENT: Parliamentary
republic
LANGUAGES: English (official),
Setswana, Kalanga,
Sekgalagadi, others
MONEY: Pula
LIFE EXPECTANCY: 54
LITERACY RATE: 85%

 The national animal of Botswana is the zebra.

BRAZIL

LOCATION: South America
CAPITAL: Brasília
AREA: 3,287,612 sq mi
(8,514,877 sq km)
POPULATION ESTIMATE (2013):
201,009,622
GOVERNMENT: Federal republic
LANGUAGES: Portuguese (official),
Spanish, German, Italian,
Japanese, English, various
Amerindian languages
MONEY: Real
LIFE EXPECTANCY: 73
LITERACY RATE: 90%

 More species of primates live in Brazil than in any other country in the world.

BRUNEI

LOCATION: Asia
CAPITAL: Bandar Seri Begawan
AREA: 2,226 sq mi
(5,765 sq km)
POPULATION ESTIMATE (2013):
415,717
GOVERNMENT: Constitutional
sultanate
LANGUAGES: Malay (official),
English, Chinese
MONEY: Bruneian dollar
LIFE EXPECTANCY: 77
LITERACY RATE: 95%

 Located on the island of Borneo, Brunei is made up of two pieces of land that are separated from one another by a strip of land that is part of Malaysia.

BULGARIA

LOCATION: Europe
CAPITAL: Sofia
AREA: 42,811 sq mi
(110,879 sq km)
POPULATION ESTIMATE (2013):
6,981,642
GOVERNMENT: Parliamentary
democracy
LANGUAGES: Bulgarian (official),
Turkish, Roma, others
MONEY: Lev
LIFE EXPECTANCY: 74
LITERACY RATE: 98%

 Bulgaria has the worst air pollution in Europe.

BURKINA FASO

LOCATION: Africa
CAPITAL: Ouagadougou
AREA: 105,870 sq mi
(274,200 sq km)
POPULATION ESTIMATE (2013):
17,812,961
GOVERNMENT: Parliamentary
republic
LANGUAGES: French (official),
native African languages
MONEY: CFA franc
LIFE EXPECTANCY: 54
LITERACY RATE: 29%

 Burkina Faso's main export is gold.

BURUNDI

LOCATION: Africa
CAPITAL: Bujumbura
AREA: 10,745 sq mi
(27,830 sq km)
POPULATION ESTIMATE (2013):
10,060,714
GOVERNMENT: Republic
LANGUAGES: Kirundi and French
(both official), Swahili
MONEY: Burundi franc
LIFE EXPECTANCY: 60
LITERACY RATE: 67%

 Burundi is one of the smallest countries in Africa, and one of the poorest countries in the world. Its largest export is coffee.

COUNTRIES

CAMBODIA

LOCATION: Asia
CAPITAL: Phnom Penh
AREA: 69,900 sq mi (181,035 sq km)
POPULATION ESTIMATE (2013): 15,205,539
GOVERNMENT: Multiparty democracy under a constitutional monarchy
LANGUAGES: Khmer (official), French, English
MONEY: Riel
LIFE EXPECTANCY: 63
LITERACY RATE: 74%

GUESS WHAT? *Angkor Wat, an ancient temple in Cambodia, is often called the eighth wonder of the world.*

CAMEROON

LOCATION: Africa
CAPITAL: Yaoundé
AREA: 183,567 sq mi (475,440 sq km)
POPULATION ESTIMATE (2013): 22,534,532
GOVERNMENT: Republic
LANGUAGES: French and English (both official), various African languages
MONEY: CFA franc
LIFE EXPECTANCY: 55
LITERACY RATE: 71%

GUESS WHAT? *The goliath frog, the world's biggest frog, comes from Cameroon. These amphibians can be more than 1 foot (30 cm) long and weigh as much as a house cat, about 7.2 pounds (3.3 kg).*

CANADA

LOCATION: North America
CAPITAL: Ottawa
AREA: 3,855,081 sq mi (9,984,670 sq km)
POPULATION ESTIMATE (2013): 34,568,221
GOVERNMENT: Parliamentary democracy, federation, and constitutional monarchy
LANGUAGES: English and French (both official), others
MONEY: Canadian dollar
LIFE EXPECTANCY: 82
LITERACY RATE: 99%

GUESS WHAT? *There are an estimated 500,000 to 1 million moose in Canada. They are found in every province of the country and live to be 15 to 25 years old.*

CAPE VERDE

LOCATION: Africa
CAPITAL: Praia
AREA: 1,557 sq mi (4,033 sq km)
POPULATION ESTIMATE (2013): 531,046
GOVERNMENT: Republic
LANGUAGES: Portuguese (official), Crioulo
MONEY: Cape Verdean escudo
LIFE EXPECTANCY: 71
LITERACY RATE: 85%

GUESS WHAT? *Cape Verde is a group of islands about 300 to 500 miles (483 to 805 km) off the coast of Senegal. The islands were formed when hot spots of bubbling magma erupted from Earth's crust.*

CENTRAL AFRICAN REPUBLIC

LOCATION: Africa
CAPITAL: Bangui
AREA: 240,534 sq mi (622,984 sq km)
POPULATION ESTIMATE (2013): 5,166,510
GOVERNMENT: Republic
LANGUAGES: French (official), Sangho, other African languages
MONEY: CFA franc
LIFE EXPECTANCY: 51
LITERACY RATE: 57%

GUESS WHAT? *Central African Republic is home to the Aka tribe—a group of Pygmy people characterized by their short height.*

CHAD

LOCATION: Africa
CAPITAL: N'Djamena
AREA: 495,752 sq mi (1,284,000 sq km)
POPULATION ESTIMATE (2013): 11,193,452
GOVERNMENT: Republic
LANGUAGES: French and Arabic (both official), Sara, others
MONEY: CFA franc
LIFE EXPECTANCY: 49
LITERACY RATE: 35%

GUESS WHAT? *After decades of war and conflict, a single movie theater reopened in Chad in 2011. The Normandy cinema had been closed for 20 years.*

CHILE

LOCATION: South America
CAPITAL: Santiago
AREA: 291,933 sq mi
(756,102 sq km)
POPULATION ESTIMATE (2013):
17,216,945
GOVERNMENT: Republic
LANGUAGES: Spanish (official),
Mapudungun, German, English
MONEY: Chilean peso
LIFE EXPECTANCY: 78
LITERACY RATE: 99%

GUESS WHAT? *The world's largest outdoor swimming pool is at Chile's San Alfonso del Mar Resort. It is 3,323 feet (1,013 m) long and 115 feet (35 m) deep and holds 66 million gallons (250 million L) of water.*

CHINA

LOCATION: Asia
CAPITAL: Beijing
AREA: 3,705,386 sq mi
(9,596,961 sq km)
POPULATION ESTIMATE (2013):
1,349,585,838
GOVERNMENT: Communist state
LANGUAGES: Chinese (Mandarin; official), Yue (Cantonese), local dialects
MONEY: Renminbi yuan
LIFE EXPECTANCY: 75
LITERACY RATE: 95%

GUESS WHAT? *Kites were invented in China 3,000 years ago and were primarily used for frightening opponents in battle.*

COLOMBIA

LOCATION: South America
CAPITAL: Bogotá
AREA: 439,735 sq mi
(1,138,910 sq km)
POPULATION ESTIMATE (2013):
45,745,783
GOVERNMENT: Republic
LANGUAGE: Spanish (official)
MONEY: Colombian peso
LIFE EXPECTANCY: 75
LITERACY RATE: 94%

GUESS WHAT? *According to legend, there is a land in South America full of gold and precious gemstones. Some thought this land, known as "El Dorado," could be found in Colombia, prompting Spanish explorers to travel to the country in the 1500s in search of fortune.*

COMOROS

LOCATION: Africa
CAPITAL: Moroni
AREA: 863 sq mi (2,235 sq km)
POPULATION ESTIMATE (2013): 752,288
GOVERNMENT: Republic
LANGUAGES: French and Arabic
(both official), Shikomoro
MONEY: Comoran franc
LIFE EXPECTANCY: 63
LITERACY RATE: 76%

GUESS WHAT? *In 1938, a fisherman captured the first known live coelacanth (seel-a-kanth), a fish previously seen only as a fossil. It had a large body, armorlike scales, and more fins than most fish. Scientists think it may be related to the first four-legged land animals. There are two types of coelacanths, and one lives in the waters around Comoros.*

CONGO, DEMOCRATIC REPUBLIC OF THE

LOCATION: Africa
CAPITAL: Kinshasa
AREA: 905,355 sq mi
(2,344,858 sq km)
POPULATION ESTIMATE (2013):
75,507,308
GOVERNMENT: Republic
LANGUAGES: French (official),
Lingala, Kingwana, Kikongo,
Tshiluba
MONEY: Congolese franc
LIFE EXPECTANCY: 56
LITERACY RATE: 67%

GUESS WHAT? *Democratic Republic of the Congo, in Central Africa, is about the size of Western Europe.*

CONGO, REPUBLIC OF THE

LOCATION: Africa
CAPITAL: Brazzaville
AREA: 132,046 sq mi
(342,000 sq km)
POPULATION ESTIMATE (2013):
4,574,099
GOVERNMENT: Republic
LANGUAGES: French (official),
Lingala, Monokutuba,
Kikongo, others
MONEY: CFA franc
LIFE EXPECTANCY: 56
LITERACY RATE: 84%

GUESS WHAT? *Cassava, a woody shrub with an edible root, is an important crop in the Republic of the Congo.*

COSTA RICA

LOCATION: Central America
CAPITAL: San José
AREA: 19,730 sq mi
(51,100 sq km)
POPULATION ESTIMATE (2013):
4,695,942
GOVERNMENT: Democratic republic
LANGUAGES: Spanish (official),
English
MONEY: Costa Rican colón
LIFE EXPECTANCY: 78
LITERACY RATE: 96%

GUESS WHAT? *There are several active volcanoes in Costa Rica. One of the most active is Arenal Volcano, in northwestern Costa Rica.*

COTE D'IVOIRE (IVORY COAST)

LOCATION: Africa
CAPITAL: Yamoussoukro
AREA: 124,502 sq mi
(322,463 sq km)
POPULATION ESTIMATE (2013):
22,400,835
GOVERNMENT: Republic
LANGUAGES: French (official),
Dioula and many other
native dialects
MONEY: CFA franc
LIFE EXPECTANCY: 58
LITERACY RATE: 57%

GUESS WHAT? *Côte d'Ivoire is the world's largest exporter of cocoa beans. Cocoa beans are used to make chocolate.*

CROATIA

LOCATION: Europe
CAPITAL: Zagreb
AREA: 21,851 sq mi
(56,594 sq km)
POPULATION ESTIMATE (2013):
4,475,611
GOVERNMENT: Parliamentary
democracy
LANGUAGES: Croatian (official),
Serbian, others
MONEY: Kuna
LIFE EXPECTANCY: 76
LITERACY RATE: 99%

GUESS WHAT? *The Dalmatian dog breed is named after Croatia's mountainous Dalmatian Coast, which runs along the Adriatic Sea.*

CUBA

LOCATION: Caribbean
CAPITAL: Havana
AREA: 42,803 sq mi
(110,860 sq km)
POPULATION ESTIMATE (2013):
11,061,886
GOVERNMENT: Communist state
LANGUAGE: Spanish (official)
MONEY: Cuban peso
LIFE EXPECTANCY: 78
LITERACY RATE: 100%

GUESS WHAT? *The bee hummingbird, which is found only in Cuba, is the world's tiniest bird. It weighs less than a dime.*

CYPRUS

LOCATION: Middle East
CAPITAL: Nicosia
AREA: 3,572 sq mi (9,251 sq km)
POPULATION ESTIMATE (2013):
1,155,403
GOVERNMENT: Republic
LANGUAGES: Greek and Turkish
(both official), English
MONEY: Euro (formerly Cyprus
pound)
LIFE EXPECTANCY: 78
LITERACY RATE: 99%

GUESS WHAT? *Archaeologists found a well-preserved cat skeleton in Cyprus that was 9,500 years old. It may be the earliest evidence ever uncovered showing that people kept cats as pets a long, long time ago.*

CZECH REPUBLIC

LOCATION: Europe
CAPITAL: Prague
AREA: 30,451 sq mi
(78,867 sq km)
POPULATION ESTIMATE (2013):
10,609,762
GOVERNMENT: Parliamentary
democracy
LANGUAGES: Czech, Slovak, others
MONEY: Koruna
LIFE EXPECTANCY: 78
LITERACY RATE: 99%

GUESS WHAT? *According to legend, the villagers who built the Charles Bridge, in Prague, mixed egg yolks into the mortar, believing it would make the bridge stronger. Built in the 1350s, it is one of the oldest structures in Europe.*

DENMARK

LOCATION: Europe
CAPITAL: Copenhagen
AREA: 16,639 sq mi
(43,094 sq km)
POPULATION ESTIMATE (2013):
5,556,452
GOVERNMENT: Constitutional
monarchy
LANGUAGES: Danish, Faroese,
Greenlandic, German
MONEY: Krone
LIFE EXPECTANCY: 79
LITERACY RATE: 99%

GUESS WHAT? *Lego bricks are made in Denmark. In 1939, the first Lego factory had only 10 employees. Today, the toy company employs about 10,000 people.*

DJIBOUTI

LOCATION: Africa
CAPITAL: Djibouti
AREA: 8,958 sq mi
(23,200 sq km)
POPULATION ESTIMATE (2013): 792,198
GOVERNMENT: Republic
LANGUAGES: Arabic and French
(both official), Somali, Afar
MONEY: Djiboutian franc
LIFE EXPECTANCY: 62
LITERACY RATE: 68%

GUESS WHAT? *Many residents of Djibouti are nomadic animal herders. That means they travel from place to place with their animals to find food and water sources.*

DOMINICA

LOCATION: Caribbean
CAPITAL: Roseau
AREA: 290 sq mi (751 sq km)
POPULATION ESTIMATE (2013):
73,286
GOVERNMENT: Parliamentary
democracy
LANGUAGES: English (official),
French patois
MONEY: East Caribbean dollar
LIFE EXPECTANCY: 76
LITERACY RATE: 94%

GUESS WHAT? *Some scenes from Pirates of the Caribbean: Dead Man's Chest and At World's End were filmed in Dominica.*

DOMINICAN REPUBLIC

LOCATION: Caribbean
CAPITAL: Santo Domingo
AREA: 18,792 sq mi
(48,670 sq km)
POPULATION ESTIMATE (2013):
10,219,630
GOVERNMENT: Democratic republic
LANGUAGE: Spanish (official)
MONEY: Dominican peso
LIFE EXPECTANCY: 78
LITERACY RATE: 90%

GUESS WHAT? *National police officers and members of the armed forces in the Dominican Republic are not allowed to vote in national elections.*

EAST TIMOR
(TIMOR-LESTE)

LOCATION: Asia
CAPITAL: Dili
AREA: 5,743 sq mi
(14,874 sq km)
POPULATION ESTIMATE (2013):
1,172,390
GOVERNMENT: Republic
LANGUAGES: Tetum and
Portuguese (both official),
Indonesian, English, other
native languages
MONEY: U.S. dollar
LIFE EXPECTANCY: 67
LITERACY RATE: 58%

GUESS WHAT? *East Timor takes up the eastern half of the island of Timor. The western half is part of Indonesia.*

ECUADOR

LOCATION: South America
CAPITAL: Quito
AREA: 109,484 sq mi
(283,561 sq km)
POPULATION ESTIMATE (2013):
15,439,429
GOVERNMENT: Republic
LANGUAGES: Spanish (official),
Quechua, other Amerindian
languages
MONEY: U.S. dollar
LIFE EXPECTANCY: 76
LITERACY RATE: 92%

GUESS WHAT? *At the festival called Año Viejo (or "old year"), Ecuadorans make puppets that represent the bad things of the past year, then burn them to welcome the new year.*

EGYPT

LOCATION: Africa
CAPITAL: Cairo
AREA: 386,660 sq mi
(1,001,450 sq km)
POPULATION ESTIMATE (2013):
85,294,388
GOVERNMENT: Republic
LANGUAGE: Arabic (official)
MONEY: Egyptian pound
LIFE EXPECTANCY: 73
LITERACY RATE: 74%

GUESS WHAT? *Ancient Egyptians worshipped cats as sacred. They believed that the animals protected households.*

EL SALVADOR

LOCATION: Central America
CAPITAL: San Salvador
AREA: 8,124 sq mi (21,041 sq km)
POPULATION ESTIMATE (2013):
6,108,590
GOVERNMENT: Republic
LANGUAGES: Spanish (official),
Nahua
MONEY: U.S. dollar
LIFE EXPECTANCY: 74
LITERACY RATE: 85%

GUESS WHAT? *Just outside the towns of Corinto and Cacaopera in El Salvador, archaeologists have discovered cave paintings dating back to 8000 B.C. The images reveal details about the lives of people who lived more than 10,000 years ago.*

EQUATORIAL GUINEA

LOCATION: Africa
CAPITAL: Malabo
AREA: 10,830 sq mi
(28,051 sq km)
POPULATION ESTIMATE (2013): 704,001
GOVERNMENT: Republic
LANGUAGES: Spanish and French
(both official), Fang, Bubi
MONEY: CFA franc
LIFE EXPECTANCY: 63
LITERACY RATE: 94%

GUESS WHAT? *Abira is a ritual practiced in Equatorial Guinea in which villagers perform a ceremony involving music and dance to protect the community from evil.*

ERITREA

LOCATION: Africa
CAPITAL: Asmara
AREA: 45,406 sq mi
(117,600 sq km)
POPULATION ESTIMATE (2013):
6,233,682
GOVERNMENT: Transitional
LANGUAGES: Tigrinya, Arabic, and
English (all official), Tigre,
Kunama, Afar, others
MONEY: Nakfa
LIFE EXPECTANCY: 63
LITERACY RATE: 69%

GUESS WHAT? *The Danakil Depression in Eritrea, Ethiopia, and Djibouti is one of the hottest places on Earth. Temperatures reach as high as 145°F (63°C).*

ESTONIA

LOCATION: Europe
CAPITAL: Tallinn
AREA: 17,463 sq mi
(45,228 sq km)
POPULATION ESTIMATE (2013):
1,266,375
GOVERNMENT: Parliamentary
republic
LANGUAGES: Estonian (official),
Russian, others
MONEY: Euro (formerly kroon)
LIFE EXPECTANCY: 74
LITERACY RATE: 100%

GUESS WHAT? *Tallinn's Old Town is one of the best-preserved medieval towns in Europe. Buildings from the 13th through the 16th centuries still stand.*

ETHIOPIA

LOCATION: Africa
CAPITAL: Addis Ababa
AREA: 426,373 sq mi
(1,104,300 sq km)
POPULATION ESTIMATE (2013):
93,877,025
GOVERNMENT: Federal republic
LANGUAGES: Amarigna, English,
and Arabic (all official),
Oromigna and Tigrigna (both
regional official), others
MONEY: Birr
LIFE EXPECTANCY: 60
LITERACY RATE: 39%

GUESS WHAT? *In 1974, parts of an ancient skeleton were found near Hadar, Ethiopia. The skeleton, known as Lucy, is of an ancestor of modern humans. It is 3.2 million years old.*

FIJI

LOCATION: Oceania
CAPITAL: Suva
AREA: 7,057 sq mi (18,274 sq km)
POPULATION ESTIMATE (2013): 896,758
GOVERNMENT: Republic
LANGUAGES: Fijian and English (both official), Hindustani
MONEY: Fijian dollar
LIFE EXPECTANCY: 72
LITERACY RATE: 94%

GUESS WHAT? *Some Fijians used to engage in cannibalism, or the eating of human flesh. A boot with teeth marks on it that supposedly belonged to the country's last victim can be seen in the Fiji Museum.*

FINLAND

LOCATION: Europe
CAPITAL: Helsinki
AREA: 130,559 sq mi (338,145 sq km)
POPULATION ESTIMATE (2013): 5,266,114
GOVERNMENT: Republic
LANGUAGES: Finnish and Swedish (both official), others
MONEY: Euro (formerly markka)
LIFE EXPECTANCY: 80
LITERACY RATE: 100%

GUESS WHAT? *Avantouinti, or ice swimming, is a popular activity in Finland. Often, a chunk of ice is cut out of a frozen lake or river, revealing an area that people can swim in. Some Finns believe ice swimming is the secret to good health.*

FRANCE

LOCATION: Europe
CAPITAL: Paris
AREA: 248,573 sq mi (643,801 sq km)
POPULATION ESTIMATE (2013): 65,951,611
GOVERNMENT: Republic
LANGUAGE: French (official)
MONEY: Euro (formerly franc)
LIFE EXPECTANCY: 82
LITERACY RATE: 99%

GUESS WHAT? *When Paris hosted the 1900 Olympic Games, winning athletes received valuable pieces of art instead of gold medals.*

GABON

LOCATION: Africa
CAPITAL: Libreville
AREA: 103,346 sq mi (267,667 sq km)
POPULATION ESTIMATE (2013): 1,640,286
GOVERNMENT: Republic
LANGUAGES: French (official), Fang, Myene, Nzebi, Bapounou/Eschira, Bandjabi
MONEY: CFA franc
LIFE EXPECTANCY: 52
LITERACY RATE: 89%

GUESS WHAT? *Gabon is one of the few countries that are home to the endangered western lowland gorilla.*

THE GAMBIA

LOCATION: Africa
CAPITAL: Banjul
AREA: 4,361 sq mi (11,295 sq km)
POPULATION ESTIMATE (2013): 1,883,051
GOVERNMENT: Republic
LANGUAGES: English (official), Mandinka, Wolof, Fula, others
MONEY: Dalasi
LIFE EXPECTANCY: 64
LITERACY RATE: 51%

GUESS WHAT? *The Gambia hosts a project every year called Wide Open Walls, in which street artists from around the world spend two weeks painting murals on walls in villages around the country.*

GEORGIA

LOCATION: Asia
CAPITAL: Tbilisi
AREA: 26,911 sq mi (69,700 sq km)
POPULATION ESTIMATE (2013): 4,942,157
GOVERNMENT: Republic
LANGUAGES: Georgian (official), Russian, Armenian, Azeri, others
MONEY: Lari
LIFE EXPECTANCY: 78
LITERACY RATE: 100%

GUESS WHAT? *The medieval cave city of Vardzia, complete with a monastery and a water system, was built into the side of a mountain in southern Georgia.*

COUNTRIES

GERMANY

LOCATION: Europe
CAPITAL: Berlin
AREA: 137,847 sq mi
(357,022 sq km)
POPULATION ESTIMATE (2013):
81,147,265
GOVERNMENT: Federal republic
LANGUAGE: German
MONEY: Euro (formerly
deutsche mark)
LIFE EXPECTANCY: 80
LITERACY RATE: 99%

GUESS WHAT? *Germany is home to many impressive castles. Neuschwanstein Castle is one of the best known. It was the inspiration for Sleeping Beauty's castle in Disneyland.*

GHANA

LOCATION: Africa
CAPITAL: Accra
AREA: 92,098 sq mi
(238,533 sq km)
POPULATION ESTIMATE (2013):
25,199,609
GOVERNMENT: Constitutional
democracy
LANGUAGES: English (official),
Ashanti, Ewe, Fante, Boron,
Dagomba, Dangme, others
MONEY: Cedi
LIFE EXPECTANCY: 65
LITERACY RATE: 72%

GUESS WHAT? *The word ghana means "warrior king" in the Ashanti language.*

GREECE

LOCATION: Europe
CAPITAL: Athens
AREA: 50,949 sq mi
(131,957 sq km)
POPULATION ESTIMATE (2013):
10,772,967
GOVERNMENT: Parliamentary
republic
LANGUAGE: Greek (official)
MONEY: Euro (formerly drachma)
LIFE EXPECTANCY: 80
LITERACY RATE: 97%

GUESS WHAT? *There are more than 2,000 Greek islands. Fewer than 200 are inhabited.*

GRENADA

LOCATION: Caribbean
CAPITAL: Saint George's
AREA: 133 sq mi (344 sq km)
POPULATION ESTIMATE (2013): 109,590
GOVERNMENT: Parliamentary
democracy
LANGUAGES: English (official),
French patois
MONEY: East Caribbean dollar
LIFE EXPECTANCY: 74
LITERACY RATE: 96%

GUESS WHAT? *Grenada is sometimes referred to as the Spice Island because it is a leading producer of many of the world's spices, especially nutmeg.*

GUATEMALA

LOCATION: Central America
CAPITAL: Guatemala City
AREA: 42,042 sq mi
(108,889 sq km)
POPULATION ESTIMATE (2013):
14,373,472
GOVERNMENT: Constitutional
democratic republic
LANGUAGES: Spanish (official),
Amerindian languages
MONEY: Quetzal
LIFE EXPECTANCY: 71
LITERACY RATE: 76%

GUESS WHAT? *September 15th is a national holiday in Guatemala. Residents celebrate the day, in 1821, when Guatemala became independent from Spain.*

GUINEA

LOCATION: Africa
CAPITAL: Conakry
AREA: 94,926 sq mi
(245,857 sq km)
POPULATION ESTIMATE (2013):
11,176,026
GOVERNMENT: Republic
LANGUAGES: French (official),
native languages
MONEY: Guinean franc
LIFE EXPECTANCY: 59
LITERACY RATE: 41%

GUESS WHAT? *Guinea is one of the wettest places on Earth. Conakry gets about 169 inches (429 cm) of rain per year!*

GUINEA-BISSAU

LOCATION: Africa
CAPITAL: Bissau
AREA: 13,948 sq mi
(36,125 sq km)
POPULATION ESTIMATE (2013):
1,660,870
GOVERNMENT: Republic
LANGUAGES: Portuguese (official),
Crioulo, African languages
MONEY: CFA franc
LIFE EXPECTANCY: 50
LITERACY RATE: 55%

GUESS WHAT? *Many farmers in Guinea-Bissau follow animism, which is the belief that everything—from rocks and hurricanes to animals and humans—has a soul.*

GUYANA

LOCATION: South America
CAPITAL: Georgetown
AREA: 83,000 sq mi
(214,969 sq km)
POPULATION ESTIMATE (2013): 739,903
GOVERNMENT: Republic
LANGUAGES: English (official),
Amerindian dialects, Creole,
Caribbean Hindustani, Urdu
MONEY: Guyanese dollar
LIFE EXPECTANCY: 68
LITERACY RATE: 92%

GUESS WHAT? *The national bird of Guyana is the hoatzin. These birds rarely fly, and babies of the species learn to swim before they fly. The hoatzin eats mostly leaves and has a stomach that is similar to that of a cow or a sheep.*

HAITI

LOCATION: Caribbean
CAPITAL: Port-au-Prince
AREA: 10,714 sq mi
(27,750 sq km)
POPULATION ESTIMATE (2013):
9,893,934
GOVERNMENT: Republic
LANGUAGES: Creole and
French (both official)
MONEY: Gourde
LIFE EXPECTANCY: 63
LITERACY RATE: 49%

GUESS WHAT? *In the late 1700s, Toussaint Louverture led more than half a million slaves in a revolt that resulted in the country declaring its independence from France in 1804.*

HONDURAS

LOCATION: Central America
CAPITAL: Tegucigalpa
AREA: 43,278 sq mi
(112,090 sq km)
POPULATION ESTIMATE (2013):
8,448,465
GOVERNMENT: Democratic
constitutional republic
LANGUAGES: Spanish (official),
Amerindian dialects
MONEY: Lempira
LIFE EXPECTANCY: 71
LITERACY RATE: 85%

GUESS WHAT? *Every year, a "rain of fish" occurs in Honduras. Six-inch (15.2 cm) fish fall from the sky. Scientists are not sure what causes this strange rain.*

HUNGARY

LOCATION: Europe
CAPITAL: Budapest
AREA: 35,918 sq mi
(93,028 sq km)
POPULATION ESTIMATE (2013):
9,939,470
GOVERNMENT: Parliamentary
democracy
LANGUAGES: Hungarian, others
MONEY: Forint
LIFE EXPECTANCY: 75
LITERACY RATE: 99%

GUESS WHAT? *Hungary is mostly made up of flat, fertile land. About two-thirds of the country is used for agriculture.*

ICELAND

LOCATION: Europe
CAPITAL: Reykjavík
AREA: 39,768 sq mi
(103,000 sq km)
POPULATION ESTIMATE (2013):
315,281
GOVERNMENT: Constitutional
republic
LANGUAGES: Icelandic, English,
Nordic languages, German
MONEY: Icelandic krona
LIFE EXPECTANCY: 81
LITERACY RATE: 99%

GUESS WHAT? *Formed from an explosion of an underwater volcano, Surtsey is one of the youngest islands on Earth. It became part of Iceland in 1963.*

INDIA

LOCATION: Asia
CAPITAL: New Delhi
AREA: 1,269,219 sq mi
(3,287,263 sq km)
POPULATION ESTIMATE (2013):
1,220,800,359
GOVERNMENT: Federal republic
LANGUAGES: Hindi, Bengali,
Telugu, Marathi, Tamil, Urdu,
Gujarati, Malayalam, Kannada,
Oriya, Punjabi, Assamese,
Kashmiri, Sindhi, and Sanskrit
(all official), English, others
MONEY: Indian rupee
LIFE EXPECTANCY: 67
LITERACY RATE: 63%

GUESS WHAT? *Indira Gandhi became prime minister of India in 1966. She was one of the first women elected to lead a nation.*

INDONESIA

LOCATION: Asia
CAPITAL: Jakarta
AREA: 735,358 sq mi
(1,904,569 sq km)
POPULATION ESTIMATE (2013):
251,160,124
GOVERNMENT: Republic
LANGUAGES: Bahasa Indonesia
(official), Dutch, English,
many local dialects
MONEY: Rupiah
LIFE EXPECTANCY: 72
LITERACY RATE: 93%

GUESS WHAT? *Indonesia is home to the Komodo dragon, the largest lizard in the world. It is also one of the most deadly animals on Earth.*

IRAN

LOCATION: Middle East
CAPITAL: Tehran
AREA: 636,372 sq mi
(1,648,195 sq km)
POPULATION ESTIMATE (2013):
79,853,900
GOVERNMENT: Theocratic republic
LANGUAGES: Persian (official),
Turkic, Kurdish, others
MONEY: Rial
LIFE EXPECTANCY: 71
LITERACY RATE: 85%

GUESS WHAT? *Nowruz, also known as the Persian New Year, is an Iranian holiday that begins in late March. During Nowruz, family and friends gather, feast, and celebrate the year that has passed and welcome the new one. Children get a two-week vacation from school.*

IRAQ

LOCATION: Middle East
CAPITAL: Baghdad
AREA: 169,235 sq mi
(438,317 sq km)
POPULATION ESTIMATE (2013):
31,858,481
GOVERNMENT: Parliamentary
democracy
LANGUAGES: Arabic and Kurdish
(official), Turkmen, Assyrian
MONEY: Iraqi dinar
LIFE EXPECTANCY: 71
LITERACY RATE: 79%

GUESS WHAT? *Some historians believe the Hanging Gardens of Babylon, one of the seven wonders of the ancient world, were located in present-day Iraq until an earthquake destroyed them.*

IRELAND

LOCATION: Europe
CAPITAL: Dublin
AREA: 27,132 sq mi
(70,273 sq km)
POPULATION ESTIMATE (2013):
4,775,982
GOVERNMENT: Republic,
parliamentary democracy
LANGUAGES: Irish (Gaelic) and
English (both official)
MONEY: Euro (formerly Irish
pound, or punt)
LIFE EXPECTANCY: 80
LITERACY RATE: 99%

GUESS WHAT? *Irish step dance is popular in Ireland. Dancers keep their upper bodies still while performing fast moves with their feet.*

ISRAEL

LOCATION: Middle East
CAPITAL: Jerusalem
AREA: 8,019 sq mi
(20,770 sq km)
POPULATION ESTIMATE (2013):
7,707,042
GOVERNMENT: Parliamentary
democracy
LANGUAGES: Hebrew (official),
Arabic, English
MONEY: New Israeli shekel
LIFE EXPECTANCY: 81
LITERACY RATE: 97%

GUESS WHAT? *The glue on Israeli postage stamps is certified kosher.*

ITALY

LOCATION: Europe
CAPITAL: Rome
AREA: 116,348 sq mi
(301,340 sq km)
POPULATION ESTIMATE (2013):
61,482,297
GOVERNMENT: Republic
LANGUAGES: Italian (official),
German, French, Slovene
MONEY: Euro (formerly lira)
LIFE EXPECTANCY: 82
LITERACY RATE: 99%

GUESS WHAT? *The Leaning Tower of Pisa was built on marshy land, which is why the building does not stand straight. It leans a tiny bit more each year.*

JAMAICA

LOCATION: Caribbean
CAPITAL: Kingston
AREA: 4,244 sq mi
(10,991 sq km)
POPULATION ESTIMATE (2013):
2,909,714
GOVERNMENT: Constitutional parliamentary democracy
LANGUAGES: English, English patois
MONEY: Jamaican dollar
LIFE EXPECTANCY: 73
LITERACY RATE: 87%

GUESS WHAT? *Jerk cooking is popular in Jamaica. Foods prepared in the jerk style are rubbed with spices such as Scotch bonnet peppers, thyme, paprika, and allspice, and then are slow-cooked in deep pits.*

JAPAN

LOCATION: Asia
CAPITAL: Tokyo
AREA: 145,914 sq mi
(377,915 sq km)
POPULATION ESTIMATE (2013):
127,253,075
GOVERNMENT: Parliamentary government with a constitutional monarchy
LANGUAGE: Japanese
MONEY: Yen
LIFE EXPECTANCY: 84
LITERACY RATE: 99%

GUESS WHAT? *Japan is an archipelago made up of more than 3,000 islands.*

JORDAN

LOCATION: Middle East
CAPITAL: Amman
AREA: 34,495 sq mi
(89,342 sq km)
POPULATION ESTIMATE (2013):
6,482,081
GOVERNMENT: Constitutional monarchy
LANGUAGES: Arabic (official),
English
MONEY: Jordanian dinar
LIFE EXPECTANCY: 80
LITERACY RATE: 96%

GUESS WHAT? *A white antelope called the Arabian oryx, native to Jordan, was declared extinct in the wild in 1972. Thanks to breeding programs, there are now more than 1,000 of these animals in the wild in the Middle East.*

KAZAKHSTAN

LOCATION: Asia
CAPITAL: Astana
AREA: 1,052,090 sq mi
(2,724,900 sq km)
POPULATION ESTIMATE (2013):
17,736,896
GOVERNMENT: Republic with authoritarian presidential rule
LANGUAGES: Russian (official),
Kazakh
MONEY: Tenge
LIFE EXPECTANCY: 70
LITERACY RATE: 100%

GUESS WHAT? *New research suggests the Botai people who settled in Kazakhstan around 6,000 years ago were the first people to domesticate horses.*

KENYA

LOCATION: Africa
CAPITAL: Nairobi
AREA: 224,081 sq mi
(580,367 sq km)
POPULATION ESTIMATE (2013):
44,037,656
GOVERNMENT: Republic
LANGUAGES: English and Kiswahili (both official), others
MONEY: Kenyan shilling
LIFE EXPECTANCY: 63
LITERACY RATE: 87%

GUESS WHAT? *After a long struggle against the British, Kenya became independent in 1963. The country's first president was Jomo Kenyatta, a leader in the independence movement.*

COUNTRIES

KIRIBATI

LOCATION: Oceania
CAPITAL: Tarawa
AREA: 313 sq mi (811 sq km)
POPULATION ESTIMATE (2013): 103,248
GOVERNMENT: Republic
LANGUAGES: English (official), I-Kiribati (Gilbertese)
MONEY: Australian dollar
LIFE EXPECTANCY: 65
LITERACY RATE: Not available

GUESS WHAT? *The islands of Kiribati sit very close to sea level. As climate change makes the world warmer, sea levels will rise, putting the country in danger of being submerged.*

KOREA, NORTH

LOCATION: Asia
CAPITAL: Pyongyang
AREA: 46,540 sq mi (120,538 sq km)
POPULATION ESTIMATE (2013): 24,720,407
GOVERNMENT: Communist state and one-man dictatorship
LANGUAGE: Korean
MONEY: North Korean won
LIFE EXPECTANCY: 70
LITERACY RATE: 100%

GUESS WHAT? *Even in North Korea's capital city, Pyongyang, there are many power shortages. When the traffic lights go out, the government has female police officers direct traffic.*

KOREA, SOUTH

LOCATION: Asia
CAPITAL: Seoul
AREA: 38,541 sq mi (99,720 sq km)
POPULATION ESTIMATE (2013): 48,955,203
GOVERNMENT: Republic
LANGUAGES: Korean, English
MONEY: South Korean won
LIFE EXPECTANCY: 80
LITERACY RATE: 98%

GUESS WHAT? *Currently, the only way to get in or out of South Korea is by boat or plane because the country's only land border, with North Korea, is closed to travelers.*

KOSOVO

LOCATION: Europe
CAPITAL: Pristina
AREA: 4,203 sq mi (10,887 sq km)
POPULATION ESTIMATE (2013): 1,847,708
GOVERNMENT: Republic
LANGUAGES: Albanian and Serbian (both official), Bosnian, Turkish, Roma
MONEY: Euro (formerly deutsche mark)
LIFE EXPECTANCY: Not available
LITERACY RATE: 92%

GUESS WHAT? *Kosovo means "field of blackbirds."*

KUWAIT

LOCATION: Middle East
CAPITAL: Kuwait City
AREA: 6,880 sq mi (17,818 sq km)
POPULATION ESTIMATE (2013): 2,695,316
GOVERNMENT: Constitutional emirate
LANGUAGES: Arabic (official), English
MONEY: Kuwaiti dinar
LIFE EXPECTANCY: 77
LITERACY RATE: 94%

GUESS WHAT? *On average, there are only about eight rainy days a year in Kuwait.*

KYRGYZSTAN

LOCATION: Asia
CAPITAL: Bishkek
AREA: 77,202 sq mi (199,951 sq km)
POPULATION ESTIMATE (2013): 5,548,042
GOVERNMENT: Republic
LANGUAGES: Kyrgyz and Russian (both official), Uzbek, others
MONEY: Som
LIFE EXPECTANCY: 70
LITERACY RATE: 99%

GUESS WHAT? *Making shyrdaks, or colorful felt carpets, is a popular craft among the nomadic people of Kyrgyzstan.*

LAOS

LOCATION: Asia
CAPITAL: Vientiane
AREA: 91,429 sq mi
(236,800 sq km)
POPULATION ESTIMATE (2013):
6,695,166
GOVERNMENT: Communist state
LANGUAGES: Lao (official), French,
English, others
MONEY: Kip
LIFE EXPECTANCY: 63
LITERACY RATE: 73%

GUESS WHAT? *The red panda, which is more closely related to the raccoon to the than giant panda, lives in the forests of Laos.*

LATVIA

LOCATION: Europe
CAPITAL: Riga
AREA: 24,938 sq mi
(64,589 sq km)
POPULATION ESTIMATE (2013):
2,178,443
GOVERNMENT: Parliamentary
democracy
LANGUAGES: Latvian (official),
Russian, Lithuanian, others
MONEY: Euro (formerly lats)
LIFE EXPECTANCY: 73
LITERACY RATE: 100%

GUESS WHAT? *According to legend, the first decorated evergreen tree to be used in a Christmas celebration was in Riga, Latvia, in 1510.*

LEBANON

LOCATION: Middle East
CAPITAL: Beirut
AREA: 4,015 sq mi
(10,400 sq km)
POPULATION ESTIMATE (2013):
4,131,583
GOVERNMENT: Republic
LANGUAGES: Arabic (official),
French, English, Armenian
MONEY: Lebanese pound
LIFE EXPECTANCY: 75
LITERACY RATE: 90%

GUESS WHAT? *Unlike many of its neighboring countries in the Middle East, Lebanon has no deserts.*

LESOTHO

LOCATION: Africa
CAPITAL: Maseru
AREA: 11,720 sq mi
(30,355 sq km)
POPULATION ESTIMATE (2013):
1,936,181
GOVERNMENT: Parliamentary
constitutional monarchy
LANGUAGES: English and Sesotho
(official), Zulu, Xhosa
MONEY: Loti
LIFE EXPECTANCY: 52
LITERACY RATE: 90%

GUESS WHAT? *Lesotho lies entirely above an altitude of 3,281 feet (1,000 m), which is why it is nicknamed the Kingdom in the Sky.*

LIBERIA

LOCATION: Africa
CAPITAL: Monrovia
AREA: 43,000 sq mi
(111,369 sq km)
POPULATION ESTIMATE (2013):
3,989,703
GOVERNMENT: Republic
LANGUAGES: English (official),
ethnic dialects
MONEY: Liberian dollar
LIFE EXPECTANCY: 58
LITERACY RATE: 61%

GUESS WHAT? *Liberia is home to the largest population of endangered pygmy hippos in the world.*

LIBYA

LOCATION: Africa
CAPITAL: Tripoli
AREA: 679,358 sq mi
(1,759,540 sq km)
POPULATION ESTIMATE (2013):
6,002,347
GOVERNMENT: Transitional
LANGUAGES: Arabic (official),
Italian, English, Berber
MONEY: Libyan dinar
LIFE EXPECTANCY: 76
LITERACY RATE: 90%

GUESS WHAT? *To supply its people with water, Libya has built the Great Man-Made River, a huge system of pipes that draw water from beneath the Sahara desert.*

COUNTRIES

LIECHTENSTEIN

LOCATION: Europe
CAPITAL: Vaduz
AREA: 62 sq mi (160 sq km)
POPULATION ESTIMATE (2013): 37,009
GOVERNMENT: Constitutional monarchy
LANGUAGES: German (official), Alemannic dialect
MONEY: Swiss franc
LIFE EXPECTANCY: 82
LITERACY RATE: 100%

GUESS WHAT? *Liechtenstein is one of the two doubly landlocked countries in the world. (Uzbekistan is the other.) It is bordered only by countries that are also landlocked, meaning that they do not have direct access to an ocean or sea.*

LITHUANIA

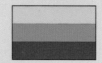

LOCATION: Europe
CAPITAL: Vilnius
AREA: 25,212 sq mi (65,300 sq km)
POPULATION ESTIMATE (2013): 3,515,858
GOVERNMENT: Parliamentary democracy
LANGUAGES: Lithuanian (official), Russian, Polish, others
MONEY: Litas
LIFE EXPECTANCY: 76
LITERACY RATE: 100%

GUESS WHAT? *The white stork is the national bird of Lithuania.*

LUXEMBOURG

LOCATION: Europe
CAPITAL: Luxembourg
AREA: 998 sq mi (2,586 sq km)
POPULATION ESTIMATE (2013): 514,862
GOVERNMENT: Constitutional monarchy
LANGUAGES: Luxembourgish, German, and French (all official)
MONEY: Euro (formerly Luxembourg franc)
LIFE EXPECTANCY: 80
LITERACY RATE: 100%

GUESS WHAT? *The University of Luxembourg and Sacred Heart University Luxembourg are the only universities in Luxembourg.*

MACEDONIA

LOCATION: Europe
CAPITAL: Skopje
AREA: 9,928 sq mi (25,713 sq km)
POPULATION ESTIMATE (2013): 2,087,171
GOVERNMENT: Parliamentary democracy
LANGUAGES: Macedonian and Albanian (both official), Turkish, others
MONEY: Macedonian denar
LIFE EXPECTANCY: 76
LITERACY RATE: 97%

GUESS WHAT? *The town of Kuklica, in northeast Macedonia, is home to 120 natural stone pillars. Some people think these rock formations look like humans.*

MADAGASCAR

LOCATION: Africa
CAPITAL: Antananarivo
AREA: 226,658 sq mi (587,041 sq km)
POPULATION ESTIMATE (2013): 22,599,098
GOVERNMENT: Republic
LANGUAGES: French and Malagasy (both official), English
MONEY: Malagasy ariary
LIFE EXPECTANCY: 65
LITERACY RATE: 65%

GUESS WHAT? *About 80% of the plants and animals found in Madagascar are endemic, meaning they don't exist naturally anywhere else. This includes the fossa, a catlike predator featured in the movie Madagascar.*

MALAWI

LOCATION: Africa
CAPITAL: Lilongwe
AREA: 45,747 sq mi (118,484 sq km)
POPULATION ESTIMATE (2013): 16,777,547
GOVERNMENT: Multiparty democracy
LANGUAGES: English (official), Chichewa, Chinyanja, Chiyao, Chitumbuka, others
MONEY: Kwacha
LIFE EXPECTANCY: 53
LITERACY RATE: 75%

GUESS WHAT? *Joyce Banda became Malawi's first female president, in 2012. She is the second woman to lead a country in Africa.*

MALAYSIA

LOCATION: Asia
CAPITAL: Kuala Lumpur
AREA: 127,355 sq mi
(329,847 sq km)
POPULATION ESTIMATE (2013):
29,628,392
GOVERNMENT: Constitutional
monarchy
LANGUAGES: Bahasa Malay
(official), English, Chinese,
Tamil, others
MONEY: Ringgit
LIFE EXPECTANCY: 74
LITERACY RATE: 93%

GUESS WHAT? *At 1,483 feet (452 m) high, the Petronas Towers are two of the world's tallest buildings. The pair of towers in Kuala Lumpur are connected by a walkway 558 feet (170 m) above the ground.*

MALDIVES

LOCATION: Asia
CAPITAL: Male
AREA: 115 sq mi (298 sq km)
POPULATION ESTIMATE (2013): 393,988
GOVERNMENT: Republic
LANGUAGES: Dhivehi (official),
English
MONEY: Rufiyaa
LIFE EXPECTANCY: 75
LITERACY RATE: 98%

GUESS WHAT? *About 80% of the Maldives sits less than 3.2 feet (1 m) above sea level.*

MALI

LOCATION: Africa
CAPITAL: Bamako
AREA: 478,841 sq mi
(1,240,192 sq km)
POPULATION ESTIMATE (2013):
15,968,882
GOVERNMENT: Republic
LANGUAGES: French (official),
Bambara, African
languages
MONEY: CFA franc
LIFE EXPECTANCY: 55
LITERACY RATE: 33%

GUESS WHAT? *The Dogon people, who live in central Mali, are known for their mythology. They re-create their myths by performing elaborate mask dances at funerals and special festivals.*

MALTA

LOCATION: Europe
CAPITAL: Valletta
AREA: 122 sq mi (316 sq km)
POPULATION ESTIMATE (2013): 411,277
GOVERNMENT: Republic
LANGUAGES: Maltese and English
(both official), others
MONEY: Euro (formerly
Maltese lira)
LIFE EXPECTANCY: 80
LITERACY RATE: 92%

GUESS WHAT? *On a child's first birthday, it is traditional for parents to play a game called il-quccija, in which a variety of objects—for example, a Bible, pen, wooden spoon, calculator, and coin—are placed in front of the child. Whichever object the child plays with is said to represent the path he or she will pursue in life.*

MARSHALL ISLANDS

LOCATION: Oceania
CAPITAL: Majuro
AREA: 70 sq mi (181 sq km)
POPULATION ESTIMATE (2013): 69,747
GOVERNMENT: Constitutional
government
LANGUAGES: Marshallese and
English (both official), others
MONEY: U.S. dollar
LIFE EXPECTANCY: 72
LITERACY RATE: 94%

GUESS WHAT? *Enewetak, a chain of coral islands in the Marshall Islands, is where the United States exploded the first hydrogen bomb, in 1952.*

MAURITANIA

LOCATION: Africa
CAPITAL: Nouakchott
AREA: 397,953 sq mi
(1,030,700 sq km)
POPULATION ESTIMATE (2013):
3,437,610
GOVERNMENT: Military junta
LANGUAGES: Arabic (official),
French, Pulaar, Soninke, others
MONEY: Ouguiya
LIFE EXPECTANCY: 62
LITERACY RATE: 59%

GUESS WHAT? *In 1981, Mauritania became one of the last countries in the world to abolish slavery.*

COUNTRIES

MAURITIUS

LOCATION: Africa
CAPITAL: Port Louis
AREA: 788 sq mi (2,040 sq km)
POPULATION ESTIMATE (2013):
1,322,238
GOVERNMENT: Parliamentary
democracy
LANGUAGES: English (official),
Creole, Bhojpuri, French,
others
MONEY: Mauritian rupee
LIFE EXPECTANCY: 75
LITERACY RATE: 89%

GUESS WHAT? *One interesting site in this island nation is known as La Roche Qui Pleure, or the Crying Rock. Strong ocean waves crashing into a cliff have carved out a shape that looks like a crying man's face.*

MEXICO

LOCATION: North America
CAPITAL: Mexico City
AREA: 758,449 sq mi
(1,964,375 sq km)
POPULATION ESTIMATE (2013):
118,818,228
GOVERNMENT: Federal republic
LANGUAGES: Spanish, native
languages
MONEY: Peso
LIFE EXPECTANCY: 77
LITERACY RATE: 94%

GUESS WHAT? *Mexico's Oaxaca (wah-hah-kah) region has preserved much of its culture from before the country was ruled by the Spanish. Two groups native to Mexico, the Mixtec and Zapotec people, still live in the area.*

MICRONESIA, FEDERATED STATES OF

LOCATION: Oceania
CAPITAL: Palikir
AREA: 271 sq mi (702 sq km)
POPULATION ESTIMATE (2013): 106,104
GOVERNMENT: Constitutional
government
LANGUAGES: English (official),
Chuukese, Kosraean,
Pohnpeian, Yapese,
Ulithian, others
MONEY: U.S. dollar
LIFE EXPECTANCY: 72
LITERACY RATE: 89%

GUESS WHAT? *Yap, one of Micronesia's four islands, is famous for using stones as money. These large, carved stones, called rai, look like wheels.*

MOLDOVA

LOCATION: Europe
CAPITAL: Chisinau
AREA: 13,070 sq mi
(33,851 sq km)
POPULATION ESTIMATE (2013):
3,619,925
GOVERNMENT: Republic
LANGUAGES: Moldovan (official),
Russian, Gagauz
MONEY: Leu
LIFE EXPECTANCY: 70
LITERACY RATE: 99%

GUESS WHAT? *Two of Moldova's most important crops are grapes and sunflower seeds.*

MONACO

LOCATION: Europe
CAPITAL: Monaco
AREA: 0.77 sq mi (2 sq km)
POPULATION ESTIMATE (2013): 30,500
GOVERNMENT: Constitutional
monarchy
LANGUAGES: French (official),
English, Italian, Monégasque
MONEY: Euro (formerly French
franc)
LIFE EXPECTANCY: 90
LITERACY RATE: 99%

GUESS WHAT? *The average person could walk across Monaco in about 56 minutes.*

MONGOLIA

LOCATION: Asia
CAPITAL: Ulaanbaatar
AREA: 603,909 sq mi
(1,564,116 sq km)
POPULATION ESTIMATE (2013):
2,912,192
GOVERNMENT: Parliamentary
LANGUAGES: Khalkha Mongol
(official), Turkic, Russian
MONEY: Togrog/tugrik
LIFE EXPECTANCY: 69
LITERACY RATE: 97%

GUESS WHAT? *Mongolia is sometimes called the Land of Blue Sky because it is sunny there nearly all year.*

MONTENEGRO

LOCATION: Europe
CAPITAL: Podgorica
AREA: 5,333 sq mi
(13,812 sq km)
POPULATION ESTIMATE (2013): 653,474
GOVERNMENT: Republic
LANGUAGES: Montenegrin
(official), Serbian, Bosnian,
Albanian, others
MONEY: Euro (formerly
deutsche mark)
LIFE EXPECTANCY: Not available
LITERACY RATE: 99%

GUESS WHAT? *The traditional folk dance of Montenegro is the* oro. *Dancers stand in a circle singing, while others dance in the center. Often it will end with young men in the circle standing on each other's shoulders.*

MOROCCO

LOCATION: Africa
CAPITAL: Rabat
AREA: 172,413 sq mi
(446,550 sq km)
POPULATION ESTIMATE (2013):
32,649,130
GOVERNMENT: Constitutional
monarchy
LANGUAGES: Arabic (official),
French, Berber dialects
MONEY: Dirham
LIFE EXPECTANCY: 76
LITERACY RATE: 67%

GUESS WHAT? *Morocco grows more peppermint than any other nation.*

MOZAMBIQUE

LOCATION: Africa
CAPITAL: Maputo
AREA: 308,642 sq mi
(799,380 sq km)
POPULATION ESTIMATE (2013):
24,096,669
GOVERNMENT: Republic
LANGUAGES: Portuguese
(official), Emakhuwa,
Xichangana, others
MONEY: Metical
LIFE EXPECTANCY: 52
LITERACY RATE: 56%

GUESS WHAT? *Mozambique became independent from Portugal in 1975. A civil war broke out two years later and lasted until 1992.*

MYANMAR (BURMA)

LOCATION: Asia
CAPITAL: Nay Pyi Taw
AREA: 261,228 sq mi
(676,578 sq km)
POPULATION ESTIMATE (2013):
55,167,330
GOVERNMENT: Parliamentary
government
LANGUAGES: Burmese (official),
minority languages
MONEY: Kyat
LIFE EXPECTANCY: 66
LITERACY RATE: 93%

GUESS WHAT? *In the ancient city of Bagan, many magnificent temples and monuments are still standing.*

NAMIBIA

LOCATION: Africa
CAPITAL: Windhoek
AREA: 318,261 sq mi
(824,292 sq km)
POPULATION ESTIMATE (2013):
2,182,852
GOVERNMENT: Republic
LANGUAGES: English (official),
Afrikaans, German, native
languages
MONEY: Namibian dollar
LIFE EXPECTANCY: 52
LITERACY RATE: 89%

GUESS WHAT? *Hoba, discovered in Namibia in the 1920s, is the largest known meteorite in the world. It is approximately 80,000 years old and weighs more than 50 tons (45 metric tons).*

NAURU

LOCATION: Oceania
CAPITAL: Yaren District
(unofficial)
AREA: 8.11 sq mi (21 sq km)
POPULATION ESTIMATE (2013):
9,434
GOVERNMENT: Republic
LANGUAGES: Nauruan (official),
English
MONEY: Australian dollar
LIFE EXPECTANCY: 66
LITERACY RATE: Not available

GUESS WHAT? *Every year, the Nauruans celebrate Angam Day, which commemorates the day in 1932 that their population reached 1,500, following a terrible flu epidemic in the 1920s.*

COUNTRIES

NEPAL

LOCATION: Asia
CAPITAL: Kathmandu
AREA: 56,827 sq mi
(147,181 sq km)
POPULATION ESTIMATE (2013):
30,430,267
GOVERNMENT: Federal democratic
republic
LANGUAGES: Nepali (official),
Maithali, Bhojpuri, Tharu,
Tamang, others
MONEY: Nepalese rupee
LIFE EXPECTANCY: 67
LITERACY RATE: 57%

GUESS WHAT? *Only about 40% of the people in Nepal have access to dependable electric power.*

NETHERLANDS

LOCATION: Europe
CAPITAL: Amsterdam
AREA: 16,040 sq mi
(41,543 sq km)
POPULATION ESTIMATE (2013):
16,805,037
GOVERNMENT: Constitutional
monarchy
LANGUAGES: Dutch and Frisian
(both official)
MONEY: Euro (formerly guilder)
LIFE EXPECTANCY: 81
LITERACY RATE: 99%

GUESS WHAT? *Almost every person in the Netherlands owns a bicycle. There are two times as many bicycles as cars in the country.*

NEW ZEALAND

LOCATION: Oceania
CAPITAL: Wellington
AREA: 103,363 sq mi
(267,710 sq km)
POPULATION ESTIMATE (2013):
4,365,113
GOVERNMENT: Parliamentary
democracy
LANGUAGES: English, Maori, and
sign language (all official),
others
MONEY: New Zealand dollar
LIFE EXPECTANCY: 81
LITERACY RATE: 99%

GUESS WHAT? *Sheep outnumber people in New Zealand, five to one.*

NICARAGUA

LOCATION: Central America
CAPITAL: Managua
AREA: 50,336 sq mi
(130,370 sq km)
POPULATION ESTIMATE (2013):
5,788,531
GOVERNMENT: Republic
LANGUAGE: Spanish (official)
MONEY: Córdoba
LIFE EXPECTANCY: 72
LITERACY RATE: 78%

GUESS WHAT? *Lake Nicaragua is the only freshwater lake in the world that is home to oceanic sharks.*

NIGER

LOCATION: Africa
CAPITAL: Niamey
AREA: 489,189 sq mi
(1,267,000 sq km)
POPULATION ESTIMATE (2013):
16,899,327
GOVERNMENT: Republic
LANGUAGES: French (official),
Hausa, Djerma
MONEY: CFA franc
LIFE EXPECTANCY: 54
LITERACY RATE: 29%

GUESS WHAT? *Niger's nickname is the Frying Pan of the World because temperatures range from 85°F (24°C) to 105°F (40°C) year-round.*

NIGERIA

LOCATION: Africa
CAPITAL: Abuja
AREA: 356,667 sq mi
(923,768 sq km)
POPULATION ESTIMATE (2013):
174,507,539
GOVERNMENT: Federal republic
LANGUAGES: English (official),
Hausa, Yoruba, Igbo, Fulani,
and more than 500 other
native languages
MONEY: Naira
LIFE EXPECTANCY: 52
LITERACY RATE: 61%

GUESS WHAT? *A 2009 United Nations report said Nigeria's film industry (known as Nollywood) made more films than the United States did. Nigeria became the second-largest movie-producing country. Only India made more films.*

NORWAY

LOCATION: Europe
CAPITAL: Oslo
AREA: 125,021 sq mi
(323,802 sq km)
POPULATION ESTIMATE (2013):
5,085,582
GOVERNMENT: Constitutional
monarchy
LANGUAGES: Two official forms
of Norwegian: Bokmal and
Nynorsk
MONEY: Krone
LIFE EXPECTANCY: 80
LITERACY RATE: 100%

GUESS WHAT? *During the summer in northern Norway, the sun shines all day and all night.*

OMAN

LOCATION: Middle East
CAPITAL: Muscat
AREA: 119,499 sq mi
(309,500 sq km)
POPULATION ESTIMATE (2013):
3,154,134
GOVERNMENT: Monarchy
LANGUAGES: Arabic (official),
English, Baluchi, Urdu,
Indian dialects
MONEY: Omani rial
LIFE EXPECTANCY: 74
LITERACY RATE: 87%

GUESS WHAT? *Oman was mostly closed to tourists until the 1980s.*

PAKISTAN

LOCATION: Asia
CAPITAL: Islamabad
AREA: 307,374 sq mi
(790,095 sq km)
POPULATION ESTIMATE (2013):
193,238,868
GOVERNMENT: Federal
republic
LANGUAGES: Urdu and English
(official), Punjabi, Sindhi,
Siraiki, Pashto, others
MONEY: Pakistani rupee
LIFE EXPECTANCY: 67
LITERACY RATE: 55%

GUESS WHAT? *The Khyber Pass is a famous mountain pass between Pakistan and Afghanistan. It cuts through the Hindu Kush mountain range. The Khyber Pass has been a major trade route for centuries.*

PALAU

LOCATION: Oceania
CAPITAL: Melekeok
AREA: 177 sq mi (459 sq km)
POPULATION ESTIMATE (2013): 21,108
GOVERNMENT: Constitutional
government
LANGUAGES: Palauan (official on
most islands), English (official),
Filipino, Chinese, others
MONEY: U.S. dollar
LIFE EXPECTANCY: 72
LITERACY RATE: 92%

GUESS WHAT? *Jellyfish Lake, located on the rocky island Eil Malk, is home to millions of golden jellyfish. These jellyfish, which do not sting, travel from one side of the lake to the other every day in order to get sunlight. They need lots of sunlight to survive.*

PANAMA

LOCATION: Central America
CAPITAL: Panama City
AREA: 29,120 sq mi
(75,420 sq km)
POPULATION ESTIMATE (2013):
3,559,408
GOVERNMENT: Constitutional
democracy
LANGUAGES: Spanish (official),
English
MONEY: Balboa, U.S. dollar
LIFE EXPECTANCY: 78
LITERACY RATE: 94%

GUESS WHAT? *If you climb to the top of Panama's Barú volcano, you can see both the Pacific Ocean and the Atlantic Ocean.*

PAPUA NEW GUINEA

LOCATION: Oceania
CAPITAL: Port Moresby
AREA: 178,703 sq mi
(462,840 sq km)
POPULATION ESTIMATE (2013):
6,431,902
GOVERNMENT: Constitutional
parliamentary democracy
LANGUAGES: Tok Pisin, English,
and Hiri Motu (all official),
about 860 native languages
MONEY: Kina
LIFE EXPECTANCY: 67
LITERACY RATE: 62%

GUESS WHAT? *More languages are spoken in Papua New Guinea than anywhere else.*

COUNTRIES

PARAGUAY

LOCATION: South America
CAPITAL: Asunción
AREA: 157,047 sq mi
(406,752 sq km)
POPULATION ESTIMATE (2013):
6,623,252
GOVERNMENT: Constitutional
republic
LANGUAGES: Spanish and Guaraní
(both official)
MONEY: Guaraní
LIFE EXPECTANCY: 77
LITERACY RATE: 94%

GUESS WHAT? *The Itaipú dam on the Paraná River is one of the largest hydroelectric power plants in the world. It generates power for Paraguay and Brazil.*

PERU

LOCATION: South America
CAPITAL: Lima
AREA: 496,225 sq mi
(1,285,216 sq km)
POPULATION ESTIMATE (2013):
29,849,303
GOVERNMENT: Constitutional
republic
LANGUAGES: Spanish and
Quechua (both official),
Aymara, others
MONEY: Nuevo sol
LIFE EXPECTANCY: 73
LITERACY RATE: 90%

GUESS WHAT? *Chan Chan is a huge mud city built between 850 and 1200 A.D. in northwestern Peru.*

PHILIPPINES

LOCATION: Asia
CAPITAL: Manila
AREA: 115,830 sq mi
(300,000 sq km)
POPULATION ESTIMATE (2013):
105,720,644
GOVERNMENT: Republic
LANGUAGES: Filipino (based on
Tagalog) and English (both
official), regional languages
MONEY: Philippine peso
LIFE EXPECTANCY: 72
LITERACY RATE: 95%

GUESS WHAT? *The endangered tamaraw, a buffalo, is found only on the island of Mindoro, in the Philippines.*

POLAND

LOCATION: Europe
CAPITAL: Warsaw
AREA: 120,728 sq mi
(312,685 sq km)
POPULATION ESTIMATE (2013):
38,383,809
GOVERNMENT: Republic
LANGUAGE: Polish (official)
MONEY: Zloty
LIFE EXPECTANCY: 76
LITERACY RATE: 100%

GUESS WHAT? *Scientist Marie Curie was born in Warsaw on November 7, 1867. She won two Nobel Prizes—one for physics (1903) and one for chemistry (1911).*

PORTUGAL

LOCATION: Europe
CAPITAL: Lisbon
AREA: 35,556 sq mi
(92,090 sq km)
POPULATION ESTIMATE (2013):
10,799,270
GOVERNMENT: Republic;
parliamentary democracy
LANGUAGES: Portuguese and
Mirandese (both official)
MONEY: Euro (formerly escudo)
LIFE EXPECTANCY: 79
LITERACY RATE: 95%

GUESS WHAT? *At 10.7 miles (17.2 km) long, the Vasco da Gama Bridge over the Tagus River, in Lisbon, is the longest bridge in Europe.*

QATAR

LOCATION: Middle East
CAPITAL: Doha
AREA: 4,473 sq mi (11,586 sq km)
POPULATION ESTIMATE (2013):
2,042,444
GOVERNMENT: Traditional
monarchy (emirate)
LANGUAGES: Arabic (official),
English
MONEY: Qatari riyal
LIFE EXPECTANCY: 78
LITERACY RATE: 96%

GUESS WHAT? *Based on averages from 1978 to 2012, the hottest day of the year in Qatar is July 6, with an average high temperature of 106°F (41°C) and an average low of 87°F (31°C). The coldest day is January 22, with an average low of 57°F (14°C) and an average high of 70°F (21°C).*

ROMANIA

LOCATION: Europe
CAPITAL: Bucharest
AREA: 92,043 sq mi
(238,391 sq km)
POPULATION ESTIMATE (2013):
21,790,479
GOVERNMENT: Republic
LANGUAGES: Romanian (official),
Hungarian, Romany
MONEY: Leu
LIFE EXPECTANCY: 74
LITERACY RATE: 98%

GUESS WHAT? *Bram Stoker based his novel Dracula on Vlad Tepes, a cruel 15th century Wallachian prince. Wallachia merged with Moldavia in 1859 and became Romania in 1862.*

RUSSIA

LOCATION: Europe and Asia
CAPITAL: Moscow
AREA: 6,601,668 sq mi
(17,098,242 sq km)
POPULATION ESTIMATE (2013):
142,500,482
GOVERNMENT: Federation
LANGUAGES: Russian (official),
many minority languages
MONEY: Ruble
LIFE EXPECTANCY: 70
LITERACY RATE: 100%

GUESS WHAT? *Russia is the largest country in the world. It covers one-eighth of the total land on Earth.*

RWANDA

LOCATION: Africa
CAPITAL: Kigali
AREA: 10,169 sq mi
(26,338 sq km)
POPULATION ESTIMATE (2013):
12,012,589
GOVERNMENT: Republic
LANGUAGES: Kinyarwanda,
French, and English
(all official), Kiswahili
MONEY: Rwandan franc
LIFE EXPECTANCY: 59
LITERACY RATE: 71%

GUESS WHAT? *Rwanda is Africa's most densely populated country.*

SAINT KITTS AND NEVIS

LOCATION: Caribbean
CAPITAL: Basseterre
AREA: 101 sq mi (261 sq km)
POPULATION ESTIMATE (2013): 51,134
GOVERNMENT: Parliamentary
democracy
LANGUAGE: English (official)
MONEY: East Caribbean dollar
LIFE EXPECTANCY: 75
LITERACY RATE: 98%

GUESS WHAT? *Both the islands of Saint Kitts and Nevis, separated by only a 1.9-mile (3.1 km) stretch of water, are home to large volcanoes. However, only Mount Nevis, located on Nevis, may still be active.*

SAINT LUCIA

LOCATION: Caribbean
CAPITAL: Castries
AREA: 238 sq mi (616 sq km)
POPULATION ESTIMATE (2013): 162,781
GOVERNMENT: Parliamentary
democracy
LANGUAGES: English (official),
French patois
MONEY: East Caribbean dollar
LIFE EXPECTANCY: 77
LITERACY RATE: 90%

GUESS WHAT? *The national tree of Saint Lucia is the calabash tree. The gooey insides of the calabash fruit are used for making medicine. The outer shells of the fruit are used as bowls, lanterns, and containers.*

SAINT VINCENT AND THE GRENADINES

LOCATION: Caribbean
CAPITAL: Kingstown
AREA: 150 sq mi
(389 sq km)
POPULATION ESTIMATE (2013):
103,220
GOVERNMENT: Parliamentary
democracy
LANGUAGES: English, French patois
MONEY: East Caribbean dollar
LIFE EXPECTANCY: 75
LITERACY RATE: 96%

GUESS WHAT? *Saint Vincent and the Grenadines is made up of 32 islands and cays (small, low-lying sandy islands).*

COUNTRIES

SAMOA

LOCATION: Oceania
CAPITAL: Apia
AREA: 1,093 sq mi (2,831 sq km)
POPULATION ESTIMATE (2013): 195,476
GOVERNMENT: Parliamentary democracy
LANGUAGES: Samoan (official), English
MONEY: Tala
LIFE EXPECTANCY: 73
LITERACY RATE: 99%

GUESS WHAT? *Tattooing is important in Samoan culture. Traditional tattoos, or pe'a, cover men's bodies from their mid-back to their knees. The patterns of women's tattoos, known as malu, are lighter and use less ink than the patterns of the men's tattoos.*

SAN MARINO

LOCATION: Europe
CAPITAL: San Marino
AREA: 24 sq mi (61 sq km)
POPULATION ESTIMATE (2013): 32,448
GOVERNMENT: Republic
LANGUAGE: Italian
MONEY: Euro (formerly Italian lira)
LIFE EXPECTANCY: 83
LITERACY RATE: 96%

GUESS WHAT? *San Marino, founded around 301 A.D., is the world's oldest republic.*

SAO TOME AND PRINCIPE

LOCATION: Africa
CAPITAL: São Tomé
AREA: 372 sq mi (964 sq km)
POPULATION ESTIMATE (2013): 186,817
GOVERNMENT: Republic
LANGUAGE: Portuguese (official)
MONEY: Dobra
LIFE EXPECTANCY: 64
LITERACY RATE: 70%

GUESS WHAT? *During the late 1400s, Portugal settled groups of former prisoners on São Tomé and Príncipe.*

SAUDI ARABIA

LOCATION: Middle East
CAPITAL: Riyadh
AREA: 830,000 sq mi (2,149,690 sq km)
POPULATION ESTIMATE (2013): 26,939,583
GOVERNMENT: Monarchy
LANGUAGE: Arabic
MONEY: Saudi riyal
LIFE EXPECTANCY: 75
LITERACY RATE: 87%

GUESS WHAT? *Mecca and Medina are the two holiest sites in the Islamic religion. Both places are in Saudi Arabia.*

SENEGAL

LOCATION: Africa
CAPITAL: Dakar
AREA: 75,955 sq mi (196,722 sq km)
POPULATION ESTIMATE (2013): 13,300,410
GOVERNMENT: Republic
LANGUAGES: French (official), Wolof, Pulaar, Jola, Mandinka
MONEY: CFA franc
LIFE EXPECTANCY: 61
LITERACY RATE: 50%

GUESS WHAT? *Lake Retba, just outside Dakar, is pink! The water is incredibly salty, and there are salt-loving algae in the lake that make the water pink.*

SERBIA

LOCATION: Europe
CAPITAL: Belgrade
AREA: 29,913 sq mi (77,474 sq km)
POPULATION ESTIMATE (2013): 7,243,007
GOVERNMENT: Republic
LANGUAGES: Serbian (official), Hungarian, others
MONEY: Serbian dinar
LIFE EXPECTANCY: 75
LITERACY RATE: 98%

GUESS WHAT? *Serbia is one of the biggest exporters of raspberries in the world. About one-third of the world's raspberries come from this small, landlocked nation.*

SEYCHELLES

LOCATION: Africa
CAPITAL: Victoria
AREA: 176 sq mi (455 sq km)
POPULATION ESTIMATE (2013): 90,846
GOVERNMENT: Republic
LANGUAGES: English (official), Creole, other
MONEY: Seychelles rupee
LIFE EXPECTANCY: 74
LITERACY RATE: 92%

GUESS WHAT? *Many believe the lost treasure of pirate Olivier Levasseur, thought to be worth around $160 million, still lies buried on the island of Mahé, which is part of the Seychelles.*

SIERRA LEONE

LOCATION: Africa
CAPITAL: Freetown
AREA: 27,699 sq mi (71,740 sq km)
POPULATION ESTIMATE (2013): 5,612,685
GOVERNMENT: Constitutional democracy
LANGUAGES: English (official), Mende, Temne, Krio
MONEY: Leone
LIFE EXPECTANCY: 57
LITERACY RATE: 43%

GUESS WHAT? *Sierra Leone is home to many rare and endangered primates, including the western chimpanzee, Diana monkey, and red colobus.*

SINGAPORE

LOCATION: Asia
CAPITAL: Singapore
AREA: 269 sq mi (697 sq km)
POPULATION ESTIMATE (2013): 5,460,302
GOVERNMENT: Parliamentary republic
LANGUAGES: Chinese (Mandarin), English, and Malay (all official); Hokkien, Tamil, Cantonese, others
MONEY: Singapore dollar
LIFE EXPECTANCY: 84
LITERACY RATE: 96%

GUESS WHAT? *Chewing gum is against the law in Singapore. The country banned the import and sale of gum to prevent litter.*

SLOVAKIA

LOCATION: Europe
CAPITAL: Bratislava
AREA: 18,933 sq mi (49,035 sq km)
POPULATION ESTIMATE (2013): 5,488,339
GOVERNMENT: Parliamentary democracy
LANGUAGES: Slovak (official), Hungarian, Roma, Ukranian
MONEY: Euro (formerly koruna)
LIFE EXPECTANCY: 76
LITERACY RATE: 100%

GUESS WHAT? *Slovakia is famous for its caves. Of the thousands of caves around the country, fewer than 20 are open to the public.*

SLOVENIA

LOCATION: Europe
CAPITAL: Ljubljana
AREA: 7,827 sq mi (20,273 sq km)
POPULATION ESTIMATE (2013): 1,992,690
GOVERNMENT: Parliamentary republic
LANGUAGES: Slovenian (official), Serbo-Croatian, Italian, Hungarian, others
MONEY: Euro (formerly Slovenian tolar)
LIFE EXPECTANCY: 78
LITERACY RATE: 100%

GUESS WHAT? *More than half of Slovenia is covered in forests.*

SOLOMON ISLANDS

LOCATION: Oceania
CAPITAL: Honiara
AREA: 11,157 sq mi (28,896 sq km)
POPULATION ESTIMATE (2013): 597,248
GOVERNMENT: Parliamentary democracy
LANGUAGES: English (official), Melanesian pidgin, more than 120 local languages
MONEY: Solomon Islands dollar
LIFE EXPECTANCY: 75
LITERACY RATE: 84%

GUESS WHAT? *Marovo Lagoon, in the New Georgia Islands (which are part of the Solomon Islands), is the world's largest saltwater lagoon. Lagoons are shallow bodies of water cut off from larger bodies, often by coral reefs.*

SOMALIA

LOCATION: Africa
CAPITAL: Mogadishu
AREA: 246,199 sq mi
(637,657 sq km)
POPULATION ESTIMATE (2013):
10,251,568
GOVERNMENT: Transitional;
parliamentary federal republic
LANGUAGES: Somali and Arabic
(both official), English, Italian
MONEY: Somali shilling
LIFE EXPECTANCY: 51
LITERACY RATE: 38%

GUESS WHAT? *Many Somalians are nomads. They travel from place to place with their animals to find food and water sources. Because camels are strong and can survive in harsh, dry climates, they are very important to nomadic Somalis.*

SOUTH AFRICA

LOCATION: Africa
CAPITALS: Pretoria (administrative),
Cape Town (legislative),
Bloemfontein (judicial)
AREA: 471,008 sq mi
(1,219,090 sq km)
POPULATION ESTIMATE (2013):
48,601,098
GOVERNMENT: Republic
LANGUAGES: Zulu, Xhosa, Sepedi,
Afrikaans, English, Setswana,
Sesotho, Tsonga, others
MONEY: Rand
LIFE EXPECTANCY: 49
LITERACY RATE: 93%

GUESS WHAT? *The Vredefort Dome, in South Africa, was formed about 2 billion years ago, when a meteorite hit Earth. It is the world's oldest meteorite scar.*

SPAIN

LOCATION: Europe
CAPITAL: Madrid
AREA: 195,124 sq mi
(505,370 sq km)
POPULATION ESTIMATE (2013):
47,370,542
GOVERNMENT: Parliamentary
monarchy
LANGUAGES: Castilian Spanish
(official), Catalan, Galician,
Basque
MONEY: Euro (formerly peseta)
LIFE EXPECTANCY: 81
LITERACY RATE: 98%

GUESS WHAT? *Spanish children are not visited by the tooth fairy. Instead, they believe a mouse named Ratoncito Pérez who will take the tooth and leave a treasure.*

SRI LANKA

LOCATION: Asia
CAPITAL: Colombo (executive and
judicial), Sri Jayewardenepura
Kotte (legislative)
AREA: 25,332 sq mi
(65,610 sq km)
POPULATION ESTIMATE (2013):
21,675,648
GOVERNMENT: Republic
LANGUAGES: Sinhala (official),
Tamil, English, others
MONEY: Sri Lankan rupee
LIFE EXPECTANCY: 76
LITERACY RATE: 91%

GUESS WHAT? *Sri Lanka's flag is one of the oldest flags in the world. It symbolizes unity and harmony among all peoples of the country.*

SUDAN

LOCATION: Africa
CAPITAL: Khartoum
AREA: 718,723 sq mi
(1,861,484 sq km)
POPULATION ESTIMATE (2013):
34,847,910
GOVERNMENT: Federal republic
LANGUAGES: Arabic and English
(both official), Nubian,
Ta Bedawie, Fur
MONEY: Sudanese pound
LIFE EXPECTANCY: 63
LITERACY RATE: 72%

GUESS WHAT? *The White Nile, which flows from South Sudan, and the Blue Nile, which flows from Ethiopia, join together in Sudan to form the main Nile River.*

SUDAN, SOUTH

LOCATION: Africa
CAPITAL: Juba
AREA: 284,777 sq mi
(644,329 sq km)
POPULATION ESTIMATE (2013):
11,090,104
GOVERNMENT: Republic
LANGUAGES: Arabic and English
(both official), others
MONEY: South Sudanese pound
LIFE EXPECTANCY: Not available
LITERACY RATE: 27%

GUESS WHAT? *South Sudan's national anthem, "South Sudan Oyee [Hurray]," was written by a group of students from the University of Juba. Their lyrics were chosen during a competition held in 2010.*

SURINAME

LOCATION: South America
CAPITAL: Paramaribo
AREA: 63,251 sq mi
(163,820 sq km)
POPULATION ESTIMATE (2013): 566,846
GOVERNMENT: Constitutional democracy
LANGUAGES: Dutch (official), English, Surinamese, Caribbean Hindustani, Javanese
MONEY: Surinamese dollar
LIFE EXPECTANCY: 71
LITERACY RATE: 95%

 Rain forests cover 80% of Suriname.

SWAZILAND

LOCATION: Africa
CAPITAL: Mbabane
AREA: 6,704 sq mi
(17,364 sq km)
POPULATION ESTIMATE (2013): 1,403,362
GOVERNMENT: Monarchy
LANGUAGES: Siswati and English (both official)
MONEY: Lilangeni
LIFE EXPECTANCY: 50
LITERACY RATE: 89%

 *The shield on the Swaziland flag is a traditional Zulu shield. Zulus are an ethnic group of Bantu-speaking people from southeastern Africa.*

SWEDEN

LOCATION: Europe
CAPITAL: Stockholm
AREA: 173,860 sq mi
(450,295 sq km)
POPULATION ESTIMATE (2013): 9,647,386
GOVERNMENT: Constitutional monarchy
LANGUAGE: Swedish
MONEY: Krona
LIFE EXPECTANCY: 81
LITERACY RATE: 99%

A smorgasbord is a traditional Scandinavian buffet meal, including many different foods. Some traditional Swedish smorgasbord dishes are smoked salmon, pickled herring, boiled potatoes, sliced meats and cheeses, and sausages.

SWITZERLAND

LOCATION: Europe
CAPITAL: Bern
AREA: 15,937 sq mi
(41,277 sq km)
POPULATION ESTIMATE (2013): 7,996,026
GOVERNMENT: Confederation (similar to a federal republic)
LANGUAGES: German, French, Italian, and Romansch (all official), others
MONEY: Swiss franc
LIFE EXPECTANCY: 82
LITERACY RATE: 99%

According to legend, yodeling was developed in the Swiss Alps as a form of long-distance communication. The high mountains allow for clear echoes.

SYRIA

LOCATION: Middle East
CAPITAL: Damascus
AREA: 71,498 sq mi
(185,180 sq km)
POPULATION ESTIMATE (2013): 22,457,336
GOVERNMENT: Republic under an authoritarian regime
LANGUAGES: Arabic (official), Kurdish, Armenian, Aramaic, Circassian, others
MONEY: Syrian pound
LIFE EXPECTANCY: 75
LITERACY RATE: 84%

Satellite images of Syria show evidence of 4,000-year-old roads.

TAIWAN

LOCATION: Asia
CAPITAL: Taipei
AREA: 13,892 sq mi
(35,980 sq km)
POPULATION ESTIMATE (2013): 23,299,716
GOVERNMENT: Multiparty democracy
LANGUAGES: Chinese (Mandarin; official), Taiwanese, others
MONEY: New Taiwan dollar
LIFE EXPECTANCY: 80
LITERACY RATE: 96%

Because this island nation is located on the edge of two tectonic plates (which are the huge sections of rock that make up Earth's crust), there are many earthquakes in Taiwan. There are also many geothermal hot springs.

COUNTRIES

TAJIKISTAN

LOCATION: Asia
CAPITAL: Dushanbe
AREA: 55,251 sq mi
(143,100 sq km)
POPULATION ESTIMATE (2013):
7,910,041
GOVERNMENT: Republic
LANGUAGES: Tajik (official),
Russian
MONEY: Somoni
LIFE EXPECTANCY: 67
LITERACY RATE: 100%

GUESS WHAT? *The Pamir mountains, which are mostly in Tajikistan, are some of the tallest in the world. They are known as the Roof of the World.*

TANZANIA

LOCATION: Africa
CAPITALS: Dar es Salaam
(commercial), Dodoma
(political)
AREA: 365,755 sq mi
(947,300 sq km)
POPULATION ESTIMATE (2013):
48,261,942
GOVERNMENT: Republic
LANGUAGES: Swahili and English
(both official), Arabic, others
MONEY: Tanzanian shilling
LIFE EXPECTANCY: 61
LITERACY RATE: 69%

GUESS WHAT? *Tanzanian hip-hop is called bongo flava. The term comes from the Swahili word for "brains," ubongo.*

THAILAND

LOCATION: Asia
CAPITAL: Bangkok
AREA: 198,117 sq mi
(513,120 sq km)
POPULATION ESTIMATE (2013):
67,497,151
GOVERNMENT: Constitutional
monarchy
LANGUAGES: Thai (Siamese),
English, regional dialects
MONEY: Baht
LIFE EXPECTANCY: 74
LITERACY RATE: 94%

GUESS WHAT? *Thailand is the only country in Southeast Asia never to have been taken over by a European power. It was known as Siam until 1939.*

TOGO

LOCATION: Africa
CAPITAL: Lomé
AREA: 21,925 sq mi
(56,785 sq km)
POPULATION ESTIMATE (2013):
7,154,237
GOVERNMENT: Republic, under
transition to multiparty
democratic rule
LANGUAGES: French (official), Ewe,
Mina, Kabye, Dagomba
MONEY: CFA franc
LIFE EXPECTANCY: 64
LITERACY RATE: 60%

GUESS WHAT? *Whether they are selling a small bunch of bananas or a big basket of chickens, Togolese vendors usually carry their goods on their heads.*

TONGA

LOCATION: Oceania
CAPITAL: Nuku'alofa
AREA: 288 sq mi (747 sq km)
POPULATION ESTIMATE (2013): 106,322
GOVERNMENT: Constitutional
monarchy
LANGUAGES: Tongan and English
(both official)
MONEY: Pa'anga
LIFE EXPECTANCY: 76
LITERACY RATE: 99%

GUESS WHAT? *In Tonga, it is illegal to be shirtless in public, unless you are at a resort.*

TRINIDAD AND TOBAGO

LOCATION: Caribbean
CAPITAL: Port-of-Spain
AREA: 1,980 sq mi (5,128 sq km)
POPULATION ESTIMATE (2013):
1,225,225
GOVERNMENT: Parliamentary
democracy
LANGUAGES: English (official),
Caribbean Hindustani, French,
Spanish, Chinese
MONEY: Trinidad and
Tobago dollar
LIFE EXPECTANCY: 72
LITERACY RATE: 99%

GUESS WHAT? *The limbo, a dance in which a person leans backward to pass under a gradually lowered horizontal pole, was first danced in Trinidad and Tobago.*

TUNISIA

LOCATION: Africa
CAPITAL: Tunis
AREA: 63,170 sq mi
(163,610 sq km)
POPULATION ESTIMATE (2013):
10,835,873
GOVERNMENT: Republic
LANGUAGES: Arabic (official),
French, Berber
MONEY: Tunisian dinar
LIFE EXPECTANCY: 75
LITERACY RATE: 79%

GUESS WHAT? *Scenes from many Hollywood films, including* **Raiders of the Lost Ark** *and* **Star Wars,** *have been filmed in Tunisia.*

TURKEY

LOCATION: Europe and Asia
CAPITAL: Ankara
AREA: 302,535 sq mi
(783,562 sq km)
POPULATION ESTIMATE (2013):
80,694,485
GOVERNMENT: Republican
parliamentary democracy
LANGUAGES: Turkish (official),
Kurdish, others
MONEY: New Turkish lira
LIFE EXPECTANCY: 73
LITERACY RATE: 94%

GUESS WHAT? *Istanbul, the largest city in Turkey, is one of the few cities in the world that straddle two continents (Europe and Asia). It was called Constantinople until the 1920s and was officially renamed in 1930.*

TURKMENISTAN

LOCATION: Asia
CAPITAL: Ashgabat
AREA: 188,455 sq mi
(488,100 sq km)
POPULATION ESTIMATE (2013):
5,113,040
GOVERNMENT: Republic with
authoritarian presidential
rule
LANGUAGES: Turkmen (official),
Russian, Uzbek, others
MONEY: Manat
LIFE EXPECTANCY: 69
LITERACY RATE: 100%

GUESS WHAT? *Nomadic farmers in Turkmenistan live in yurts, collapsible tents built on wooden frames.*

TUVALU

LOCATION: Oceania
CAPITAL: Funafuti
AREA: 10 sq mi (26 sq km)
POPULATION ESTIMATE (2013): 10,698
GOVERNMENT: Parliamentary
democracy
LANGUAGES: Tuvaluan and English
(both official), Samoan, Kiribati
MONEY: Australian dollar,
Tuvaluan dollar
LIFE EXPECTANCY: 65
LITERACY RATE: Not available

GUESS WHAT? *Although it is surrounded by water, Tuvalu has no rivers, lakes, or streams. People rely on rain for their drinking water. Also, a water-treatment facility there can remove salt from ocean water to make it drinkable.*

UGANDA

LOCATION: Africa
CAPITAL: Kampala
AREA: 93,065 sq mi
(241,038 sq km)
POPULATION ESTIMATE (2013):
34,758,809
GOVERNMENT: Republic
LANGUAGES: English (official),
Luganda, other Niger-Congo
languages, Nilo-Saharan
languages, Swahili, Arabic
MONEY: Ugandan shilling
LIFE EXPECTANCY: 54
LITERACY RATE: 73%

GUESS WHAT? *On the Ugandan flag, the red color represents the brotherhood of man. Black represents the African people, and yellow stands for the sun.*

UKRAINE

LOCATION: Europe
CAPITAL: Kiev
AREA: 233,032 sq mi
(603,550 sq km)
POPULATION ESTIMATE (2013):
44,573,205
GOVERNMENT: Republic
LANGUAGES: Ukrainian (official),
Russian, others
MONEY: Hryvnia
LIFE EXPECTANCY: 69
LITERACY RATE: 100%

GUESS WHAT? *Ukraine is known as the Breadbasket of Europe because its soil is rich in nutrients and its climate is good for growing healthy crops. It produces wheat, barley, rye, oats, beets, and other crops that help feed the entire region.*

COUNTRIES

UNITED ARAB EMIRATES

LOCATION: Middle East
CAPITAL: Abu Dhabi
AREA: 32,278 sq mi
(83,600 sq km)
POPULATION ESTIMATE (2013):
5,473,972
GOVERNMENT: Federation
LANGUAGES: Arabic (official),
Persian, English, Hindi, Urdu
MONEY: U.A.E. dirham
LIFE EXPECTANCY: 77
LITERACY RATE: 90%

GUESS WHAT? *The Mall of the Emirates, in Dubai, features an indoor ski slope. The slope is more than 1,300 feet (396 m) high. It uses 6,000 tons (5,443 metric tons) of snow.*

UNITED KINGDOM

LOCATION: Europe
CAPITAL: London
AREA: 94,058 sq mi
(243,610 sq km)
POPULATION ESTIMATE (2013):
63,395,574
GOVERNMENT: Constitutional
monarchy
LANGUAGES: English, Scots,
Scottish Gaelic, Welsh, Irish
MONEY: British pound
LIFE EXPECTANCY: 80
LITERACY RATE: 99%

GUESS WHAT? *British English and American English are a little different. In the United Kingdom, french fries are called "chips," potato chips are called "crisps," sweaters are referred to as "jumpers," and sneakers are known as "trainers."*

UNITED STATES

LOCATION: North America
CAPITAL: Washington, D.C.
AREA: 3,794,100 sq mi
(9,826,675 sq km)
POPULATION ESTIMATE (2013):
316,438,601
GOVERNMENT: Constitution-based
federal republic
LANGUAGES: English, Spanish
(spoken by a sizable minority)
MONEY: U.S. dollar
LIFE EXPECTANCY: 79
LITERACY RATE: 99%

GUESS WHAT? *The average child in the United States spends more than seven hours a day looking at a screen. Kids are spending more time using computers or mobile phones, watching TV, or playing video games every week than they spend in school.*

URUGUAY

LOCATION: South America
CAPITAL: Montevideo
AREA: 67,960 sq mi
(176,015 sq km)
POPULATION ESTIMATE (2013):
3,324,460
GOVERNMENT: Constitutional
republic
LANGUAGES: Spanish (official),
Portuñol, Brazilero
MONEY: Uruguayan peso
LIFE EXPECTANCY: 76
LITERACY RATE: 98%

GUESS WHAT? *About 93% of Uruguayans live in cities, and one-third of those live in the capital.*

UZBEKISTAN

LOCATION: Asia
CAPITAL: Tashkent
AREA: 172,741 sq mi
(447,400 sq km)
POPULATION ESTIMATE (2013):
28,661,637
GOVERNMENT: Republic with
authoritarian presidential rule
LANGUAGES: Uzbek (official),
Russian, Tajik, others
MONEY: Uzbekistani som
LIFE EXPECTANCY: 73
LITERACY RATE: 99%

GUESS WHAT? *Uzbekistan has a very dry climate. Much of the country is desert.*

VANUATU

LOCATION: Oceania
CAPITAL: Port-Vila
AREA: 4,706 sq mi
(12,189 sq km)
POPULATION ESTIMATE (2013): 261,565
GOVERNMENT: Parliamentary
republic
LANGUAGES: Bislama, English, and
French (all official); most people
speak one of more than 100 local
languages;
MONEY: Vatu
LIFE EXPECTANCY: 72
LITERACY RATE: 83%

GUESS WHAT? *Vanuatu is an archipelago. It is made up of more than 80 islands, known as the New Hebrides. Most feature mountains, tropical rain forests, and active volcanoes. People live on most of the islands.*

VATICAN CITY (HOLY SEE)

LOCATION: Europe
CAPITAL: Vatican City
AREA: 0.17 sq mi (0.44 sq km)
POPULATION ESTIMATE (2013): 839
GOVERNMENT: Ecclesiastical
LANGUAGES: Italian, Latin, French
MONEY: Euro
LIFE EXPECTANCY: Not available
LITERACY RATE: 100%

GUESS WHAT? *Vatican City is the smallest country in the world. The post office there issues official Vatican City stamps.*

VENEZUELA

LOCATION: South America
CAPITAL: Caracas
AREA: 352,143 sq mi (912,050 sq km)
POPULATION ESTIMATE (2013): 28,459,085
GOVERNMENT: Federal republic
LANGUAGES: Spanish (official), native languages
MONEY: Bolívar
LIFE EXPECTANCY: 74
LITERACY RATE: 96%

GUESS WHAT? *Venezuela is home to many stunning mesas, or table-top mountains. Known as tepuis, these mountains have steep sides and a flat top.*

VIETNAM

LOCATION: Asia
CAPITAL: Hanoi
AREA: 127,881 sq mi (331,210 sq km)
POPULATION ESTIMATE (2013): 92,477,857
GOVERNMENT: Communist state
LANGUAGES: Vietnamese (official), French, English, Khmer, Chinese
MONEY: Dong
LIFE EXPECTANCY: 73
LITERACY RATE: 93%

GUESS WHAT? *Instead of counting their ages by their birthdays, people in Vietnam all turn one year older on Têt, the Vietnamese New Year.*

YEMEN

LOCATION: Middle East
CAPITAL: Sanaa
AREA: 203,850 sq mi (527,968 sq km)
POPULATION ESTIMATE (2013): 25,338,458
GOVERNMENT: Republic
LANGUAGE: Arabic
MONEY: Yemeni rial
LIFE EXPECTANCY: 64
LITERACY RATE: 65%

GUESS WHAT? *The Romans called Yemen Arabia Felix, or Happy Arabia, in 26 B.C., because the area was beautiful, rich, and powerful. Much of its wealth came from growing spices.*

ZAMBIA

LOCATION: Africa
CAPITAL: Lusaka
AREA: 290,587 sq mi (752,618 sq km)
POPULATION ESTIMATE (2013): 14,222,233
GOVERNMENT: Republic
LANGUAGES: Bemba, Nyanja, Tonga, Lozi, Lunda, Kaonde, Luvale, and English (all official), others
MONEY: Kwacha
LIFE EXPECTANCY: 52
LITERACY RATE: 61%

GUESS WHAT? *Zambia got its name from the Zambezi River, which is an important source of energy, fish, and water for crops. Zambezi comes from the local word yambezhi, which translates to "heart of all."*

ZIMBABWE

LOCATION: Africa
CAPITAL: Harare
AREA: 150,872 sq mi (390,757 sq km)
POPULATION ESTIMATE (2013): 13,182,908
GOVERNMENT: Parliamentary democracy
LANGUAGES: English (official), Shona, Ndebele (Sindebele), tribal dialects
MONEY: U.S. dollar, South African rand, and six other currencies
LIFE EXPECTANCY: 54
LITERACY RATE: 84%

GUESS WHAT? *Great Zimbabwe is the name of an ancient stone-walled city in southeastern Zimbabwe. Its ruins still stand.*

AMAZING PLACES
AROUND THE WORLD

TAIPEI 101,
TAIWAN

VICTORIA FALLS,
ZAMBIA

MACHU PICCHU,
PERU

DOME OF THE ROCK,
ISRAEL

STONEHENGE,
UNITED KINGDOM

COUNTRIES

From Victoria Falls in Zambia to Taipei 101 in Taiwan, countless landmarks, buildings, and monuments are found around the world. Each of these sites, whether natural or man-made, offers visitors something. You might learn about geology and wildlife at a massive canyon or uncover the mysteries of ancient people in the ruins of an old city. If you can't visit the world's most stunning places, no problem. Find a book in your school library, or check out TIME For Kids Around the World, at *timeforkids.com/atw*.

TOP 5 NEWEST COUNTRIES IN THE WORLD

By seceding, splitting up, or declaring independence, some regions have become new nations. South Sudan seceded from Sudan. Kosovo, Serbia, and Montenegro were once a single country (Yugoslavia). Here are the most recent additions to the map.

1. SOUTH SUDAN JULY 9, 2011

2. KOSOVO FEBRUARY 17, 2008

3. SERBIA JUNE 5, 2006

| 2002 | 2003 | 2004 | 2005 | 2006 | 2007 | 2008 | 2009 | 2010 | 2011 |

4. MONTENEGRO JUNE 3, 2006

5. EAST TIMOR (TIMOR-LESTE) MAY 20, 2002

GUESS WHAT?
When the Soviet Union broke up in 1991, 15 countries became independent: Armenia, Azerbaijan, Belarus, Estonia, Georgia, Kazakhstan, Kyrgyzstan, Latvia, Lithuania, Moldova, Russia, Tajikistan, Turkmenistan, Ukraine, and Uzbekistan.

Women in Juba, the capital of South Sudan, celebrate the one-year anniversary of the country's independence.

TIME FOR KIDS

GAME

JUMBLED GEOGRAPHY

In the sentences below, the names of the countries have gotten scrambled. Can you get the letters back in the right order?

The Muslim emperor Shah Jahan built the Taj Mahal, in Agra, **DNIIA**, as a tomb for his beloved wife Mumtaz Mahal.

1. _____

CIAHN is the country that has the most people.

2. _____

If you want to see the Sphinx and the Great Pyramids, you'll have to travel to **GTEYP**, in North Africa.

3. _____

For the past few years, Maximilian and Alexander have been two of the most popular names for boys in **YGMNERA**.

4. _____

The very first Olympics took place in **EERGEC**.

5. _____

Bonjour is how you say hello in **AFNREC**.

6. _____

Ring-tailed lemurs and fossas are found only on the island nation of **DASMACARGA**.

7. _____

The country located to the north of the United States is **ACDNAA**.

8. _____

The country **CELIH** should not be confused with a spicy bean-filled stew.

9. _____

At 5,369 feet (1,636 m) deep, Lake Baikal is the deepest lake in the world. It is located in Siberia, **SISRAU**.

10. _____

Venice, **YTILA**, is famous for its canals, or man-made waterways.

11. _____

COUNTRIES

Answers on page 276

ENERGY

A new kind of farm can be found out at sea. **Page 115**

ENERGY IS EVERYWHERE!

Energy can be found in many different forms: in light, heat, motion, and more. There is energy in everything, even in a book sitting on a table. All energy can be lumped into one of two categories:

POTENTIAL ENERGY

KINETIC ENERGY

ENERGY ON THE WAY

Potential energy is stored energy. Here are some of the many types of potential energy.

Mechanical energy depends on position. If you stretch a rubber band as far as it can go, it has the potential to fly farther than if you'd barely stretched it at all.

Natural gas and **coal** have lots of potential energy. When we burn them, they are converted to thermal energy, or heat.

There is a great deal of **nuclear energy** stored in the nucleus of an atom. (An atom is the smallest particle of matter. All things are made up of atoms.) When atoms are split at a nuclear power plant, huge amounts of energy are released.

The **food** we eat has lots of potential energy. After we eat it, it is converted into chemical energy. People get the energy they need to run, jump, laugh, and breathe from the chemical energy stored in food.

Like mechanical energy, **gravitational energy** depends on the position of an object. The higher up an object goes, the more gravitational energy it has. When you let the object go, its potential energy will immediately be converted to kinetic, or motion, energy.

ENERGY ON THE MOVE

Kinetic energy **is the energy of motion. Moving people or objects have kinetic energy. Electrical, heat, sound, and light energy are types of kinetic energy.**

The **electrical energy** that flows from power plants through wires and into outlets in your home is kinetic energy.

Heat is kinetic energy. Everything on Earth is made up of miniscule particles called atoms and molecules. When something heats up, its atoms and molecules begin to move faster and faster. There is motion there, even if it is microscopic and you can't see it.

Sound travels as vibrations in the air. When a musician strums the strings of a guitar, the strings vibrate and send vibrations through the air.

Your eardrum picks up these vibrations and detects the sounds. Here again, there is motion in the air, even though you cannot see it.

Transferring Energy

Energy cannot be created or destroyed. Instead, it changes form. When an object is held above the ground, it has potential energy. The second the object starts to fall or roll, potential energy changes to kinetic energy. As the object speeds up, its kinetic energy increases and its potential energy decreases. Upon impact, kinetic energy suddenly drops. The energy in the object is converted to other forms of energy, such as heat energy or sound energy. And some of the kinetic energy transfers to other objects upon impact. This is what happens when an archer shoots an arrow into a target.

When an archer draws back the arrow on a bow, the arrow has potential energy.

When the archer lets go, the potential energy in the arrow is converted into kinetic energy.

When the arrow hits the target, the kinetic energy is transferred to the target. Some of it is converted to heat energy and sound energy.

113

NONRENEWABLE ENERGY

Many millions of years ago, animals and plants died and broke down. This decaying matter was buried under many layers of earth. Over time, it underwent changes and was transformed into new substances: coal, natural gas, and petroleum (crude oil). Known as fossil fuels, these substances are major sources of energy around the world. Unfortunately, fossil fuels are a nonrenewable energy source. One day, they will run out.

Often workers will use huge machines to dig deep into the ground in search of fossil fuels.

♦ Collecting coal, natural gas, and oil causes pollution. These fuels must be dug, drilled, or pushed out of the ground. Mining for them can release gases and chemicals that are harmful to the environment. It is also dangerous for the workers.

♦ To convert most fossil fuels into electricity, they must be burned. Burning fuel pollutes the air, which can make people sick. It also releases chemicals that contribute to global warming and cause acid rain.

♦ Accidents like oil spills can be devastating to wildlife and ecosystems.

♦ In addition to coal, natural gas, and petroleum, nuclear power is a nonrenewable energy source. Unlike power plants that use fossil fuels, nuclear power plants do not rely on burning fuel for energy. Instead, nuclear power plants use the element uranium. In a process called fission, atoms of uranium are split. This gives off great amounts of heat that can be used to create electricity.

The Importance of Turbines

A turbine is a machine that changes the energy of a moving substance (water or air) into energy that can be used for electricity. The turbine has a set of blades that rotate like the blades of a fan. Making electricity in many power plants is all about boiling water. Most power plants burn a fuel, such as coal or oil. The heat from the burning fuel boils water. When the water boils, it produces steam. The steam pushes against the turbine's blades. The blades spin, which turns the shaft of the turbine. The shaft then moves a generator that makes electric current. Running water and wind can also turn the turbines of electric power plants.

RENEWABLE ENERGY

Renewable energy sources have unlimited supplies. Wind, running water, solar power, the Earth's heat, and (believe it or not!) trash are renewable energy sources because we will never run out of them.

☼ The amount of **wind energy** Americans use to make electricity is growing. In some places, thousands of wind turbines stand together in what are called wind farms. You can find wind farms in places where winds are strong and steady. Many wind farms are on wide plains or in windy mountain passes. Others are being built offshore, in lakes and oceans. Winds can be steadier and stronger over water than over land, so offshore wind farms may generate more power than ones on land. But experts want to make sure that the wind turbines do not harm migrating birds.

☼ Water power is also known as **hydroelectric power,** or **hydropower.** Waterfalls and fast-running rivers are major sources of hydropower. Another way to harness hydropower is the storage method, in which dams are used to trap water in large reservoirs. When power is needed, the dams are opened and the water flows out. The water pressure created is then converted into energy. About 7% of the electricity used in the United States comes from hydroelectric power.

☼ We will never run out of **solar energy.** Energy from the sun is free and constant. Solar furnaces use mirrors to direct the sun's energy to boil water or another fluid. The steam then spins a turbine at a power plant.

☼ **Geothermal energy** is heat from within Earth. Some geothermal power plants use natural steam from deep underground to drive turbines. At other plants, Earth's heat boils water to make steam.

☼ **Burning trash** is one way to get rid of garbage and create energy. But waste-to-energy plants are expensive to build, and they release pollution. In 2011, 30 million tons (27 million metric tons) of garbage were burned for energy in the United States.

GUESS WHAT?

Wind power has been the fastest-growing energy source worldwide since 1990.

YOU Have the Power!

Just Kick for Light

A special soccer ball can be turned into a lamp. All you need to do is kick the ball around for a while.

Here's how it works: A pendulum swings back and forth inside the moving ball, gathering up kinetic energy. The pendulum takes that energy and uses it to turn on a small generator inside the ball. The generator is connected to a rechargeable battery. That's where the energy gets stored.

When you're done playing soccer, you can then plug the ball into the LED lamp that comes with the ball. After 30 minutes of play, there should be enough energy in the battery to light the lamp for up to three hours.

A group of former Harvard University students invented this amazing soccer ball, which they call the Socccket. They hope it will help give cheap off-grid power to people living in low-income areas around the world.

Charge by Hand

Several companies have invented smartphone chargers that use kinetic energy. You plug the charger into a phone and then use a manual crank to recharge the phone's battery. With some hand-operated chargers, the motion of your arm makes the handle spin around, which produces the energy. These devices are handy to take on camping or hiking trips. But they were mainly designed for emergency situations when electricity is suddenly not available, such as after an earthquake or flood. Being able to charge a phone in that kind of situation can help save lives.

Some chargers will work for any device with a USB plug.

Rocking-Chair Power

A designer in San Francisco has built a rocking chair that powers its own reading light. The back-and-forth rocking motion that you make while sitting in the chair creates kinetic energy. That energy is picked up from sensors on the bottom of the chair's rockers. It's then stored in a small battery hidden inside the chair. When enough energy is in the battery, it lights an LED lamp that's attached to the chair.

Footfalls for Fuel

"Foot power" can be converted into electricity! In Britain, for example, paving tiles made out of recycled rubber are being used to run low-voltage lighting and other electronic equipment. When a person steps on one of these tiles, the rubber gets pushed down a tiny bit—about 0.2 inches (0.5 cm). That motion creates kinetic energy, which is then collected and stored in a battery within the tile. When enough footsteps have fallen on the tile, the battery can be used to produce electricity.

In Canterbury, England, these incredible tiles are being used to light a school hallway. The tiles are doing the same for a tunnel in a London subway station. Elsewhere in London, a sidewalk of tiles generates enough electricity to light up the entrance to a shopping mall.

Uphill? No Problem.

Wouldn't it be great if you could coast uphill on your bike? Well, a newly invented bicycle wheel can help you do that. The wheel collects the kinetic energy that is released when you push on your bicycle's brakes. That energy charges a battery inside the wheel's hub. When the battery is charged enough, you can use its stored energy to "drive" you and your bike up a hill— without pedaling!

ENVIRONMENT

Learn about Siberian tigers returning to the forests of China. **Page 125**

⚠ SO HERE'S THE BAD NEWS ⚠

EXPANDING DESERTS

More than 40% of the world's landmasses are drylands—areas that have high temperatures and low rainfall. Although they are not as biologically diverse as rain forests and other habitats, drylands are home to millions of unique species of plants and animals that have adapted to living where it is hot and water is scarce.

Drylands are under increasing threats, however. Global warming and misuse of the lands by humans are turning parts of them into deserts. Scientists call this process desertification. Overgrazing by cattle and sheep, for example, can quickly destroy grasses and other plants. When those plants are gone, the land's thin layer of nutrient-rich topsoil blows away. What's left behind is dust and sand.

Drylands are turning into deserts at a rate of 20,000 square miles (51,800 sq km) each year. Environmentalists around the world are trying to halt the destruction of drylands. They are replanting them with trees, shrubs, and grasses. They are also teaching people to raise livestock and crops in ways that don't harm these fragile lands.

GUESS WHAT? The destruction of drylands causes huge dust storms. Many of these storms can be seen from space. In 2010, a dust storm rose up from the arid grasslands of Mongolia in northern China. The yellow dust blew east for thousands of miles, even as far away as South Korea and Japan.

A Sudanese woman rakes the ground to collect dry grasses that can be fed to livestock.

SEAS ON THE RISE

Sea levels have been rising about 0.14 inches (3.5 mm) every year since the early 1990s. That's twice as fast as during the previous 80 years.

The speed at which the seas are rising has many people very worried. Even a small increase can have a devastating impact on the world's coastal regions. Every inch that the sea level rises causes an average of 50 inches (1.27 m) of beach to disappear.

Scientists believe global warming is responsible for the rising seas. When the Earth's temperature rises, the water in its oceans gets warmer. As the water warms, it expands, causing sea levels to rise. Global warming also causes polar ice caps to melt. The melted ice fills the Earth's oceans with more water and causes the temperature of the oceans to keep rising. Here's why: Polar ice is white and super-bright. It reflects sunlight back into the atmosphere. But when the ice is gone, the sunlight gets absorbed into the dark ocean, further warming it up.

People are working hard to keep sea levels from rising even faster and higher. The most important step is to reduce the amount of carbon dioxide and other heat-trapping gases that get released into the Earth's atmosphere.

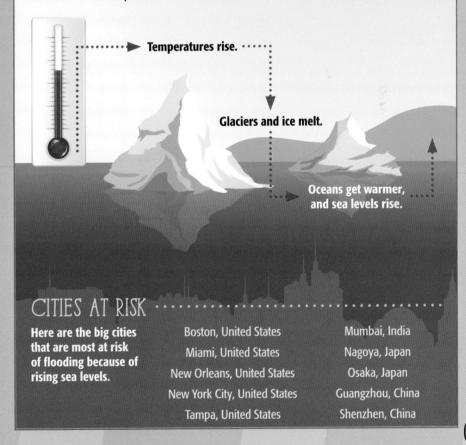

Temperatures rise.

Glaciers and ice melt.

Oceans get warmer, and sea levels rise.

CITIES AT RISK

Here are the big cities that are most at risk of flooding because of rising sea levels.

Boston, United States

Miami, United States

New Orleans, United States

New York City, United States

Tampa, United States

Mumbai, India

Nagoya, Japan

Osaka, Japan

Guangzhou, China

Shenzhen, China

NEW YORKERS ARE BREATHING EASIER

The air in New York City is cleaner than it's been in 50 years. Sulfur dioxide levels in the city's air, for example, dropped 69% between 2008 and 2013. Sulfur dioxide is a colorless gas that can harm the lungs if breathed in over a long period of time.

New York City's air is cleaner mainly because of a program that encourages building owners to heat their buildings with natural gas instead of heating oil. Certain types of heating oil produce high levels of sulfur dioxide.

POLAR BEARS ARE HEALTHIER

Baby polar bears and their mothers have much lower levels of toxic chemicals called polychlorinated biphenyls (PCBs) in their bodies than they did a decade ago. Researchers took blood samples from polar bears that live in Svalbard, a remote group of Norwegian islands. They found that the PCB levels of mother bears had dropped by 55% over a period of 10 years. PCB levels in cubs dropped by 59%.

That's great news for polar bears! PCBs can affect the chemistry in their bodies in ways that make it difficult for young bears to grow and thrive.

PCBs were once widely used to make many different products, including paints and plastic items. They've been banned for years, but are still found in the environment. Scientists say the drop in PCBs in polar bears is evidence that the international ban on these chemicals is working.

GIANT TURTLES ARE RETURNING

Leatherbacks, the world's largest living turtles, are making a comeback in some regions of the Atlantic Ocean. A single beach in the Caribbean country of Trinidad, for example, now has about 500 female leatherback turtles nesting there each year. Environmental biologists say the protection of nesting beaches has made a big difference. Changes in fishing methods have also been made, so the turtles don't get caught in big nets.

Though the leatherback population is growing, these turtles are still considered "critically endangered." In the Pacific Ocean, their numbers have fallen a stunning 98% since the 1980s.

A leatherback turtle can weigh up to 2,000 pounds (907 kg). That's as much as a small car!

HIDDEN HABITATS

Tucked away in this grid are the 12 words from the list below. They may go up, down, across, or diagonal. Can you find them all?

cactus
desert
forest
fox
frog
grassland
monkey
ocean
rabbit
tundra
turtle
zebra

F	K	E	O	R	H	F	C	E	T	M	G
R	A	B	B	I	T	O	T	C	A	O	V
O	Y	W	T	M	J	S	A	A	T	N	I
G	Z	O	D	E	E	B	N	C	E	K	B
D	E	S	E	R	T	U	R	T	L	E	E
A	B	E	O	K	U	E	A	U	R	Y	Z
R	R	F	H	V	N	G	F	S	V	M	E
E	A	A	L	O	D	A	O	C	E	A	N
C	T	E	I	M	R	Q	X	B	H	K	O
A	N	G	G	R	A	S	S	L	A	N	D

Answer on page 276

BIOMES

The landmasses on Earth consist of six different kinds of large regions called biomes. The environment of each biome reflects the climate, temperature, and geographical features that exist there. The wildlife found in each biome has adapted over millions of years to survive and thrive.

TROPICAL FORESTS

Tropical rain forests are hot, humid, and rainy. More kinds of trees exist in rain forests than anywhere else in the world. Rain forests in Africa, Asia, and South America also have many species of animals.

WILDLIFE

Jaguar

Howler monkey

Tree boa

Toucan

At the start of 2013, the Republic of Congo set aside 1,765 square miles (4,572 sq km) of its tropical forest as a national park. The main purpose of the new Ntokou-Pikounda National Park is to protect endangered animals, especially the 15,000 western lowland gorillas that live there.

The government of Ecuador announced in 2013 that it was going to allow companies to drill for oil in Yasuni National Park. Environmentalists oppose the drilling. They say the construction of roads, drilling platforms, and pipelines will cause terrible environmental damage to the park's rain forest. The Yasuni National Park is one of the most biologically diverse areas in the world. In fact, 2.5 acres (1 hectare) of the park have as many different types of trees and insects as are contained in all of the United States and Canada combined!

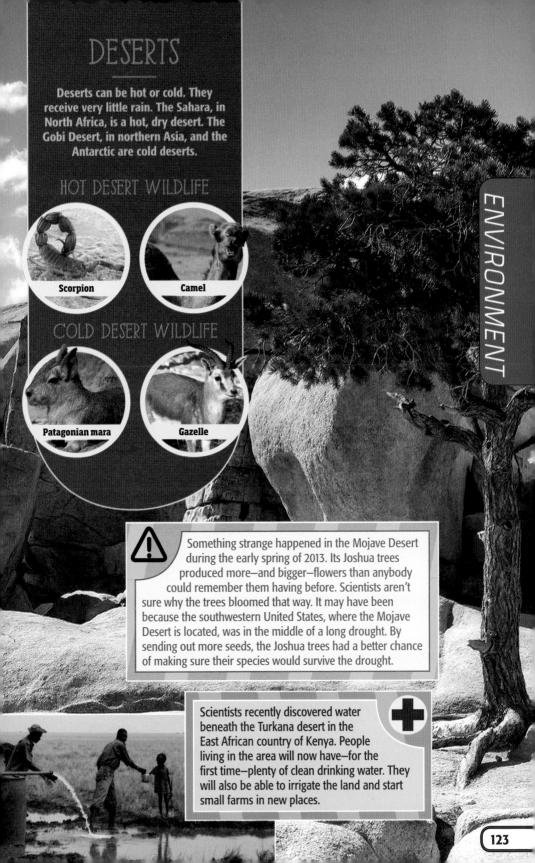

DESERTS

Deserts can be hot or cold. They receive very little rain. The Sahara, in North Africa, is a hot, dry desert. The Gobi Desert, in northern Asia, and the Antarctic are cold deserts.

HOT DESERT WILDLIFE

Scorpion

Camel

COLD DESERT WILDLIFE

Patagonian mara

Gazelle

ENVIRONMENT

⚠ Something strange happened in the Mojave Desert during the early spring of 2013. Its Joshua trees produced more—and bigger—flowers than anybody could remember them having before. Scientists aren't sure why the trees bloomed that way. It may have been because the southwestern United States, where the Mojave Desert is located, was in the middle of a long drought. By sending out more seeds, the Joshua trees had a better chance of making sure their species would survive the drought.

Scientists recently discovered water beneath the Turkana desert in the East African country of Kenya. People living in the area will now have—for the first time—plenty of clean drinking water. They will also be able to irrigate the land and start small farms in new places.

GRASSLANDS

There are several types of grassland, including the savannas of South America, the prairies of North America, and the steppes of central Asia. Grass is the main type of plant because there isn't enough rain to support many shrubs or trees.

The central Asian country of Mongolia has one of the largest remaining grassland areas in the world. But heavy grazing by sheep and goats is turning the grassland into desert. Over the past 25 years, the number of livestock in Mongolia has more than doubled, to 45 million animals.

WILDLIFE

Ostrich

Coyote

Pronghorn

Meerkat

The tigrina is a small wildcat (about the size of a house cat) that prowls the grasslands and forests of Brazil. Scientists used to think there was only one species of tigrina. But they recently discovered that the tigrinas living in the grasslands were genetically different from those living in the forests. Environmentalists are now working to make sure that both species thrive in their habitats.

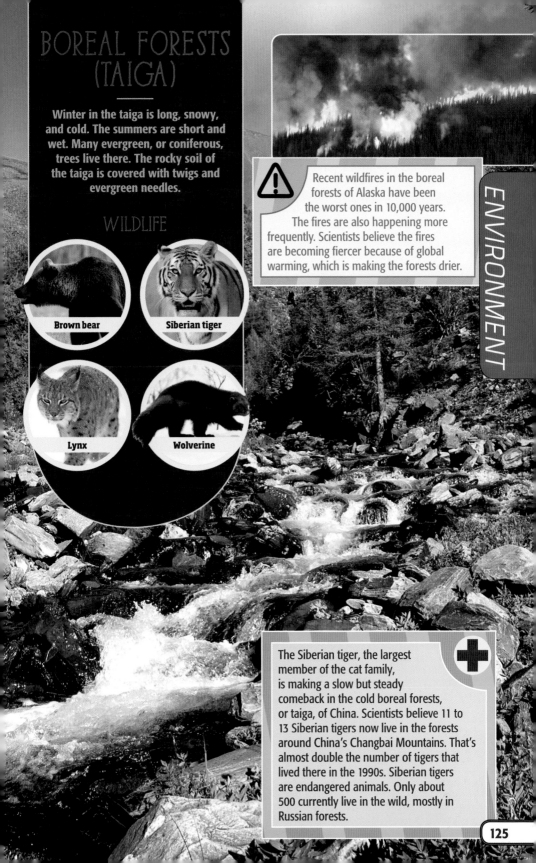

BOREAL FORESTS (TAIGA)

Winter in the taiga is long, snowy, and cold. The summers are short and wet. Many evergreen, or coniferous, trees live there. The rocky soil of the taiga is covered with twigs and evergreen needles.

WILDLIFE

Brown bear

Siberian tiger

Lynx

Wolverine

⚠️ Recent wildfires in the boreal forests of Alaska have been the worst ones in 10,000 years. The fires are also happening more frequently. Scientists believe the fires are becoming fiercer because of global warming, which is making the forests drier.

The Siberian tiger, the largest member of the cat family, is making a slow but steady comeback in the cold boreal forests, or taiga, of China. Scientists believe 11 to 13 Siberian tigers now live in the forests around China's Changbai Mountains. That's almost double the number of tigers that lived there in the 1990s. Siberian tigers are endangered animals. Only about 500 currently live in the wild, mostly in Russian forests.

TEMPERATE FORESTS

In temperate forests, also known as deciduous forests, there are four seasons and a moderate amount of rain. Many hardwood trees, such as maple and oak, grow in temperate forests. Other plant life includes mushrooms, moss, and lichen.

WILDLIFE

Squirrel

Mountain lion

Deer

Porcupine

A $280 million project to save the world's remaining forests was started in November 2013. Three countries—the United States, Britain, and Norway—donated the money. The project will try to stop forests from being cut down to make room for farming and ranching. Instead, people will be encouraged to use forests to create products that don't require destroying these important biomes.

A deadly fungus is threatening to kill off an entire species of frogs that lives in the temperate forests of Chile. When the fungus infects the frogs, it causes a deadly disease called chytridiomycosis.

The species of frogs are known as Darwin's frogs. They were named by the British naturalist Charles Darwin when he visited Chile, in 1834.

TUNDRA

It is very cold year-round in the tundra, and there is almost no rain or snow. The soil is permanently frozen, preventing trees and most plant life, aside from moss, lichen, and grasses, from growing. During the short, cool summers, some flowering plants flourish.

WILDLIFE

Arctic fox

Seal

Owl

Wolf

⚠️ The shallow lakes of Canada's northern tundra are drying up. Scientists believe global warming is the reason. Winters on the tundra have been getting warmer and drier. So there is less water from melting snow to fill the lakes in the spring.

In 2013, crews of government workers finally hauled away dozens of 55-gallon (189 L) fuel drums and hundreds of other metal containers from a wilderness park on the Alaska tundra. The rusted containers had been left there by the United States military more than 50 years ago. The cleanup project cost $300,000 and took several weeks to finish.

GEOGRAPHY

Where is the deepest canyon in the United States? **Page 133**

ALL AROUND THE
WORLD

Geography is the study of the surface of Earth. There is plenty to study: mountains, valleys, oceans, and rivers. There are dry deserts, rainy tropical forests, flat plains, heavily populated areas, places with very few people, lands filled with precious minerals, and landscapes covered with trees. These many characteristics have an impact on what occurs in any area of the world. Many things—the jobs that people have, the types of homes they build, the food they eat, and the weather they encounter—are affected by the geography of a place.

GUESS WHAT?

The majority of people live on only 10% of the planet's surface.

Bodies of Water

More than 70% of the surface of Earth is water. The five oceans cover much of the planet. Here are Earth's other bodies of water.

A **sea** is a branch of one of the five oceans. A sea is partially enclosed by land. For example, the Indian Ocean is divided in two by the country of India, forming the Arabian Sea on one side and the Bay of Bengal on the other.

A **river** is a channel of moving water, traveling from a higher altitude to a lower altitude, propelled by gravity. A small, narrow river is a **stream.** Rivers usually end in oceans, but streams may end in a lake.

A **lake** is a body of water that is completely surrounded by land. Some lakes have the word *sea* in their names, but they're really lakes. A lake filled with salt water is usually called a sea. The Dead Sea is one example.

A **pond** is a very small lake that is not moving and is shallow enough to support plants with roots.

Earth's **Five Oceans**

One enormous body of water covers the planet. You can sail in a boat and reach every ocean without ever taking the boat out of the water. But it is generally recognized that there are five oceans: Pacific, Atlantic, Indian, Southern, and Arctic. The Pacific is the biggest and covers about one-third of the Earth's surface. The Arctic is the smallest and is frozen all the time, except at its edges.

ARCTIC OCEAN
Area: 6,007,000 square miles (15,558,000 sq km)

Average depth: 3,953 feet (1,205 m)

ATLANTIC OCEAN
Area: 32,870,000 square miles (85,133,000 sq km)

Average depth: 11,962 feet (3,646 m)

INDIAN OCEAN
Area: 27,243,000 square miles (70,560,000 sq km)

Average depth: 12,274 feet (3,741 m)

PACIFIC OCEAN
Area: 62,456,000 square miles (161,760,000 sq km)

Average depth: 13,386 feet (4,080 m)

SOUTHERN OCEAN
Area: 8,479,000 square miles (21,960,000 sq km)

Average depth: 10,728 feet (3,270 m)

SOURCE: NOAA NATIONAL GEOPHYSICAL DATA CENTER

GEOGRAPHY

TOP 5

Deepest Lakes

1. Lake Baikal, Russia
5,369 feet (1,636 m) deep

2. Lake Tanganyika, Burundi, Democratic Republic of the Congo, Tanzania, and Zambia
4,826 feet (1,471 m) deep

3. Caspian Sea, Azerbaijan, Iran, Kazakhstan, Russia, and Turkmenistan
3,362 feet (1,025 m) deep

4. Vostok Lake, Antarctica
At least 2,950 feet (899 m) deep

5. Lake O'Higgins/San Martín, Argentina and Chile
2,742 feet (836 m) deep

SOURCE: NATIONAL PARK SERVICE

THE 7 CONTINENTS

	AFRICA	ANTARCTICA	ASIA (including the Middle East)
How **Big** Is It?	11,608,000 square miles (30,065,000 sq km)	5,100,000 square miles (13,209,000 sq km)	17,212,000 square miles (44,579,000 sq km)
Highest Point	Mount Kilimanjaro 19,340 feet (5,895 m)	Vinson Massif 16,066 feet (4,897 m)	Mount Everest 29,035 feet (8,850 m)
Lowest Point	Lake Assal 512 feet (156 m) below sea level	Bentley Subglacial Trench 8,383 feet (2,555 m) below sea level	Dead Sea 1,365 feet (416 m) below sea level

Earth's **Crust**

Earth is approximately 4.5 billion years old. In its lifetime, it has changed a lot. Although we do not feel the land shifting beneath our feet, it is moving. The ground we walk on is the outer layer of the Earth, or the Earth's crust. Soon after the Earth formed, this rocky crust hardened. But the crust is not a single solid layer of rock. It's broken into many plates that move across, under, and over one another.

The **crust** is, on average, about 20 miles (32 km) thick.

The **mantle** is a heavy, rocky layer.

The outer core is liquid. It is made up of molten rock—like lava.

Earth's inner core is a solid ball of mostly iron and nickel.

AUSTRALIA/ OCEANIA	EUROPE	NORTH AMERICA (including Central America and the Caribbean)	SOUTH AMERICA
3,132,000 square miles (8,112,000 sq km)	3,841,000 square miles (9,947,000 sq km)	9,449,000 square miles (24,474,000 sq km)	6,880,000 square miles (17,819,000 sq km)
Mount Wilhelm 14,794 feet (4,509 m)	Mount Elbrus 18,481 feet (5,633 m)	Mount McKinley 20,322 feet (6,194 m)	Mount Aconcagua 22,831 feet (6,959 m)
Lake Eyre 52 feet (16 m) below sea level	Caspian Sea 92 feet (28 m) below sea level	Death Valley 282 feet (86 m) below sea level	Laguna del Carbón 344 feet (105 m) below sea level

GEOGRAPHY

One **Giant** Landmass

Many scientists believe the seven continents we have today were once part of a single gigantic supercontinent, which they call Pangaea, a Greek word that means "all the Earth." According to this theory, Pangaea began to break apart about 200 million to 250 million years ago. Today, the Earth's crust is broken up into seven or eight major plates. There are also other, smaller plates. Volcanoes form where plates meet—both aboveground and deep underwater.

 The continents are still drifting very slowly—about 0.4 to 4 inches (1 to 10 cm) per year.

The **Dinosaurs** Say So!

Scientists have found fossils that support the theory of Pangaea. They have found the fossilized remains of animals that lived more than 200 million years ago in areas that are now separated by enormous oceans. When the animals were alive, these areas would have been right next to each other.

The cynognathus was a reptile that lived during the Triassic period (about 245 million to 251 million years ago). Cynognathus fossils have been found in South America and Africa in areas that once would have been connected by land.

FROM
TIME
FOR KIDS
MAGAZINE

A Devastating Earthquake BY CAMERON KEADY WITH AP REPORTING

A magnitude 7.7 earthquake rocked Pakistan's Awaran district in September 2013. The quake created widespread damage. The hard-hit district was made up of mostly mud and handmade brick houses that quickly collapsed with the Earth's tremors. But along with destruction came creation. After the quake, a small landmass of mud appeared off the coast of Pakistan.

Arawan is located in Pakistan's Balochistan province. The area's mountainous landscape makes it a prime location for earthquakes. Three tectonic plates come together there. Tectonic plates are the pieces that make up Earth's crust. They are slowly but constantly shifting. Earthquakes occur when these plates bump, slip, and slide. The tremors from this quake were so intense they were felt across the border, in New Delhi, India.

EARTHQUAKE ISLAND

The force of this earthquake created an island in the middle of the Arabian Sea. Extreme tectonic activity can cause mud from under the sea to rise to the surface. Combined with natural gases, the mud can gather to form a landmass. "When such a strong earthquake builds pressure, there is the likelihood of such islands emerging," says Zahid Rafi, head of the Geological Survey of Pakistan. "That big shock beneath the Earth causes a lot of disturbance."

According to Pakistani oceanographers, the small new island is about 60 feet (18 m) high, 100 feet (30 m) long, and 250 feet (76 m) wide. It sits in an area of the sea that is only about 23 feet (7 m) deep. Officials are not yet sure whether the island will dissolve over time, or if it is a permanent addition to the Arabian Sea. Scientists will study the mud it is made of to try to predict if it will stay where it is or eventually sink back into the ocean.

Volcanic Islands

Earthquakes can cause islands to form, and volcanoes can too. Beginning in November 2013, a new island, referred to as **Niijima,** appeared. It is located next to the tiny Japanese island Nishino Shima, in the Pacific Ocean. Underwater volcanic activity released steam, rocks, and ash, which led to the creation of the new land. Over the next weeks, Niijima merged with Nishino Shima. Some scientists predict that the new land will remain above water for at least several years. But just as islands can appear, they can disappear too.

Where in the World?

THE DEEPEST CANYON IN THE UNITED STATES
Carved by the Snake River, Hells Canyon on the border of Idaho, Washington, and Oregon is more than 8,000 feet (2,438 m) deep.

THE HIGHEST PLACE ON EARTH
Mount Everest, in Nepal, the world's tallest mountain, stands 29,035 feet (8,850 m) above sea level.

THE DEEPEST PLACE ON EARTH
Deep in the Pacific Ocean is the Mariana Trench, which is 35,827 feet (10,920 m) below sea level.

THE LARGEST SALTWATER LAKE ON EARTH
The landlocked Caspian Sea has a volume of water greater than any other lake, including all freshwater lakes.

THE LARGEST RAIN FOREST ON EARTH
The Amazon in South America covers parts of Brazil, Bolivia, Ecuador, Peru, Colombia, Venezuela, Suriname, French Guiana, and Guyana.

THE LARGEST ACTIVE VOLCANO ON EARTH
At about 50,000 feet (15,240 m) above its base, Mauna Loa, in Hawaii, is actually taller than Mount Everest. But most of the volcano is under the sea.

THE TALLEST TREE ON EARTH
Hyperion, a redwood in Redwood National Park, California, stands at 379 feet (115.5 m).

THE TALLEST WATERFALL ON EARTH
Angel Falls (Salto Angel), in Venezuela's Canaima National Park, has a 3,287-foot (1,002 m) drop.

THE DRIEST PLACE ON EARTH
Arica, Chile, gets just 0.03 inches (0.8 cm) of rainfall a year.

THE HOTTEST PLACE ON EARTH
On July 10, 1913, the temperature reached 134°F (56.7°C) in Death Valley, California.

THE COLDEST PLACE ON EARTH
The East Antarctic Plateau reached a low of −136°F (−93.2°C) on August 10, 2010.

GEOGRAPHY

THE LONGEST RIVER
The Nile runs for 4,160 miles (6,695 km).

GOVERNMENT

Read Sandra Day O'Connor's smart advice for kids. **Page 140**

Constitution Q&A BY GLENN GREENBERG

The U.S. Constitution may be more than 225 years old, but it's certainly not showing its age. This document is as important to the country today as it was when it was first signed on September 17, 1787. The Constitution established our national government and lists the rights of U.S. citizens. Jeffrey Rosen, the president of the National Constitution Center in Philadelphia, Pennsylvania, spoke with TIME FOR KIDS about what the document means and why it should be celebrated.

TFK: How would you describe the U.S. Constitution?

JEFFREY ROSEN: The Constitution is our fundamental law. It both empowers and limits our government. The part of the Constitution that limits government is most notably the Bill of Rights, the first 10 amendments to the Constitution, which includes rights like freedom of speech, freedom of religion, and rights against unreasonable searches and seizures. Those rights make clear that government can't do certain things and has to respect the basic rights of the people.

TFK: Why is the Constitution so important?

ROSEN: The Constitution is the most important document in American history. It expresses our basic values as a people: our commitment to democracy, popular sovereignty, free speech, and limited government. It expresses who we are as a people. We as Americans are united by our attachment to the basic rights and values expressed in the Constitution. It's the most inspiring and beautiful document there is.

TFK: Americans celebrate Constitution Day every year on September 17. What is the best way to celebrate the Constitution on Constitution Day?

ROSEN: Of course, the very best way would be to come to the National Constitution Center! We are a center of constitutional education and debate. But if you're not able to do that, the best way would be to learn about the Constitution and debate it. Having citizens actively debate the meaning of the Constitution is what ultimately determines its meaning in the 21st century and beyond. Read the Bill of Rights, pick an amendment, such as freedom of speech, and discuss with your friends what you think it means.

The National Constitution Center, which opened in 2003, has interactive exhibits.

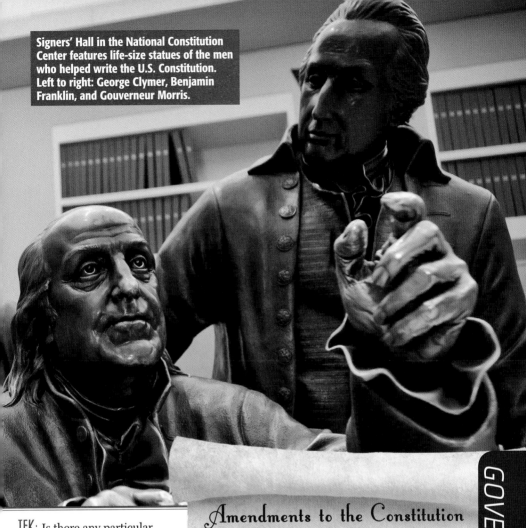

Signers' Hall in the National Constitution Center features life-size statues of the men who helped write the U.S. Constitution. Left to right: George Clymer, Benjamin Franklin, and Gouverneur Morris.

TFK: Is there any particular exhibit at the National Constitution Center that you would recommend to visitors?

ROSEN: I would go right up our beautiful marble stairs to Signers' Hall. There, you'll find beautifully rendered, historically accurate life-size statues of all the framers of the Constitution. Ben Franklin is the most popular. People love to touch him. You'll see how short Alexander Hamilton was! The excitement of seeing the framers all in one place is something that visitors always love and it's definitely a great place to experience Constitution Day.

Amendments to the Constitution

The framers of the U.S. Constitution always knew it would be a document that could grow and change as the nation changed. In the years since the Bill of Rights was ratified, 27 amendments have been added to the U.S. Constitution. Here are a few.

The **6th Amendment** (1791) says citizens have the right to a speedy, public trial by jury and the right to have an attorney during a trial.

The **13th Amendment** (1865) abolishes slavery.

The **19th Amendment** (1920) extends the right to vote to women.

The **22nd Amendment** (1951) says that a person cannot be elected president of the United States more than twice.

The **26th Amendment** (1971) lowers the voting age from 21 to 18.

FROM
TIME
FOR KIDS
MAGAZINE

The **3** Branches of the U.S. Government

The U.S. government is divided into three branches:

The **LEGISLATIVE** branch makes the laws. It is made up of a bicameral, or two-chambered, legislature. The two chambers are the Senate and the House of Representatives. To become a law, a bill must be approved by both chambers. Both chambers have the power to hold hearings to gather information on the bills they are considering.

The **EXECUTIVE** branch carries out the laws made by the legislative branch. This branch is made up of the president, the vice president, and the cabinet.

The **JUDICIAL** branch determines whether the laws created by the legislature and enforced by the executive branch are constitutional. The judicial branch is made up of the Supreme Court and federal courts around the country.

The purpose of this structure is to provide a separation of powers among three equally important branches. The three branches of government have different responsibilities, but they work together to keep any one branch from becoming too powerful.

FOR EXAMPLE, the legislative branch creates laws, but the judicial branch can strike down a law if it conflicts with the spirit of the Constitution.

Two Powerful Houses

The U.S. Congress is made up of two houses.
Together, they make the nation's laws.

THE HOUSE OF REPRESENTATIVES

This chamber includes 435 representatives. The larger a state's population, the more representatives it has. Representatives are elected to two-year terms. The speaker of the House presides over the sessions.

The House of Representatives has the following special powers and responsibilities:

Create bills that allow the government to collect taxes.

Create bills that empower the government to spend money.

Elect the president in the event that no candidate receives a majority of electoral votes.

Vote to impeach the president, vice president, or other elected official. This means to formally charge a public official with wrongdoing.

GUESS WHAT? To run for the House of Representatives, a candidate must be at least 25 years old.

THE SENATE

This chamber includes 100 senators, two for each state. Senators are elected to six-year terms, with one-third of the Senate being elected every even-numbered year. The vice president (or president pro tempore, in the vice president's absence) presides over the sessions.

GUESS WHAT? To run for the Senate, a person must be at least 30 years old.

The Senate has the following special powers and responsibilities:

Ratify, or approve, treaties made by the president. This requires a two-thirds vote of all senators.

Accept or reject (by majority vote of all senators) the president's appointments of Supreme Court justices and federal judges, ambassadors, and other high-level executive-branch officials.

Hold trials of officials impeached by the House of Representatives and convict or acquit them. A two-thirds vote of all senators is needed for conviction.

GOVERNMENT

Together, the president, the vice president, and the cabinet make up the executive branch of the government.

The **PRESIDENT** is the leader of the nation and the commander in chief of the U.S. Armed Forces. To learn more about what the president does, go to page 190.

The **VICE PRESIDENT** presides over the Senate but casts a vote only in the event of a tie. If the president dies, resigns, or is removed from office, the vice president assumes the office of president. Like the president, the vice president must be a native-born U.S. citizen, must be at least 35 years old, and must have lived in the United States for at least 14 years.

The **CABINET** is made up of 15 department heads who advise the president. Today, the president's cabinet consists of the vice president plus 15 secretaries. Cabinet secretaries are nominated by the president, then each nominee is questioned by the Senate. These interviews are known as confirmation hearings. Each nominee must be confirmed, or approved, by a majority of 51 or more senators. Here are the cabinet departments, along with their Web addresses.

 Agriculture usda.gov

 Commerce commerce.gov

 Defense defense.gov

 Education ed.gov

 Energy energy.gov

 Health and Human Services hhs.gov

 Homeland Security dhs.gov

 Housing and Urban Development hud.gov

 Interior doi.gov

 Justice (Attorney General) justice.gov

 Labor dol.gov

 State state.gov

 Transportation dot.gov

 Treasury treasury.gov

 Veterans Affairs va.gov

The U.S. Supreme Court and federal courts interpret the way an established law must be carried out.

There are many **federal courts** around the country. Known as the lower courts, these include U.S. district courts, courts of appeals, bankruptcy courts, and others. There are also special courts, some of which handle appeals for veterans and members of the armed services. The **Supreme Court** is the highest court in the country. Most of the cases that the Supreme Court hears come from the lower courts. A person with a legal claim can petition, or ask, the Supreme Court to review a decision from a lower court. The Supreme Court also hears cases in which one state sues another or a state sues the national government.

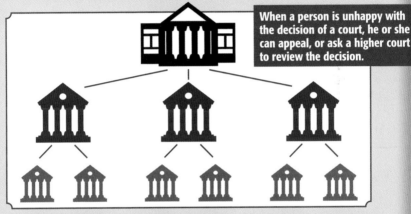

When a person is unhappy with the decision of a court, he or she can appeal, or ask a higher court to review the decision.

The Supreme Court has the power to declare a law unconstitutional. The court consists of eight associate justices and a chief justice. All decisions are made by a majority vote of the justices.

Supreme Court justices and federal judges are appointed by the president and confirmed by the Senate. They serve for life or until they decide to resign or retire.

Elena Kagan is the newest justice. She joined the Supreme Court in 2010.

Sonia Sotomayor   Stephen G. Breyer   Samuel A. Alito Jr.   Elena Kagan

Clarence Thomas   Antonin Scalia   Chief Justice John G. Roberts   Anthony M. Kennedy   Ruth Bader Ginsberg

GOVERNMENT

A Chat with Sandra Day O'Connor BY TFK KID REPORTER BRIDGET BERNARDO

In 1981, Sandra Day O'Connor made history when she became the first woman on the United States Supreme Court. Justice O'Connor retired in 2005, but she remains very active. She has written a book about the history of the high court, *Out of Order: Stories from the History of the Supreme Court.* Over lunch, we discussed the justice's life after the court and what she describes as her most important project: a Web-based program called iCivics that was designed to teach kids about how federal, state, and local governments work.

TFK: You said iCivics is the most important thing you've ever done. Why?

O'CONNOR: Because it is teaching, I hope, several generations of young people how they are going to be good citizens. I think that's the most important thing there is.

TFK: Why should kids learn about civics?

O'CONNOR: Because I think it's critically important that everybody understand how our government works and how we're each part of it. . . . It matters and it matters for your whole life, so I just think it's very, very important.

TFK: One of the games on iCivics is called Executive Command, where you can be the president. If you were president and your chief justice had just retired, what qualities would you look for in a nominee for the new chief justice?

O'CONNOR: I would want somebody who had considerable experience so I could look back and see what kind of job they do. I want to know what kind of opinions they write, what decisions they're making. You would find out everything you could. You'd want to check all the newspaper reports about the person and all the information you can get from respected leaders. That's an important appointment.

TFK: You retired from the Supreme Court in 2005. Why are you still so busy?

O'CONNOR: Because I have a lot of energy. That's why.

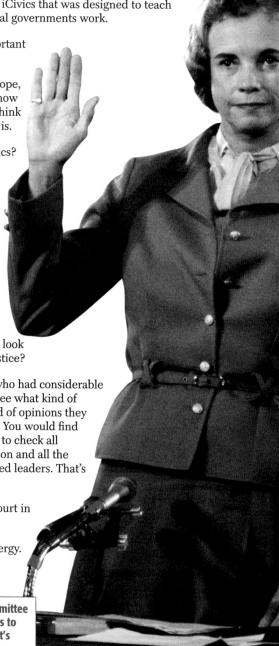

O'Connor testifies before a Senate committee in 1981. The Senators use these hearings to decide if they will confirm the president's appointment of a Supreme Court judge.

TFK: I watched Chief Justice Roberts' introduction to his confirmation hearing, and he compared being a judge to being an umpire.

O'CONNOR: There is a lot more to being a judge than being an umpire. You have to make very challenging decisions sometimes. Sometimes based on facts, sometimes on the law, and . . . it's hard. Umpires just have to make instant calls: You're in or you're out, he hit it or he didn't. A judge [has] to weigh options and weigh arguments on both sides and make very technical, complicated decisions.

TFK: What is your advice to kids?

O'CONNOR: Learn all you can. Be a good reader. There is no limit to what you can learn if you're a good reader.

TFK: What was the biggest challenge you faced as a Supreme Court justice?

O'CONNOR: The biggest challenge is to be able to feel that you have performed well. That you've been able to do the work in a fair and decent way and that you've helped the cause of justice. That's what you want—to have a good feeling about what you've done. That's true of anything you try to do. You want to feel at the end of the day you've done the best you could and have really performed as well as could be expected.

TFK: Who is your favorite Founding Father?

O'CONNOR: Madison. Because he wrote the Constitution. He was the best by far.

MYSTERY PERSON

I was a lawyer and a civil rights activist who was born in Baltimore, Maryland, in 1908. I argued *Brown v. Board of Education* in front of the nation's top court in 1954. In deciding the case, the court declared racial segregation in public schools to be illegal. I was the first African American to be appointed to the U.S. Supreme Court.

WHO AM I?

Answer on page 276

O'Connor speaks before a Senate committee, about the importance of civics education.

GOVERNMENT

HISTORY

The Spanish-American War was fought in which year? **Page 151**

A TIME LINE OF PREHISTORY

The period before human beings began keeping records is called prehistory. Scientists examine fossils and rock formations to make educated guesses about what happened on Earth.

PRECAMBRIAN ERA

4.5 BILLION YEARS AGO Earth is formed from the dust and debris thrown off by an exploding star.

3.8 BILLION YEARS AGO The first rocks on Earth—chunks of Earth's crust—appear. There is evidence of bacteria in these rocks.

2.5 BILLION YEARS AGO Single-celled cynobacteria use the sun's power to create oxygen. The process is similar to the way plants create oxygen in photosynthesis.

This straight-shelled nautiloid was common during the Ordovician period.

PALEOZOIC ERA

CAMBRIAN PERIOD

570 MILLION YEARS AGO Very simple creatures appear. Made of just a few cells, they have shells and can move about. Over the next 20 to 30 million years, early fish, shellfish, and corals are born.

ORDOVICIAN PERIOD

440–450 MILLION YEARS AGO A mass extinction occurs during the Ordovician period. Many scientists think Earth may have suddenly cooled, killing off huge amounts of marine life (animals and plants that live in water).

SILURIAN PERIOD

430 MILLION YEARS AGO The first plants start growing in water. Later, they develop root systems that allow them to live on dry land.

DEVONIAN PERIOD

370 MILLION YEARS AGO Fish leave the water and begin to breathe on land. These early amphibians look a little like crocodiles. Some insects come into existence.

CARBONIFEROUS PERIOD

300–360 MILLION YEARS AGO During the Carboniferous period, all the land areas on Earth join into one supercontinent known as Pangaea. The land is mostly marshy swamp, covered with plants such as tree ferns, mosses, cycads, and giant trees. This vegetation absorbs lots of carbon dioxide and creates an oxygen-rich atmosphere.

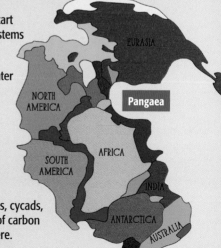

EURASIA

NORTH AMERICA

Pangaea

SOUTH AMERICA

AFRICA

INDIA

ANTARCTICA

AUSTRALIA

251–300 MILLION YEARS AGO
The first reptiles appear. They evolve slowly into sluggish creatures, some with odd-looking sails on their backs.

245–251 MILLION YEARS AGO The Great Dying occurs during the Triassic period. About 95% of marine life and 70% of the plants and animals on land are wiped out. Some scientists think that the climate may have changed because of volcanic eruptions or gases released from the ocean floor.

200–240 MILLION YEARS AGO The first dinosaurs appear. The earliest are about the size of kangaroos and are called prosauropods. Diplodocus, stegosaurus, and brachiosaurus are some of the dinosaurs that lived during this time. During this period, Pangaea breaks into separate continents, with oceans and seas between them.

An early reptile with a sail on its back was the dimetrodon.

145–200 MILLION YEARS AGO During the Jurassic period, the landscape is lush and green, with palm trees and lots of shrubs. Plant-eating dinosaurs, like the apatosaurus and the seismosaurus, thrive and become gigantic. The seismosaurus is about 148 feet (45 m) long. It has a tiny head and swallows rocks to help process all the leaves it eats. Meat-eating dinosaurs also roam the Earth, eating everything in sight. Cryolophosaurus is the fastest. Gasosaurus has incredibly powerful jaws.

65–145 MILLION YEARS AGO There are even more dinosaurs in the Cretaceous period than in the Jurassic period. Different dinosaurs develop different features that help protect them from predators and help them kill their prey. For example, the horns on a triceratops's head could gore other dinosaurs. The biggest and most fierce of all Cretaceous meat eaters is the *Tyrannosaurus rex,* or T. rex.

The fossilized bones of an Albertosaurus, a meat eater

65 MILLION YEARS AGO About 65 million years ago, something happens that kills all the dinosaurs. Some think that deadly germs were to blame. Others believe that dinosaurs killed and ate each other. There is also a theory that a huge asteroid slammed into Earth and created walls of water and dust that killed the dinosaurs. It's one of the great mysteries of world history.

65 MILLION YEARS AGO–THE PRESENT The continents reach their current positions. New life evolves. Many mammals, including humans, appear in this period. Around 6,000 years ago, humans start leaving records, which marks the end of prehistory and the beginning of history.

Saber-toothed cats became extinct about 12,000 years ago.

PERMIAN PERIOD

TRIASSIC PERIOD

MESOZOIC ERA

JURASSIC PERIOD

CRETACEOUS PERIOD

CENOZOIC ERA

ANCIENT HISTORY

5000–3500 B.C. Sumer, located in what is now Iraq, becomes the earliest known civilization. Sumerians develop a written alphabet, among other innovations.

3500–2600 B.C. People settle in the Indus River Valley, in what is now India and Pakistan.

2600 B.C. Minoan civilization begins on the island of Crete, in the Mediterranean Sea.

CIRCA 2560 B.C. The Egyptian king Khufu finishes building the Great Pyramid at Giza. The Great Sphinx is completed soon after by Khufu's son Khaefre.

2000 B.C. Babylonians develop a system of mathematics.
 • The kingdom of Kush, in Africa, becomes a major center of trade and learning.

1792 B.C. Hammurabi becomes the ruler of Babylonia. He creates the first set of laws, now known as Hammurabi's Code.

CIRCA 1600–1050 B.C. The Shang Dynasty is the first Chinese dynasty to leave written records.

551 B.C. Chinese philosopher Confucius is born. His teachings on honesty, humanity, and how people should treat one another are the foundations of Confucianism.

510 B.C. Democracy is established in Athens, Greece.

500 B.C. Carthage, in modern-day Tunisia, becomes an important trading center on the Mediterranean coast. During the Punic Wars (264 to 146 B.C.), Carthage battles with Rome. In 219, Hannibal, Carthage's leader, leads an army of troops and elephants across the Alps into Italy but is eventually defeated.

438 B.C. Construction of the Parthenon temple on the Acropolis (the highest hill in Athens) is completed.

431 B.C. The Peloponnesian War breaks out between Sparta and Athens. In 404 B.C., Sparta finally wins the war and takes over Athens.

334 B.C. Macedonian king Alexander the Great invades Persia. He eventually conquers lands from Greece to India. He even crosses into North Africa.

The Trojan War

1200 B.C. The Trojan War is fought between the Greeks and the Trojans.

814 B.C. The city of Carthage, located in what is now Tunisia, is founded by the Phoenicians.

753 B.C. According to legend, Rome is founded by Romulus.

563 B.C. Siddhartha Gautama, who becomes the Buddha, or Enlightened One, is born. He will become the founder of the Buddhist religion.

100 B.C. The great city of Teotihuacán flourishes in Mexico.

58 B.C. Julius Caesar leaves Rome for Gaul (France) and spends nine years conquering much of central Europe. He is murdered in 44 B.C.

27 B.C. Octavian becomes the first Roman emperor, ushering in a long period of peace. He is also known by the title Augustus.

WORLD HISTORY

CIRCA 1 A.D. Jesus Christ is born. He is crucified by the Romans around 30 A.D.

66 Jews rebel against Roman rule. The revolution is put down by the Romans, who destroy Jerusalem (in present-day Israel) in 70 A.D. and force many Jews into slavery.

79 Mount Vesuvius erupts, destroying the city of Pompeii (in present-day Italy).

122 Construction on Hadrian's Wall begins. It spans northern England and offers protection from the tribes to the north.

CIRCA 250 The classic period of Mayan civilization begins. It lasts until about 900. The Maya erect impressive stone buildings and temples in areas that are now part of Mexico and Central America.

330 Constantine the Great chooses Byzantium as the capital of the Roman Empire, and the city becomes known as Constantinople.

476 The Roman Empire collapses.

622 Muhammad, the founder of Islam, flees from Mecca to Medina in what is now Saudi Arabia. This journey is called the Hegira. After the death of Muhammad in 632, Muslims conquer much of North Africa and the Middle East. In 711, Muslims also conquer Spain.

700–800 Ghana is the major empire in Africa south of the Sahara desert. The kingdom, which controls the gold trade, reaches its peak in the 11th century before being defeated by Almoravids of Morocco.

800 Charlemagne is crowned the first Holy Roman Emperor by Pope Leo III.

960 The Song Dynasty begins in China. This dynasty is known for its advances in art, poetry, and philosophy.

CIRCA 1000–1300 During the classic period of their culture, Anasazi people build homes and other structures in the sides of cliffs in what is now the southwestern United States.

1066 At the Battle of Hastings, the Norman king William the Conqueror invades England and defeats English king Harold II.

1095 Pope Urban II delivers a speech urging Christians to capture the Holy Land from the Muslims. The fighting between 1096 and 1291 is known as the Crusades.

CIRCA 1200 The Inca Empire begins, and elaborate stone structures are eventually built in Cuzco and Machu Picchu, Peru. The Incas flourish until Francisco Pizarro, a Spaniard, conquers them in 1533.

1206 A Mongolian warrior named Temujin is proclaimed Genghis Khan. He expands his empire so that it includes most of Asia.

1215 A group of barons in England force King John to sign the Magna Carta, a document limiting the power of the king.

1271–1295 Marco Polo, a Venetian merchant, travels throughout Asia. His book, *Il Milione* (*The Million*), is a major European source of information about Asia.

1273 The Habsburg Dynasty begins in Eastern Europe. It remains a powerful force in the region until World War I.

1325 Aztecs begin building Tenochtitlán on the site of modern Mexico City.

1337 The Hundred Years' War starts between the English and French. France finally wins in 1453.

1347 The Black Death, or bubonic plague, breaks out in Europe. It spreads quickly, killing more than one-third of Europe's population.

1368 The Ming Dynasty is founded in China by Buddhist monk Zhu Yuanzhang (or Chu Yuan-Chang).

Aztec art

1434 Portuguese explorer Gil Eannes sails past Cape Bojador, in western Africa, which was thought to be the end of the world.

1453 Constantinople falls to the Ottoman Turks, ending the Byzantine Empire.

1455 Johannes Gutenberg invents the printing press. The Gutenberg Bible is the first book printed on the press.

1464–1591 Based in what is now Mali, Songhai is an important empire in Africa. When it is destroyed by armies from Morocco, the great culture of Timbuktu is lost.

1478 The Spanish Inquisition begins.

1487–1488 Bartholomeu Dias of Portugal leads the first European expedition around the Cape of Good Hope, at the southern tip of Africa, opening up a sea route to Asia.

1492 Christopher Columbus leaves Spain, hoping to sail to the East Indies. Instead, he and his crew land in the Bahamas and visit Cuba, Hispaniola (which is now Haiti and the Dominican Republic), and other small islands.

1497–1499 Portuguese explorer Vasco da Gama leads the first European expedition to India by sea via the Cape of Good Hope.

Francisco Pizarro

1517 Martin Luther protests the abuses of the Catholic Church, which leads to a religious split and the rise of the Protestant faith.

1519 While exploring Mexico, Spanish adventurer Hernán Cortés conquers the Aztec Empire.

1519–1522 Portuguese explorer Ferdinand Magellan's expedition circumnavigates, or sails around, the globe.

1532–1533 Spanish explorer Francisco Pizarro conquers the Inca Empire in South America.

1543 Polish astronomer Copernicus shares his theory that the sun, not the Earth, is the center of the universe.

1547 Ivan the Terrible becomes the first czar, or ruler, of Russia.

1588 The English defeat the Spanish Armada, or fleet of warships, when Spain attempts to invade England.

1618 The Thirty Years' War breaks out between Protestants and Catholics in Europe.

1620 English Pilgrims aboard the *Mayflower* land at Plymouth Rock, in present-day Massachusetts.

1632 Italian astronomer Galileo, the first person to use a telescope to look into space, confirms Copernicus's theory that Earth revolves around the sun.

1642 The English Civil War, sometimes called the Puritan Revolution, begins in Britain.

1688 The Glorious Revolution, or Bloodless Revolution, takes place in England. James II is removed from the throne, and William and Mary become the heads of the country.

1721 Peter the Great becomes czar of Russia.

1789 An angry mob storms the Bastille, a prison in Paris, setting off the French Revolution.

1803 Denmark becomes the first country in Europe to ban slave trading. Four years later, Britain does the same. The U.S. bans the slave trade in 1808.

1819 Simón Bolívar crosses the Andes to launch a surprise attack against the Spanish, liberating New Granada (now Colombia, Venezuela, Panama, and Ecuador) from Spain.

1824 Mexico becomes independent from Spain.

1845 A blight ruins the potato crop in Ireland. More than 1 million Irish starve to death, and an additional million leave for the United States to escape the Irish potato famine.

1848 This is known as the year of revolutions in Europe, as there is upheaval in France, Italy, Germany, Hungary, and elsewhere.

1859 Charles Darwin publishes *On the Origin of Species,* which introduces the scientific theory of evolution.

1871 A group of independent states unifies, creating the German Empire.

1876 Alexander Graham Bell invents the telephone.

1884–1885 During the Berlin Conference, European leaders divide up Africa into areas of control.

1892 The diesel engine is invented by Parisian Rudolf Diesel.

1893 New Zealand becomes the first country to give women the right to vote.
• The Columbian Exposition, also known as the Chicago World's Fair, is held.

1894 The Sino-Japanese War breaks out between China and Japan, who are fighting for control of Korea. An 1895 treaty declares Korea independent.

1898 The Spanish-American War begins.

1899 During the Boxer Rebellion, the Chinese fight against Christian and foreign influences in their country. American, Japanese, and European forces help stop the fighting by 1901.

1904 Japan declares war on Russia, beginning the Russo-Japanese War. The countries clash over influence in Manchuria and Korea. Japan wins the conflict and becomes a world power.

1909 Robert Peary is credited as being the first to reach the North Pole, although recent evidence suggests he might have reached only as far as 30 to 60 miles (48 to 97 km) away.

1911 Roald Amundsen, the first man to travel the Northwest Passage, reaches the South Pole.

1914 Austro-Hungarian archduke Franz Ferdinand is assassinated, setting off the chain of events that starts World War I.

1917 The United States enters World War I.
• Led by socialist Vladimir Lenin, the Russian Revolution begins. The czarist government is overthrown, and in 1922, the Soviet Union is formed.

1918 A flu epidemic spreads quickly around the world, killing more than 20 million people.

1919 The Treaty of Versailles ends World War I.

1927 Philo Farnsworth invents the television.

1928 Alexander Fleming discovers penicillin accidentally, after leaving a dish of staphylococcus bacteria uncovered and finding mold.

1929 The U.S. stock market collapses, beginning the Great Depression.

1933 Adolf Hitler becomes chancellor of Germany.
• Frequency modulation, or FM, radio is developed by Edwin Armstrong.

1936 The Spanish Civil War breaks out.

1939 World War II begins when Germany invades Poland. Britain responds by declaring war on Germany. The United States declares neutrality.

1941 The Japanese launch a surprise attack on the United States, bombing U.S. ships docked in Hawaii's Pearl Harbor. In response, the United States declares war on Japan, and both Germany and Italy declare war on the U.S.

1945 Germany surrenders on May 7, ending the war in Europe. In August, the United States drops two atomic bombs on the Japanese cities Hiroshima and Nagasaki. Japan surrenders, ending World War II.

The Boxer Rebellion

WORLD HISTORY

1947 India and Pakistan become free of British colonial rule.

1948 Israel becomes a nation.

1949 Following China's civil war, Mao Zedong sets up the Communist People's Republic of China.
• South Africa enacts apartheid laws, which make discrimination against nonwhite people part of public policy.

1950 North Korean communist forces invade South Korea, beginning the Korean War. U.S. forces support South Korea. China backs North Korea. The war ends three years later.
• Frank McNamara develops the first credit card, Diners Club.

1952 The hydrogen bomb is developed by Edward Teller and a team at a laboratory in Los Alamos, New Mexico.

1953 Edmund Hillary and Tenzing Norgay climb to the top of Mount Everest.

1955 Jonas Salk's polio vaccine is introduced.

1957 Ghana is the first territory in sub-Saharan Africa to regain its independence from a European power. Over the next 20 years, most African countries also become independent.

1961 A group of Cuban exiles, supported by the United States, invades Cuba at the Bay of Pigs. The invasion fails, and U.S.-Cuban relations worsen.
• Aboard the Vostok spacecraft, Yuri Gagarin becomes the first human in space.

1962 The Cuban Missile Crisis, a conflict between the United States, the Soviet Union, and Cuba, brings the world to the brink of nuclear war.

1963 U.S. President John F. Kennedy is assassinated on November 22, 1963. Vice President Lyndon B. Johnson is inaugurated.

1965 The United States begins officially sending troops to Vietnam to aid South Vietnam in its civil war with North Vietnam.

1967 The Six-Day War breaks out between Israel and neighboring Arab nations Egypt, Syria, and Jordan. Israel seizes the Golan Heights, the Gaza Strip, the Sinai Peninsula, and part of the West Bank of the Jordan River.

1969 Neil Armstrong is the first person to walk on the surface of the moon.

1973 The Paris Peace Accords end the Vietnam War. North Vietnam later violates the terms of the treaty and, in 1975, takes control of Saigon, the capital of South Vietnam.
• Egypt and Syria launch a surprise attack on Israel, beginning the Yom Kippur War.

1978 U.S. President Jimmy Carter, Israeli President Menachem Begin, and Egyptian President Anwar Sadat sign the Camp David Accords in an attempt to achieve peace in the Middle East.

1979 Religious leader Ayatollah Khomeini declares Iran to be an Islamic republic.

1989 The Chinese army crushes a demonstration in Tiananmen Square, in Beijing, killing hundreds, possibly thousands, of students and protesters.
• The Berlin Wall is torn down, and the city of Berlin, Germany, is reunified.

1990 Apartheid ends in South Africa. Four years later, Nelson Mandela is elected president in the country's first free, multiracial elections.
• The Persian Gulf War begins when Iraq invades Kuwait.

1991 The Soviet Union dissolves.
• Croatia, Slovenia, and Macedonia declare independence from Yugoslavia. The next year, the country of Bosnia and Herzegovina also declares independence, but war breaks out and does not end until 1995.
• Tim Berners-Lee develops the World Wide Web.

1994 Tensions between the Hutu majority and the Tutsi minority in Rwanda, Africa, lead to a genocide, or systematic killing of a racial or ethnic group. About 800,000 Tutsis are killed.

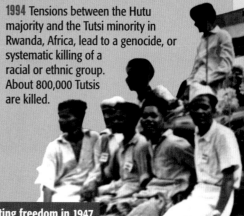

Indians celebrating freedom in 1947

1999 Honda releases the two-door Insight, the first hybrid car marketed to the masses in the United States. A year later, the Toyota Prius, the first hybrid four-door sedan, is released.

2001 After the September 11 terrorist attacks in New York City and Washington, D.C., the United States declares an international War on Terror, attacking the Taliban government in Afghanistan and searching for Osama bin Laden and al-Qaeda.

2003 With the aid of Britain and other allies, the United States invades Iraq. Though the government falls quickly, resistance and fighting continue. In 2006, Saddam Hussein is executed for crimes against humanity.
• War in the Darfur region of Sudan begins, leading to a humanitarian crisis.

2004 A powerful tsunami kills nearly 300,000 people in Indonesia, Sri Lanka, India, Thailand, and other Asian countries.

2006 Ellen Johnson-Sirleaf becomes president of Liberia. She is Africa's first elected female leader.

2008 A global economic crisis leads to loss of jobs and homes, and to a downturn in trade.

2010 A devastating earthquake hits Haiti.
• An oil rig in the Gulf of Mexico explodes, causing one of the largest oil spills in history.

2011 Protests erupt in the Middle East and North Africa, toppling leaders in Tunisia and Egypt. There is instability throughout the region.
• A massive earthquake strikes Japan, triggering a powerful tsunami.
• After intense fighting in Libya, rebels gain control of most of the country. Libyan president Muammar Gaddafi is killed. The National Transitional Council (NTC) struggles to form a stable government.
• The world population officially exceeds 7 billion on October 31. It continues to rise.

2012 In Syria, demonstrators demand the resignation of President Bashar al-Assad and the overthrow of the government. The government deploys its army to quash the uprising and kills thousands.

2013 Pope Benedict XVI steps down as the head of the Catholic Church. He is the first pope to step down in nearly 600 years. Jorge Mario Bergoglio, of Argentina, becomes the new pope, taking on the name Francis.
• Prince George is born to Britain's Prince William and Catherine, Duchess of Cambridge.
• The United Nations (U.N.) confirms that chemical weapons were used in the Syrian civil war. Leaders around the world demand that Syrian officials give up their stockpiles of chemical weapons. U.N. workers begin destroying the chemicals in October.

MYSTERY PERSON

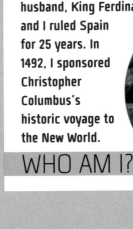

I was born in Castile in 1451. My husband, King Ferdinand II, and I ruled Spain for 25 years. In 1492, I sponsored Christopher Columbus's historic voyage to the New World.

WHO AM I?

Answer on page 276

1524 Italian explorer Giovanni da Verrazano is the first European to reach New York Harbor.

1540 In search of gold, Spanish explorer Francisco Vásquez de Coronado travels north from Mexico. One of his lieutenants is the first European to spot the Grand Canyon.

1541 Spaniard Hernando de Soto crosses the Mississippi River.

1579 Sir Francis Drake of England explores California's coastline.

1607 English settlers found Jamestown in Virginia. The colony's leader, John Smith, is captured by Native Americans. According to legend, he is saved by Pocahontas.

1609–1611 Henry Hudson visits the Chesapeake Bay, Delaware Bay, and New York Bay and becomes the first European to sail up the Hudson River.

1620 Pilgrims land at Plymouth, Massachusetts.

1626 Dutchman Peter Minuit buys the island of Manhattan from the Canarsie tribe.

1692 In Massachusetts, accusations of witchcraft lead to the Salem witch trials and the executions of 20 people.

1770 Tensions between British soldiers and colonists erupt in the Boston Massacre, when British troops kill five men.

1773 Colonists protest a tax on tea by dressing up as Native Americans, boarding ships, and dumping tea into Boston Harbor. Known as the Boston Tea Party, the protest angers the British, who pass other harsh taxes.

1775 Paul Revere warns the colonists that the British are coming. The Battle of Lexington and Concord is the first fight of the American Revolution. The British surrender at Yorktown, Virginia, in 1781.

1776 Drafted by Thomas Jefferson, the Declaration of Independence is signed, and the United States is formed.

1787 The U.S. Constitution is written and submitted to the states for ratification. By the end of the year, Delaware, Pennsylvania, and New Jersey have accepted it.

1789 George Washington becomes the first President of the United States.

1791 The Bill of Rights, written mostly by James Madison, becomes part of the Constitution.

1803 President Thomas Jefferson buys the Louisiana Territory from France, adding 885,000 square miles (2,292,139 sq km) to the United States.

1804–1806 Meriwether Lewis and William Clark explore the Louisiana territory. They reach the Pacific Ocean in 1805.

1812 The War of 1812 breaks out between the United States and Britain because of trade and border disputes, as well as disagreements about freedom of the seas. The Treaty of Ghent ends the war in 1814.

1823 President James Monroe issues the Monroe Doctrine, warning that the Americas are not open for colonization.

1836 Texas declares independence from Mexico. In response, the Mexican army attacks and kills the 189 Texans defending the Alamo.

1838 In what is known as the Trail of Tears, the U.S. government forces 16,000 Cherokees to leave their land in Georgia and relocate to a reservation in Oklahoma. Roughly a quarter of the Cherokees die.

George Washington

1846 The Mexican-American War begins. At the end of the fighting, in 1848, Mexico gives California and New Mexico (which also includes present-day Arizona, Utah, and Nevada) to the United States. In return, the United States agrees to pay Mexico $15 million.

1848 John Sutter strikes gold in California, kicking off the California gold rush.

1860 Tensions between the North and the South over slavery, taxes, and representation reach a boiling point, and South Carolina secedes from the United States.

1861 Mississippi, Florida, Alabama, Georgia, Louisiana, and Texas secede from the Union, and the Confederate government is formed. The first shots of the American Civil War are fired by Confederate soldiers at Fort Sumter, in South Carolina's Charleston Harbor. Virginia, Arkansas, Tennessee, and North Carolina also secede from the Union.

1862 The Homestead Act promises 160 acres (647,497 sq m) of land to anyone who remains on the land for five years. This law encourages settlers to move west.

1863 President Abraham Lincoln issues the Emancipation Proclamation, which frees all slaves in the Confederate states. The Battle of Gettysburg is fought. It is the bloodiest battle of the Civil War.

1865 General Robert E. Lee of the Confederacy surrenders to Union General Ulysses S. Grant at Appomattox Court House, in Virginia, ending the Civil War.
• President Lincoln is assassinated at Ford's Theater by John Wilkes Booth, and Andrew Johnson becomes President.
• The 13th Amendment, which puts an end to slavery, is ratified.

1869 The transcontinental railroad is completed.

1890 The Battle of Wounded Knee is the last major defeat for Native American tribes.

1898 The Spanish-American War is fought. At the end of the war, Cuba is independent, and Puerto Rico, Guam, and the Philippines become territories of the United States.

1903 Wilbur and Orville Wright complete their first airplane flight at Kitty Hawk, North Carolina.

1908 Henry Ford, founder of the Ford Motor Company, builds the Model T and sells it for $825, making automobiles much more affordable than ever before.

1917 The United States enters World War I.

1920 With the passage of the 19th Amendment, women get the right to vote.

1929 The U.S. stock market crashes, and the Great Depression begins.

1941 In a surprise attack, Japan bombs the U.S. fleet at Pearl Harbor, in Hawaii. The United States declares war on Japan. Germany and Italy declare war on the United States.

1945 Germany surrenders on May 7, ending the war in Europe. In August, the U.S. aircraft *Enola Gay* drops an atomic bomb on Hiroshima, Japan. Three days later, a U.S. plane drops an atomic bomb on the city of Nagasaki. The effects are devastating. Six days later, Japan surrenders, ending World War II.

The Spanish-American War

1946 The first bank-issued credit card is developed by John Biggins for the Flatbush National Bank of Brooklyn, in New York City.

1950 North Korean communist forces invade South Korea. U.S. forces enter the Korean War to defend South Korea. Despite three years of bitter fighting, little land changes hands.

1954 In *Brown v. Board of Education of Topeka, Kansas,* the U.S. Supreme Court declares that segregated schools are unconstitutional.

1955 Rosa Parks is arrested for refusing to give up her bus seat to a white person, leading to a boycott of the entire bus system in Montgomery, Alabama.

1962 The United States discovers that the Soviet Union has installed missiles on the island of Cuba that are capable of reaching the United States. Known as the Cuban Missile Crisis, this event brings the United States and the Soviet Union to the brink of nuclear war. After two weeks of extremely tense negotiations, the crisis comes peacefully to an end.

1963 Martin Luther King Jr. delivers his famous "I Have a Dream" speech to a crowd of more than 250,000 people in Washington, D.C.
 • President John F. Kennedy is assassinated.

1965 Civil rights advocate and black militant leader Malcolm X is killed.
 • A race riot in the Watts section of Los Angeles, California, is one of the worst in history.
 • President Lyndon B. Johnson authorizes air raids over North Vietnam.

MYSTERY PERSON

I was born on January 26, 1880, in Little Rock, Arkansas. In 1903, I graduated from the U.S. Military Academy at West Point. I was in charge of American forces in the South Pacific during World War II.

WHO AM I?

Answer on page 277

1968 James Earl Ray shoots and kills Martin Luther King Jr., in Memphis, Tennessee. Riots break out across the country.

1969 Neil Armstrong and Buzz Aldrin, astronauts from NASA's *Apollo 11,* are the first two people to walk on the moon.

1973 The Vietnam War ends when peace accords are signed. Two years later, North Vietnam takes over Saigon (now Ho Chi Minh City), the capital of South Vietnam.

1974 After his involvement in the Watergate scandal, President Richard Nixon resigns. Gerald Ford becomes president.

Buzz Aldrin walked on the moon in 1969.

1979 Islamic militants storm the U.S. embassy in Tehran, Iran, and 52 Americans are held hostage for 444 days.

1991 After Iraq invades Kuwait, the United States begins bombing raids. The first Persian Gulf War ends quickly as Iraqi forces are driven from Kuwait.

1999 President Bill Clinton is acquitted of impeachment charges.

2000 The election race between Democrat Al Gore and Republican George W. Bush is very close, and there are allegations of voter fraud. The U.S. Supreme Court determines the outcome, and Bush is declared the winner.

2001 On September 11, two passenger planes are hijacked and flown into the World Trade Center, in New York City, causing the buildings to collapse. Another plane is flown into the Pentagon, near Washington, D.C. A fourth hijacked plane crashes into a field in Pennsylvania. The United States and Britain respond by attacking the Taliban government in Afghanistan for harboring Osama bin Laden, the alleged mastermind of the attacks. The U.S. government declares the War on Terror.

2003 Along with its allies—Britain and other countries—the United States goes to war in Iraq. Saddam Hussein's government falls quickly, but resistance and fighting continue.

2005 Hurricane Katrina hits the Gulf Coast, destroying parts of Mississippi and Louisiana, and areas along the coast of the southeastern United States. About 80% of New Orleans, Louisiana, is flooded.

2008 A global economic crisis causes a sharp rise in unemployment. Many U.S. homeowners lose their homes.

2009 Barack Obama becomes America's first African-American president.

2010 A federal law is enacted to overhaul the U.S. health-care system and extend health insurance to the 32 million Americans who did not have it before.
 • An oil rig in the Gulf of Mexico explodes, causing one of the largest oil spills in history.

2011 The U.S. secretary of defense announces that the war in Iraq is officially over and that all remaining U.S. troops will leave Iraq by the end of 2011. During the conflict, nearly 4,500 U.S. troops lose their lives in Iraq, and about 30,000 are wounded.

2013 Because of disagreements over the costs of the Affordable Care Act, Congress fails to pass a federal budget. This leads to a 16-day shutdown of the federal government. Some essential services, like mail delivery and military protection, remain up and running.

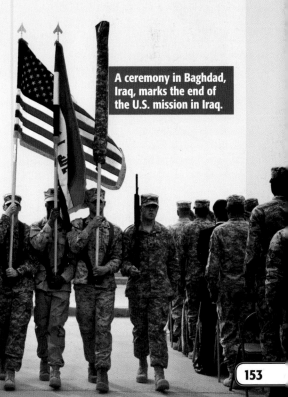

A ceremony in Baghdad, Iraq, marks the end of the U.S. mission in Iraq.

INVENTIONS AND TECHNOLOGY

One inventor has more patents than all the rest. **Page 160**

Lighting the Way BY TFK STAFF

Meet three young inventors whose bright ideas are improving communities around the world.

Kelvin Doe works on his FM radio transmitter.

LONG-LASTING BATTERY

In parts of Freetown, the capital of Sierra Leone, in West Africa, the lights come on only once a week. When he was 13, Kelvin Doe set out to light his neighborhood. He built a rechargeable battery that provides power for homes in his area. It took several attempts before Kelvin came up with the right formula for a long-lasting battery. "The lesson I learned is perseverance," Kelvin told TFK. "To try and fail is no disgrace. I kept pushing until I got the battery to work."

Sierra Leone is an extremely poor nation. It is beginning to recover from a decade-long civil war. More than 70% of the country's 5.6 million people live in poverty. There are many things Kelvin can't afford. He spends nights figuring out how to build those things. Now, at 16, Kelvin runs a radio station in Freetown. It plays music and broadcasts news. And, yes, Kelvin built the music mixer as well as the generator that powers the radio station. He made both using items he found in the trash.

When Kelvin first began tinkering with trash, some people laughed at him. They said he was wasting his time. Now his work is inspiring other young people who want to improve life for the people in their communities. "The obstacles are many, but these are part of everyday life," he says. "I never let problems get me down."

A boy's simple invention is helping farmers in Kenya—and saving the lives of lions.

A SIMPLE SOLUTION

Ann Makosinski is one smart young woman. The 15-year-old from British Columbia, Canada, has invented a flashlight that works without batteries. Ann's invention won her the top prize for her age group at the 2013 Google Science Fair. "This experience was life-changing," Ann told TFK.

A desire to help friends in the Philippines sparked Ann's bright idea. The kids struggled with their schoolwork because their families could not afford electricity. They had no lights to study by at night. Ann wanted to solve this problem. "People radiate so much energy," Ann says. "Why not capture and use some of it?"

The flashlight is built with a hollow aluminum tube in its center. The flashlight's handle has tiles on it. They combine heat from your hand and the temperature of the surrounding air to create energy. This energy powers the flashlight's bulbs.

Ann would like her "hollow flashlights" to become available to people who live in poor countries. Her next step is to put the finishing touches on her flashlight's design. The busy teenager is also working on hands-free headlamps for kids. "So many people encounter problems with something we take for granted," Ann says. "I want to provide a solution."

LION LIGHTS

It all began one night when Richard Turere was 9. He was walking around on his family's farm, in Kenya, Africa, carrying a flashlight to check on the cattle. He made an interesting discovery: Lions run away from moving lights. With that realization, Richard was able to develop an answer to a very big problem.

The Turere family's farm is located on the edge of Nairobi National Park. The area is home to many wild animals, including lions. These big cats are not afraid to sneak into farms at night for an easy cattle meal. Because of that, "I grew up hating lions," Richard, now 13, said during a recent presentation.

To protect their livestock, farmers in the area killed thousands of lions. In the past 10 years, Kenya's lion population has dropped from 15,000 to fewer than 2,000.

Using what he knew about lions, Richard came up with an idea to harmlessly keep the cats away. He attached flashing lights to the outside of his farm's cowshed. "The lights flash and trick the lions into thinking that I'm walking around the cowshed," says Richard. He calls his invention Lion Lights.

There are now more than 75 Lion Lights systems in Kenya. The invention protects livestock as well as the endangered lion population. Lions, cattle, and humans have Richard to thank.

Coolest Inventions of 2013

What makes an invention great? Some inventions help people. Others solve a problem. Sometimes, an invention makes life more fun. Here, TIME For Kids takes a look at some of 2013's coolest inventions. Which one is your favorite?

CITY SPLASH

The **PLUS POOL** will do two things at once: clean river water and give New Yorkers a place to swim. A filter scrubs water from the East River as it moves through the floating pool. Planners hope to open the pool by 2016.

POP ART

Shapes pop off the page with the **3DOODLER.** This special pen can draw objects, not just pictures of objects. It works like a 3D printer, melting and cooling plastic to make designs in any shape a doodler can dream up.

BUILT FOR SPEED

ANKI DRIVE is a $200 racing game in which toy cars can drive themselves. The cars have sensors that send information to an iPhone or iPad. Players use these devices to control the speed and position of their cars.

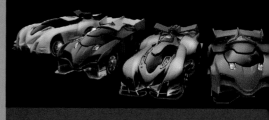

GOOD DOGGIE

Do you miss your dog when you're not home? The **ICPOOCH** helps people and pups stay in touch. A 13-year-old invented the tool. It lets dog owners video-chat with their pets and give them a treat.

RIBBIT! RIBBIT!

It's back! Scientists in Australia have used frozen tissue samples to bring back the **GASTRIC-BROODING FROG.** It has been extinct since 1983. The creatures are unusual because the female frog gives birth through its mouth. Project leader Mike Archer hopes to bring back the extinct Tasmanian tiger next.

TO THE RESCUE

The **ATLAS ROBOT** is tough and smart. The machine can use tools, crawl on rough and uneven land, and locate objects by using cameras and lasers. The robot will do the same type of work that human rescuers do. It was made with money from the military.

Boston Dyn

PICTURE THIS

Imagine your favorite video game. Now imagine feeling as if you're inside the game. The **OCULUS RIFT** makes this idea a reality. The headset lets a user play games in 3D in his or her head!

TECHNOLOGY

As engineers and inventors turn their ideas into machines and devices that can be sold and used around the world, they think a lot about the people whose lives could be improved with their inventions. How might these three new products save or change people's lives?

LOOK, MA! NO DRIVER!

Many car manufacturers are designing and testing driverless cars. These cars are equipped with advanced sensors and computer software that lets them drive on their own, even in stop-and-go city traffic. Driverless cars brake, accelerate, and turn without the help of a human driver. They even park themselves! All passengers in the car—including the "driver"—can just relax and enjoy the ride. Some people believe driverless cars are safer than cars driven by humans because driverless cars never get sleepy or distracted. These cars may start appearing regularly on our streets as early as in 2017.

Nissan's Autonomous Drive vehicle has five laser scanners and five video cameras that monitor all sides of the car.

A FANTASTIC VOYAGE

In 2010, four driverless vans made an 8,000-mile (12,875 km) trip from Parma, Italy, to Shanghai, China. The trip took 100 days. Researchers rode in the vans in case of an emergency. They had to take over the controls only at tollbooths and once when the vans got stuck in traffic in the Russian city of Moscow.

The driverless vans were equipped with four laser scanners and seven video cameras.

NOW SEE THIS!

A new invention, called Argus II, is helping some blind people see. A special set of electrodes (objects that conduct electricity) are placed in the retina of the blind person's eye. The retina is the light-sensitive area at the back of the eye where images are processed. A blind person wears an eyeglasslike device that sends visual information to the retinal implant. Once the information reaches the electrodes, it quickly travels up through the optic nerve to the brain.

People who have used the Argus II say it helps them see rough shapes and track the movements of objects. Some are even able to read large writing. The device, however, can only help people whose blindness is caused by a damaged retina.

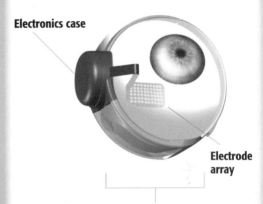

Argus II retinal implant

Electronics case

Electrode array

Receiver

GUESS WHAT? Argus II is named after Argus Panoptes, a giant in Greek mythology. He had 100 eyes and was said to be "all-seeing."

INVENTIONS AND TECHNOLOGY

BOUNCING BALLS TO THE RESCUE

Searching for survivors in collapsed buildings after an earthquake is very difficult—and dangerous. A new baseball-shaped device, called the Bounce Imaging Explorer, may soon make such searches quicker and safer. It contains six cameras, clusters of bright LED lights, and a microphone. These devices make it possible for workers to see and listen inside dark, closed spaces. It also has equipment that can test for toxic chemicals, like methane, and for dangerously high temperatures.

Search-and-rescue teams and other emergency workers, such as firefighters and policemen, can toss the Explorer into a danger area. The ball immediately sends back information about the area to a computer or smartphone.

The Explorer was invented by two graduate students at the Massachusetts Institute of Technology, Francisco Aguilar and Dave Young. They were motivated to build the device after reading about the devastating 2010 earthquake in Haiti. They wanted to help future search-and-rescue teams find people more quickly.

Types of Inventions by Thomas Edison

The first person to come up with an invention can apply for a patent. The inventor sends a drawing and a description of the invention to the U.S. government. If the person is granted a patent, then for 20 years, only he or she can make or sell that item. Thomas Edison received 1,093 U.S. patents—more than any other inventor. Here are the top five types of patents that Edison submitted.

1. ELECTRIC LIGHT AND POWER
424 patents

2. PHONGRAPHS AND SOUND RECORDINGS
199 patents

5. MINING AND GRINDING ORE
53 patents

3. TELEGRAPHS AND TELEPHONES
186 patents

4. BATTERIES
147 patents

SOURCE: THE THOMAS EDISON PAPERS AT RUTGERS UNIVERSITY

Thomas Edison and an early version of a phonograph

RIDDLE ME THIS

Read each riddle below. Draw a line from the riddle to a group of scrambled letters to help figure out the answer. The shape of the letters is a clue!

1. Pick me up, hold me to your ear.
   Talk to someone far or near.

   WHICH INVENTION AM I?

   _____

2. Give me food and drinks to hold.
   Come back later, they'll be cold.

   WHICH INVENTION AM I?

   _____

3. Climb on me and pedal fast.
   Feel the breeze as the world speeds past.

   WHICH INVENTION AM I?

   _____

4. I have teeth, but I don't bite.
   I keep your coat closed on a winter's night.

   WHICH INVENTION AM I?

   _____

Answers on page 277

MYSTERY PERSON

I was born in 1942 in New York City. I am an eye surgeon. I invented a tool that is used to fix an eye condition called cataracts. I also cofounded the American Institute for the Prevention of Blindness.

WHO AM I?

Answer on page 277

MAPS

AFRICA

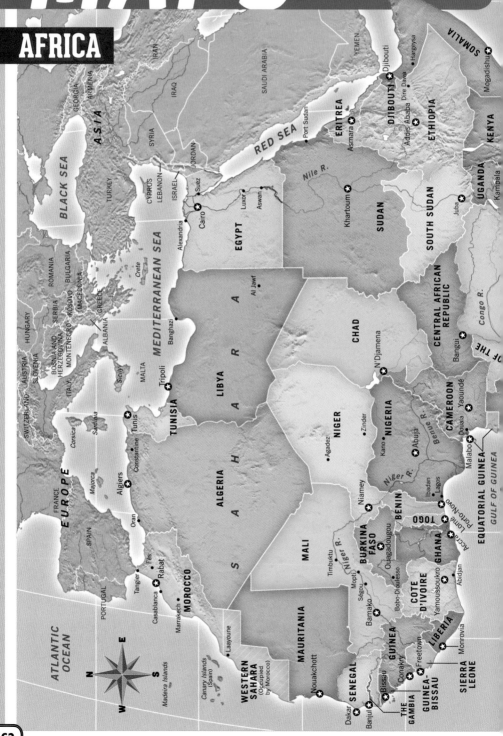

ASIA

BLACK SEA

GEORGIA
ARMENIA
IRAN
IRAQ
SYRIA
TURKEY
CYPRUS
LEBANON
ISRAEL
JORDAN
SAUDI ARABIA
YEMEN

RED SEA

SOMALIA
Mogadishu
DJIBOUTI
Djibouti
Dire Dawa
Hargeysa
ERITREA
Asmara
ETHIOPIA
Addis Ababa
KENYA
Kampala
UGANDA

EUROPE
FRANCE
SWITZERLAND
AUSTRIA
HUNGARY
SLOVENIA
ITALY
BOSNIA AND
HERZEGOVINA
MONTENEGRO
SERBIA
KOSOVO
MACEDONIA
ALBANIA
GREECE
ROMANIA
BULGARIA

MEDITERRANEAN SEA

Crete
Sicily
MALTA
Corsica
Sardinia
Majorca
Minorca

SPAIN
PORTUGAL

ATLANTIC
OCEAN

Madeira Islands
Canary Islands
(Spain)

N
W   E
S

Port Sudan
Nile R.
Khartoum
SUDAN
SOUTH SUDAN
Juba
Luxor
Aswan
EGYPT
Al Jawf
Cairo
Suez
Alexandria
Banghazi
Tripoli
LIBYA
TUNISIA
Tunis
Constantine
Algiers
Oran
Fès
Rabat
Casablanca
Tangier
Marrakech
MOROCCO

S   A   H   A   R   A
ALGERIA
MALI
Timbuktu
Mopti
Ségou
Bamako
Niger R.
Laayoune
WESTERN
SAHARA
(Occupied
by Morocco)
Nouakchott
MAURITANIA
Dakar
SENEGAL
Banjul
THE GAMBIA
Bissau
GUINEA-
BISSAU
Conakry
GUINEA
Freetown
SIERRA
LEONE
Monrovia
LIBERIA

CHAD
N'Djamena
NIGER
Agadez
Zinder
Niamey
NIGERIA
Kano
Abuja
Ibadan
Lagos
Benue R.
Niger R.
BENIN
Porto-Novo
Lomé
TOGO
1060
Ouagadougou
BURKINA
FASO
Bobo-Dioulasso
COTE
D'IVOIRE
Yamoussoukro
Abidjan
GHANA
Accra
Abidjan

CENTRAL AFRICAN
REPUBLIC
Bangui
Congo R.
Douala
CAMEROON
Yaoundé
Malabo
EQUATORIAL GUINEA
GULF OF GUINEA
OF THE

162

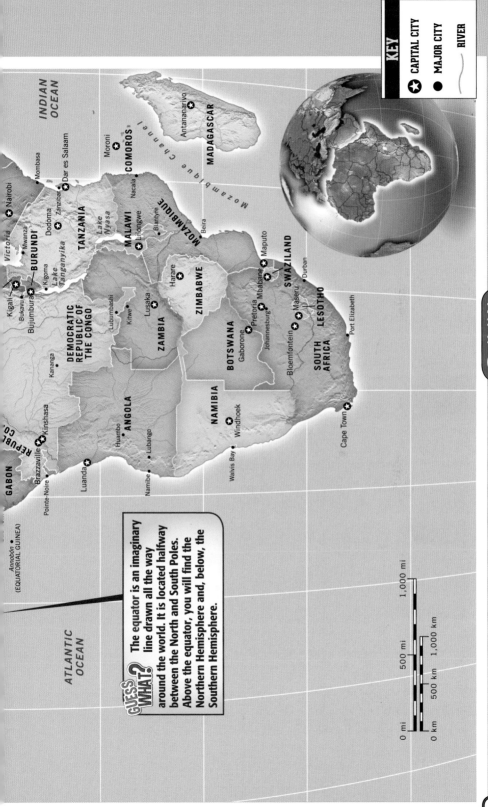

INDIAN OCEAN

MADAGASCAR

Antananarivo

Moroni
COMOROS

Mozambique Channel

Mombasa
Natrobi
Dar es Salaam
Zanzibar
Dodoma
TANZANIA
Lake Nyasa
MALAWI
Lilongwe
Blantyre
Nacala
Beira
MOZAMBIQUE

Victoria
Mwanza
BURUNDI
Kigoma
Lake Tanganyika

Kigali
Bukavu
Bujumbura
DEMOCRATIC REPUBLIC OF THE CONGO
Lubumbashi
Kitwe
ZAMBIA
Lusaka
Harare
ZIMBABWE
Maputo
SWAZILAND
Mbabane
Durban
Pretoria
Johannesburg
Maseru
LESOTHO
Port Elizabeth

Kananga

Kinshasa
REPUBL... CO...
Brazzaville
GABON

Pointe-Noire
Annobón
(EQUATORIAL GUINEA)

Luanda
Namibe
Lubango
Huambo
ANGOLA
NAMIBIA
Windhoek
Walvis Bay

BOTSWANA
Gaborone

SOUTH AFRICA
Bloemfontein
Cape Town

ATLANTIC OCEAN

GUESS WHAT? The equator is an imaginary line drawn all the way around the world. It is located halfway between the North and South Poles. Above the equator, you will find the Northern Hemisphere and, below, the Southern Hemisphere.

0 mi   500 mi   1,000 mi
0 km   500 km   1,000 km

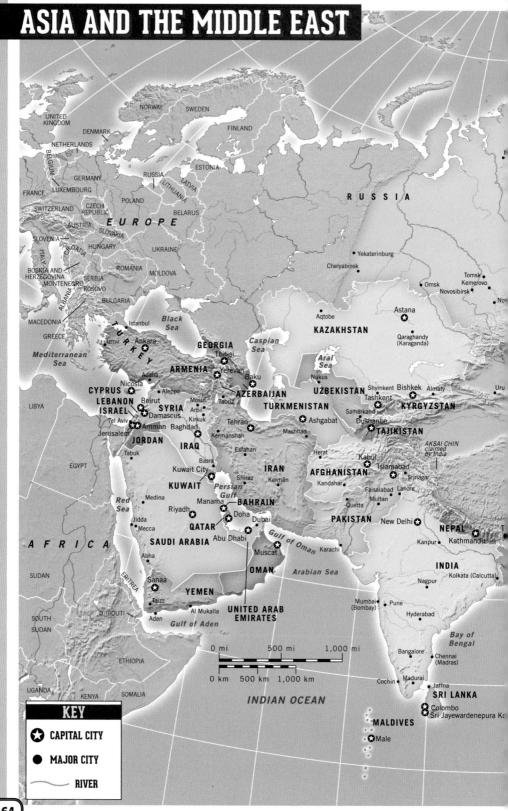

UNITED
KINGDOM
NORWAY
SWEDEN
DENMARK
FINLAND
NETHERLANDS
BELGIUM
GERMANY
RUSSIA
FRANCE
LUXEMBOURG
ESTONIA
SWITZERLAND
CZECH
REPUBLIC
POLAND
LATVIA
LITHUANIA
BELARUS
AUSTRIA
E U R O P E
SLOVAKIA
SLOVENIA
HUNGARY
UKRAINE
ITALY
CROATIA
BOSNIA AND
HERZEGOVINA
ROMANIA
MOLDOVA
MONTENEGRO
SERBIA
KOSOVO
ALBANIA
BULGARIA
MACEDONIA
GREECE

R U S S I A

• Yekaterinburg
Chelyabinsk •
• Omsk
Tomsk
Kemerovo
Novosibirsk •
• No

• Aqtobe
• Astana
Qaraghandy
(Karaganda)

KAZAKHSTAN

Istanbul
Black
Sea
Izmir • Ankara •
Adana •
Nicosia
CYPRUS
LEBANON
ISRAEL
Tel Aviv
Jerusalem
Aleppo •
Beirut •
Damascus •
SYRIA
Mosul •
Arbil •
Kirkuk •
Baghdad •
Amman •
JORDAN
Tabuk •
IRAQ
Basra •
Kuwait City •
KUWAIT
Medina •
Riyadh •
Manama •
QATAR
Jidda •
Mecca •
SAUDI ARABIA
Abha •
Sanaa •
YEMEN
Taizz •
Aden •

Mediterranean
Sea

LIBYA

Red
Sea

A F R I C A

SUDAN

SOUTH
SUDAN

ETHIOPIA

UGANDA
KENYA
SOMALIA

DJIBOUTI
ERITREA

Al Mukalla •
Gulf of Aden

GEORGIA
Tbilisi •
ARMENIA
Yerevan •
Baku •
AZERBAIJAN

Caspian
Sea

Aral
Sea
Nukus •

Shymkent •
Tashkent
UZBEKISTAN
Samarkand •
TURKMENISTAN
Ashgabat •
Dushanbe •
TAJIKISTAN

Bishkek •
Almaty •
KYRGYZSTAN

Uru

Tabriz •
Tehran •
Kermanshah •
Esfahan •
Shiraz •
Kermān •
IRAN

Mashhad •

Herat •
Kabul •
AFGHANISTAN
Islamabad •
Kandahar •

AKSAI CHIN
claimed
by India

Srinagar •

Faisalabad •
Multan •
Lahore •
Quetta •
PAKISTAN
New Delhi •
Karachi •

Nagpur •

NEPAL
Kathmandu •
Kanpur •
T

INDIA

Kolkata (Calcutta) •

Persian
Gulf
BAHRAIN
Doha •
Dubai •
Abu Dhabi •
UNITED ARAB
EMIRATES
Muscat •
OMAN

Gulf of Oman

Arabian Sea

Mumbai •
(Bombay)
Pune •
Hyderabad •

Bay of
Bengal

0 mi   500 mi   1,000 mi

0 km   500 km 1,000 km

Bangalore •
Chennai
(Madras) •
Cochin •
Madurai •
Jaffna •

INDIAN OCEAN

SRI LANKA
Colombo •
Sri Jayewardenepura Ko

MALDIVES

• Male

KEY

⭐ CAPITAL CITY

● MAJOR CITY

〰 RIVER

ARCTIC OCEAN

Tiksi

Cherskiy

Verkhoyansk

Magadan

Bering Sea

Kamchatka Peninsula

Yakutsk

S I B E R I A

Sea of Okhotsk

Petropavlovsk-Kamchatskiy

rasnoyarsk

uznetsk

Irkutsk

Ulaanbaatar

Sakhalin

Khabarovsk

MONGOLIA

Gobi Desert

Harbin

Sapporo

Changchun

Vladivostok

Shenyang

NORTH KOREA

JAPAN

Hohhot

Beijing

P'yongyang

Tokyo

Tianjin

Seoul

Nagoya

Kyoto

Taiyuan

Jinan

SOUTH KOREA

Taegu

Kobe

Osaka

Pusan

Hiroshima

Qingdao

Fukuoka

Lanzhou

Xi'an

Nagasaki

CHINA

Hefei

Shanghai

PACIFIC OCEAN

Chengdu

Wuhan

Chongqing

hasa

Naha

mphu

Fuzhou

BHUTAN

Taipei

Xiamen

BANGLADESH

Liuzhou

TAIWAN

Dhaka

Nanning

Guangzhou

Kao-hsiung

Mandalay

Macao

Hong Kong (special admin. region)

Chittagong

(special admin. region)

MYANMAR (BURMA)

Hanoi

Nay Pyi Taw

LAOS

Chiang Mai

Vientiane

Baguio

South China Sea

Quezon City

THAILAND

Da Nang

Manila

Bangkok

VIETNAM

PHILIPPINES

CAMBODIA

Cebu

Phnom Penh

Ho Chi Minh City

Davao

Phuket

Songkhla

Bandar Seri Begawan

Ipoh

BRUNEI

Kota Kinabalu

Manado

Manokwari

Medan

M A L A Y S I A

Serong

Jayapura

Kuala Lumpur

Kuching

Borneo

Palu

New Guinea

SINGAPORE

Pontianak

Samarinda

Celebes

Singapore

Sumatra

I N D O N E S I A

Banjarmasin

Palembang

Makassar

Andaman Sea

United States

N
W   E
S

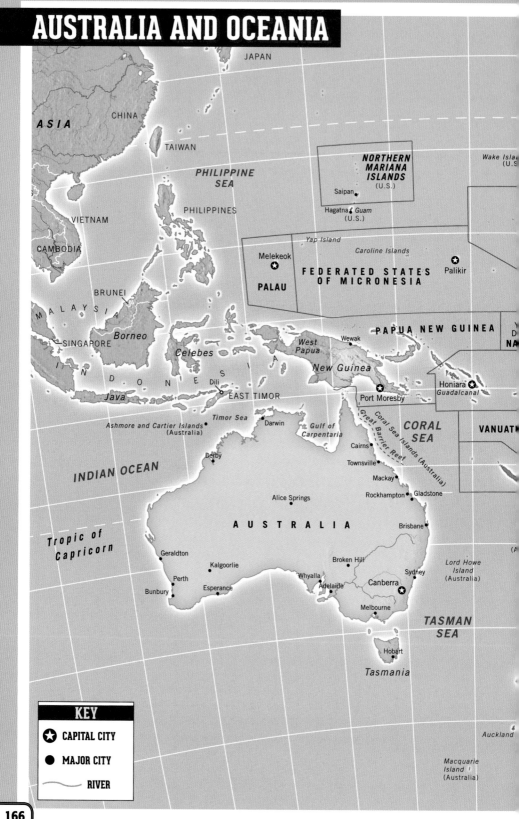

AUSTRALIA AND OCEANIA

ASIA

CHINA

JAPAN

TAIWAN

PHILIPPINE SEA

NORTHERN MARIANA ISLANDS (U.S.)

Saipan

Wake Isla (U.S

Hagatna Guam (U.S.)

PHILIPPINES

VIETNAM

CAMBODIA

Yap Island

Caroline Islands

Melekeok

FEDERATED STATES OF MICRONESIA

Palikir

PALAU

MALAYSIA

BRUNEI

SINGAPORE

Borneo

Celebes

I N D O N E S I A

Java

Dili

EAST TIMOR

West Papua

New Guinea

Wewak

PAPUA NEW GUINEA

N A

Port Moresby

Honiara

Guadalcanal

Ashmore and Cartier Islands (Australia)

Timor Sea

Darwin

Gulf of Carpentaria

INDIAN OCEAN

Derby

Cairns

Townsville

Mackay

Coral Sea Islands (Australia)

Great Barrier Reef

CORAL SEA

VANUAT

Alice Springs

A U S T R A L I A

Rockhampton

Gladstone

Brisbane

Tropic of Capricorn

Geraldton

Kalgoorlie

Broken Hill

Sydney

Lord Howe Island (Australia)

Perth

Whyalla

Esperance

Adelaide

Canberra

Bunbury

Melbourne

TASMAN SEA

Hobart

Tasmania

Auckland

Macquarie Island (Australia)

KEY

⭐ **CAPITAL CITY**

● **MAJOR CITY**

〰 **RIVER**

N
W   E
S

Tropic of Cancer

Honolulu
Hilo
Hawaii
(U.S.)

Johnston Atoll (U.S.)

ARSHALL ISLANDS

⊛ Majuro

PACIFIC OCEAN

Kingman Reef (U.S.)
Palmyra Atoll (U.S.)

⊛ Tarawa

Howland Island (U.S.)
Baker Island (U.S.)

*Jarvis
Island*
(U.S.)

Line Islands

Equator

*Gilbert
Islands*

K I R I B A T I

Phoenix Islands

**SOLOMON
ISLANDS**

⊛ Funafuti

TOKELAU (New Zealand)

Mata-Utu

SAMOA

TUVALU

**WALLIS AND
FUTUNA**
(France)

Pago
Pago

Apia ⊛

COOK ISLANDS
(New Zealand)

*Marquesas
Islands*

**AMERICAN
SAMOA**

⊛ Port-Vila

Suva ⊛

TONGA

Alofi

Papeete

*Society
Islands* • Tahiti

Tuamotu Archipelago

Nuku'alofa ⊛

FIJI

NIUE
(New Zealand)

Raritonga

oumēa

**NEW
CALEDONIA**
(France)

• Norfork Island
ston
ralia)

Kermadec Islands
(New Zealand)

FRENCH POLYNESIA (France)

Adamstown

**PITCAIRN
ISLANDS**
(U.K.)

International Date Line

NEW ZEALAND

Auckland

Hastings

Wellington

• Christchurch

Chatham Islands

• Dunedin
• Invercargill

Stewart Island

*Antipodes
Island*

ands

Campbell Island

0 mi   500 mi   1,000 mi

0 km   1,000 km

EUROPE

N W E S

Reykjavík
ICELAND

ARCTIC OCEAN

Arctic Circle

FAROE ISLANDS
(Denmark)
Torshavn

NORWEGIAN
SEA

Trondheim

0 mi   300 mi   600 mi
0 km   300 km   600 km

SHETLAND ISLANDS

ORKNEY
ISLANDS

HEBRIDES

Bergen

NORWAY

Oslo

Gavle

Stavanger

SWEDEN

Aberdeen
Glasgow

Edinburgh

Belfast

**UNITED
KINGDOM**

NORTH
SEA

Goteborg

DENMARK
Ålborg

Copenhagen
Malmo

BALT
SEA

Dublin

IRELAND

Liverpool   Leeds
Manchester
Sheffield

Birmingham

London

NETHERLANDS

Amsterdam
The Hague
Rotterdam

Hamburg
Bremen

Gdansk

Berlin

Poznan

GUERNSEY (U.K.)
JERSEY (U.K.)

Calais Lille
Le Havre   Brussels
Paris

Antwerp Essen
Düsseldorf
Cologne
Bonn   Frankfurt

GERMANY

Wroclaw

BELGIUM
LUXEMBOURG
Luxembourg

Prague

**CZECH
REPUBLIC**

Brno

ATLANTIC OCEAN

Nantes

Strasbourg
Dijon

Stuttgart

Vienna

Bratislav

B

BAY OF
BISCAY

FRANCE

Zürich
Bern
Geneva
SWITZERLAND

LIECHTENSTEIN
Munich
Vaduz

AUSTRIA

HUNGARY

Bordeaux

Lyon

Turin
Milan

Ljubljana
SLOVENIA
Venice Trieste

Zagreb

CROATIA

Porto

Bilbao

Toulouse

Genoa

PORTUGAL

Madrid

Andorra
la Vella

Marseille

ANDORRA

Monaco
MONACO

Florence

**SAN
MARINO**

**BOSNIA AND
HERZEGOVINA**
Sarajevo

Lisbon

SPAIN

Barcelona
Valencia   Majorca

Bastia

Corsica

ITALY

Rome

MONTENE
Podgoric

K

Faro
Seville

**VATICAN
CITY
(HOLY SEE)**

Bari

Tirana

Málaga
Palma

Gibraltar
(U.K.)

MEDITERRANEAN SEA

Sardinia
Cagliari

Naples

ALB

Kerkira

**TYRRHENIAN
SEA**

Palermo
Messina
Sicily

IONIAN
SEA

MOROCCO

ALGERIA

Valletta
MALTA

A F R I C A

TUNISIA

MEDITE

KEY

⭐ CAPITAL CITY

● MAJOR CITY

〜 RIVER

Murmansk

Pechora

ASIA

Arkhangel'sk

Oulu

FINLAND

Tampere

RUSSIA

Izhevsk

ku Helsinki

St. Petersburg

Tallinn

Kazan

ESTONIA

Nizhniy Novgorod

Riga

LATVIA

Samara

Moscow

HUANIA

Vilnius

Smolensk

Minsk

Lipetsk

Saratov

BELARUS

Voronezh

KAZAKHSTAN

Homyel'

Brest

Kiev

Kharkiv

Volgograd

Lviv

Luhansk

Derazhnya

Gorlovka

UKRAINE

Makeyevka

Mariupol

Rostov

Chisinau

CASPIAN
SEA

Iasi

Odessa

Mykolayiv

MOLDOVA

Kerch

Grozny

Simferopol

ROMANIA

de

Craiova

Bucharest

Sevastopol

Constanta

BLACK SEA

Sofia

tina

Varna

BULGARIA

kopje

CEDONIA

Istanbul

essaloniki

Volos

TURKEY

EECE

AEGEAN
SEA

Athens

SYRIA

IRAN

Crete

CYPRUS

IRAQ

LEBANON

AN SEA

169

Greenland Sea

Tasiilaq
(Ammassalik)

Narsarsuaq

Labrador
Sea

Island of
Newfoundland

GREENLAND
(Denmark)

Happy Valley
Goose Bay

Davis Strait

Nuuk (Godthab)

Qaanaaq (Thule)

Baffin Bay

Iqaluit

CANADA

Baffin Island

Chisasibi
(Fort George)

Alert

HUDSON
BAY

Moosonee

Queen Elizabeth Islands

Quaqtaq (Resolute)

Arctic Circle

Churchill

Winnipeg

N
E
S
W

ARCTIC
OCEAN

Victoria Island

Banks Island

Beaufort
Sea

Echo Bay

Yellowknife

Saskatoon

Regina

Bismarck

Barrow

Prudhoe Bay

Inuvik

Edmonton

Helena

Calgary

RUSSIA

Alaska (U.S.)

Fairbanks

Whitehorse

Boise

Anchorage

Valdez

Juneau

Vancouver

Seattle

Victoria

Nome

Portland

Bethel

Olympia

Salem

Kodiak

Bering
Sea

Aleutian Islands

KEY

⭐ CAPITAL CITY
● MAJOR CITY
〜 RIVER

ATLANTIC OCEAN

BERMUDA (U.K.)
Hamilton

Halifax

Montreal
Montpelier
Concord
Augusta
Ottawa
Albany
Boston
Toronto
Buffalo
Hartford
Providence
Lansing
Detroit
Cleveland
New York
Milwaukee
Toledo
Pittsburgh
Harrisburg
Philadelphia
Chicago
Indianapolis
Columbus
Baltimore
Dover
Springfield
Cincinnati
Washington, D.C.
Madison
Des Moines
Saint Louis
Louisville
Frankfort
Richmond
Norfolk
Minneapolis
St. Paul
Omaha
Lincoln
Jefferson City
Nashville
Raleigh
Kansas City
Topeka
Memphis
Columbia
Charleston
Cheyenne
Denver
Wichita
Little Rock
Birmingham
Atlanta
Savannah
Oklahoma City
Dallas
Jackson
Montgomery
Tallahassee
Santa Fe
Jacksonville
Salt Lake City
Austin
Baton Rouge
New Orleans
Phoenix
El Paso
San Antonio
Houston
Ciudad Juárez
Hermosillo
Tampico
Los Angeles
San Diego
Tijuana
Monterrey
Veracruz
Mérida
Cancún
Puerto Vallarta
León
Guadalajara
Mexico City
Puebla
Oaxaca
Mazatlán
Acapulco
La Paz

UNITED STATES

MEXICO

Gulf of California

Tropic of Cancer

PACIFIC OCEAN

GULF OF MEXICO

Freeport
Nassau
THE BAHAMAS
Miami
Havana
CUBA
Camagüey
Montego Bay
Guantánamo Bay
CAYMAN ISLANDS (U.K.)
George Town
JAMAICA
Kingston

TURKS AND CAICOS ISLANDS (U.K.)
Grand Turk
HAITI
Port-au-Prince
DOMINICAN REPUBLIC
Santiago
Santo Domingo
PUERTO RICO (U.S.)
San Juan

VIRGIN ISLANDS (U.S., U.K.)
SAINT MAARTEN/ SAINT MARTIN (Netherlands)/(France)
ANGUILLA (U.K.)
SAINT BARTHELEMY (France)
ANTIGUA AND BARBUDA
SAINT KITTS AND NEVIS
MONTSERRAT (U.K.)
GUADELOUPE (France)
DOMINICA
MARTINIQUE (France)
SAINT LUCIA
BARBADOS
SAINT VINCENT AND THE GRENADINES
GRENADA

CURAÇAO (Neth.)
ARUBA (Neth.)
BONAIRE (Neth.)

CARIBBEAN SEA

TRINIDAD AND TOBAGO
GUYANA
VENEZUELA
COLOMBIA

SOUTH AMERICA

Belize City
BELIZE
Belmopan
Guatemala City
GUATEMALA
San Salvador
EL SALVADOR
Tegucigalpa
HONDURAS
Managua
NICARAGUA
San José
COSTA RICA
Panama City
PANAMA

1,000 mi
1,000 km
500 mi
500 km
0 mi
0 km

SOUTH AMERICA

N
W   E
S

MEXICO
CUBA
HAITI
DOMINICAN REPUBLIC
Puerto Rico (U.S.)
ANTIGUA AND BARBUDA
BELIZE
JAMAICA
SAINT KITTS AND NEVIS
GUADELOUPE
HONDURAS
DOMINICA
CARIBBEAN SEA
SAINT LUCIA
BARBADOS
NICARAGUA
GRENADA
SAINT VINCENT AND THE GRENADINES
ATLANTIC OCEAN

COSTA RICA
PANAMA
Barranquilla
Cartagena
Maracaibo
Lake Maracaibo
Caracas
TRINIDAD AND TOBAGO

Medellín
Orinoco River
Ciudad Guayana
VENEZUELA
GUYANA
Georgetown
Paramaribo

Cali
Bogotá
SURINAME
Cayenne
FRENCH GUIANA
(France)

Esmeraldas
COLOMBIA
Negro River
Macapá

Equator
Quito
ECUADOR
Putumayo River
Manaus
Amazon River
Belém
São Luís
Parnaíba

Guayaquil
Benjamín Constant
Iquitos
Santarém
Fortaleza

Piura
PERU
Amazon River
AMAZON BASIN
Natal

Cruzeiro do Sul
Rain Forest
Madeira River
Xingu River
Recife

Trujillo
Ucayali River
Pôrto Velho
BRAZIL
Maceió

Lima
Cobija
Riberalta
Tocantins River

Cuzco
Araguaia River
São Francisco River
Salvador

Lake Titicaca
BOLIVIA
La Paz

Arequipa
Cochabamba
Brasília

Arica
Santa Cruz
Sucre
Brazilian Highlands
Belo Horizonte

Iquique

Antofagasta
PACIFIC OCEAN
PARAGUAY
São Paulo
Rio de Janeiro

Asunción
Ciudad del Este
Curitiba

Formosa
Paraná River

San Miguel de Tucumán
Resistencia
Encarnación
Andes Mts.
Pôrto Alegre

CHILE
Córdoba
Paraná River
Salto

Valparaíso
Rosario
URUGUAY
ATLANTIC OCEAN

Santiago
Buenos Aires
Montevideo

Concepción
ARGENTINA
Río de la Plata

Bahía Blanca
Mar del Plata

Puerto Montt

Comodoro Rivadavia

Strait of Magellan
Río Gallegos
Stanley

Punta Arenas
Falkland Islands (Islas Malvinas)
Ushuaia
(Administered by U.K.; claimed by Argentina)

Cape Horn

KEY

⭐ CAPITAL CITY

● MAJOR CITY

〰 RIVER

0 mi   500 mi   1,000 mi

0 km   500 km   1,000 km

172

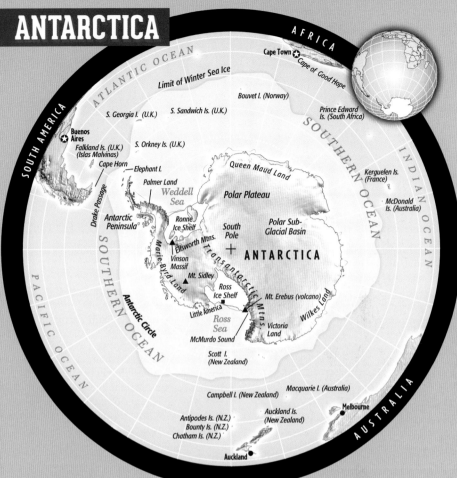

MUDDLED MAPS

Unscramble the letters below to find the names of three continents, two oceans, the northernmost place on Earth, and three types of lines found on a map. Then write the letters in the circles in order to answer the riddle below.

DIAINN NOEAC   (_)_ _ _ _ _   _ _ _ _ _

OUSHT CEMAIRA   _ _ _ _ _   _ _(_)_

ENGLODUIT   _ _ _ _ _ _ _ _ _

TROHN LOPE   _ _ _ _ _ _ _(_)_

CPIAIFC CEANO   _ _(_)_ _ _   _ _ _ _ _

RATOQUE   _ _ _(_)_ _ _

EERPOU   _ _ _(_)_ _

TDIELATU   _ _ _ _ _ _ _ _

LUSARATAI   _ _(_)_ _ _ _ _

WHAT DO PENGUINS WEAR ON THEIR HEADS?

◯◯◯   ◯◯◯◯

Answers on page 277

MOVIES AND TV

Which TV award did *The Voice* take home in 2013? **Page 178**

A Chat with Willow Shields BY KELLI PLASKET

In *The Hunger Games* (2012), Katniss Everdeen, played by Jennifer Lawrence, volunteers to compete in the Hunger Games to save her younger sister, Prim, played by Willow Shields. The sisters return in *The Hunger Games: Catching Fire* (2013), *The Hunger Games: Mockingjay, Part 1* (2014), and *The Hunger Games: Mockingjay, Part 2* (2015).

TFK spoke to Willow after the release of *Catching Fire*. The film finds Prim following in her mother's footsteps by training to become a healer while supporting Katniss on her journey. "Prim is growing up quite a bit," Willow told TFK. "She is there for Katniss a lot in *Catching Fire*." The 13-year-old actress, who likes to read and take dance classes when she's not working, shared what it's like filming with Jennifer Lawrence and how having a twin helps her relate to the sisters from District 12.

TFK: How do you relate to Prim?

WILLOW: Obviously, we live in two totally different worlds, but it's easier to relate to her because we are growing up together throughout the series. Prim is always there for her family, and she also has a real love for animals. I have always grown up around them. It's easy to connect with her.

TFK: You have a twin sister named Autumn. Does your relationship with her help you relate to Prim and Katniss?

WILLOW: Yeah. It helps you get into the mindset of filming the reaping [scene where the tributes are chosen] and thinking about the fact that your sister is going to the Hunger Games and may not come back. When you actually think about what if that happened in real life, it helps to connect with the facts and connect with the character and act better.

TFK: How are you and Autumn alike and different?

WILLOW: We are actually very different. I'm into acting, and she's more into art. She's a little bit shyer than I am. I'm probably the more outgoing sister. We have different interests in books and hobbies.

TFK: What do you like to do during your downtime on set?

WILLOW: Well, what I *have* to do during my downtime is school. Other than that, I hang out with Jen between scenes on set. But when I'm in my trailer, you'll find me doing school.

Willow Shields

5 Things You Might Not Know About **Jennifer Lawrence**

1. Jennifer grew up in Louisville, Kentucky.
2. She was voted "most talkative" in the seventh grade.
3. Before deciding to be an actor, she wanted to be a doctor.
4. She auditioned for the role of Bella Swan in *Twilight*.
5. She graduated from high school after only two years.

GUESS WHAT? *The Hunger Games* films are based on the best-selling book series by Suzanne Collins.

TFK: Do you find it difficult to balance doing work and school?

WILLOW: It's a little bit difficult because some days I might not be able to get math and reading in, so the next day, I need to double up on it, but it's worth it. It can take a little getting used to. It's a self-discipline thing that I have learned over the past two years.

TFK: What's your favorite subject to study?

WILLOW: I think my favorite is reading. I read all the time.

TFK: Most of your scenes are filmed with Jennifer Lawrence. What's it like working with her?

WILLOW: I could not ask for a better person to work with. She is so sweet, she's hilarious, she's like a big sister on set, and I always have a blast filming with

her. There's no one else who could play Katniss. She always has a good grasp on the characters she's playing.

TFK: You also filmed scenes with Prim's cat, Buttercup. What was that like?

WILLOW: It's fun. The cat that they cast as Buttercup is perfect. It's really a weird-looking cat. But the cat is super sweet, and it's fun to be on set with the trainer. They teach you to work with the cat.

TFK: Next, you'll film *Mockingjay: Part 1*. What are you looking forward to most?

WILLOW: It will be interesting because of the fact that [Prim will be] in a different place, so there's different wardrobe and different set design. It's always been District 12. It will be fun to have something different.

FROM TIME FOR KIDS MAGAZINE

The **Movie Winners** Are...

The Teen Choice Awards, People's Choice Awards, and Golden Globes are just a few of the award shows that recognize excellence in movie-making. Here are some of the big winners in 2013 and 2014.

Steve Carell lent his voice to *Despicable Me 2*, which took home the Favorite Family Movie award at the People's Choice Awards on January 8, 2014.

For his work in *Iron Man 3*, Robert Downey Jr. won the Choice Actor, Action Movie award at the Teen Choice Awards on August 11, 2013. He also nabbed the Favorite Action Movie Star award at the People's Choice Awards. This superhero flick was named Choice Action Movie at the Teen Choice Awards, and Favorite Action Movie at the People's Choice Awards.

Frozen was named Best Animated Feature Film at the Golden Globe Awards on January 12, 2014. This wintry tale stars Kristen Bell as the voice of Anna.

Adam Sandler won a Nickelodeon Kids' Choice Award on March 23, 2013. He was picked as the Favorite Voice from an Animated Movie. He played Dracula in the spooky-yet-silly animated film *Hotel Transylvania*. Audiences also picked Sandler as their Favorite Comedic Movie Actor at the People's Choice Awards.

TV **Favorites**

The Primetime Emmy Awards are given out every year to recognize the best TV shows, as chosen by members of an organization called the Academy of Television Arts and Sciences. Other awards for television shows and actors are presented at the Teen Choice Awards, the People's Choice Awards, and the Nickelodeon Kids' Choice Awards.

At the Nickelodeon Kids' Choice Awards in 2013, Selena Gomez and Ross Lynch were named Favorite TV Actress and Actor.

The Voice was selected as the Outstanding Reality-Competition Program at the 2013 Primetime Emmy Awards. The show also won the 2014 People's Choice Award for Favorite Competition TV Show.

At the People's Choice Awards, fans picked Queen Latifah as their Favorite New Talk Show Host and Ellen DeGeneres as their Favorite Daytime TV Host.

Cast of *The Big Bang Theory*

The 2013 Primetime Emmy Award for Outstanding Lead Actor in a Comedy Series went to Jim Parsons (second from right), of *The Big Bang Theory.* Parsons was also named Choice TV Actor in a Comedy at the Teen Choice Awards. At the People's Choice Awards, the show was chosen to be the Favorite Network TV Comedy.

Demi Lovato and Simon Cowell were picked as the Choice Female and Male TV Personalities at the Teen Choice Awards. They are both hosts of *The X Factor,* which won Choice TV Reality Competition Show at the Teen Choice Awards.

MOVIES AND TV

MUSIC

See who won big at the American Music Awards. **Page 183**

A Magical Experience BY TFK KID REPORTER PHOEBE WEINTRAUB

I have loved *Matilda*, by Roald Dahl, for many years, so I was very excited to see the new Broadway musical based on the book. As I took my seat, my eyes focused on the striking set in front of me. Surrounding the stage were hundreds of blocks, each with a letter of the alphabet, giving the audience a taste of the whimsical performance to come. Before the show even started, I had a feeling that I was going to love it.

Throughout *Matilda the Musical*, there are often children singing and dancing onstage. Watching these talented young performers was a highlight for me. Four young actresses take turns playing the role of Matilda, a clever little girl who stands up to cruel adults. Matilda's parents, the scheming Mr. Wormwood and his superficial wife, Mrs. Wormwood, treat their daughter as if she belongs to another family. But the actors who portray them bring a dose of comedy to their roles.

The musical is true to the plot of the book that Dahl created. It follows the ups and downs of Matilda and her classmates at Crunchem Hall Primary School and the ghastly treatment they receive at the hands of their headmistress, Miss Trunchbull. The only light in Matilda's life is her teacher, Miss Honey, who is the only one who understands Matilda.

For me, the most surprising thing about the show was that one of my favorite characters, Miss Trunchbull, is played by a man—the extremely entertaining Bertie Carvel. Trunchbull intimidates the children in the show with her over-the-top temper and unusual forms of discipline. If I were Amanda Thripp, a student who is bullied by Trunchbull because of her braids, I couldn't get out of that school fast enough!

The audience at the performance that I attended was made up of kids, teenagers, and adults. I think people of all ages, whether they are already fans of Roald Dahl or not, will love this musical.

Matilda the Musical on Broadway

TOP 5 LONGEST-RUNNING BROADWAY SHOWS

1. The Phantom of the Opera
10,839 performances*

2. Cats
7,485 performances

3. Chicago (Revival)
7,165 performances*

4. The Lion King
6,769 performances*

5. Les Misérables
6,680 performances

*Still running as of February 2014

MYSTERY PERSON

I was born on April 10, 1984. After seeing the musical *Oklahoma!* as a child, I knew I wanted to be a singer. I released my first record, *So Real*, when I was 15.

WHO AM I?

Answer on page 277

SOURCE: PLAYBILL.COM, FEBRUARY 2014

GRAMMY AWARDS

JANUARY 26, 2014

Album of the Year: *Random Access Memories,* Daft Punk

Song of the Year: "Royals," Lorde

Best New Artist: Macklemore & Ryan Lewis

Best Pop Solo Performance: "Royals," Lorde

Best Pop Vocal Album: *Unorthodox Jukebox,* Bruno Mars

Best Dance Recording: "Clarity," Zedd featuring Foxes

Best Dance/Electronica Album: *Random Access Memories,* Daft Punk

Best Traditional Pop Vocal Album: *To Be Loved,* Michael Bublé

Best Rock Performance: "Radioactive," Imagine Dragons

Best Rock Song: "Cut Me Some Slack," Paul McCartney, Dave Grohl, Krist Novoselic, and Pat Smear

Best Rock Album: *Celebration Day,* Led Zeppelin

Best Alternative Music Album: *Modern Vampires of the City,* Vampire Weekend

Best R&B Performance: "Something," Snarky Puppy featuring Lalah Hathaway

Best Traditional R&B Performance: "Please Come Home," Gary Clark Jr.

Best Urban Contemporary Album: *Unapologetic,* Rihanna

Best R&B Album: *Girl on Fire,* Alicia Keys

Best Rap Album: *The Heist,* Macklemore & Ryan Lewis

Best Country Solo Performance: "Wagon Wheel," Darius Rucker

Best Country Duo/Group Performance: "From This Valley," The Civil Wars

Best Country Song: "Merry Go 'Round," Kacey Musgraves

Best Country Album: *Same Trailer Different Park,* Kacey Musgraves

Best Children's Album: *Throw a Penny in the Wishing Well,* Jennifer Gasoi

Lorde

Bruno Mars

AMERICAN MUSIC AWARDS
NOVEMBER 24, 2013

Artist of the Year: Taylor Swift

New Artist of the Year: Ariana Grande

Single of the Year: "Cruise," Florida Georgia Line featuring Nelly

Favorite Pop/Rock Female Artist: Taylor Swift

Favorite Pop/Rock Male Artist: Justin Timberlake

Favorite Pop/Rock Band, Duo, or Group:
One Direction

Favorite Pop/Rock Album: *Take Me Home,*
One Direction

Favorite Soul/R&B Female Artist: Rihanna

Favorite Soul/R&B Male Artist: Justin Timberlake

Favorite Soul/R&B Album: *The 20/20 Experience,*
Justin Timberlake

Favorite Country Female Artist: Taylor Swift

Favorite Country Male Artist: Luke Bryan

Favorite Country Band, Duo, or Group:
Lady Antebellum

Favorite Country Album: *Red,* Taylor Swift

Top Soundtrack: *Pitch Perfect*

Favorite Latin Artist: Marc Anthony

One Direction

Rihanna

COUNTRY MUSIC AWARDS

NOVEMBER 6, 2013

Entertainer of the Year: George Strait
Male Vocalist of the Year: Blake Shelton
Female Vocalist of the Year: Miranda Lambert
Vocal Group of the Year: Little Big Town
Album of the Year: *Based on a True Story,* Blake Shelton
New Artist of the Year: Kacey Musgraves
Vocal Duo of the Year: Florida Georgia Line
Single of the Year: "Cruise," Florida Georgia Line

Kacey Musgraves

Blake Shelton

MTV VIDEO MUSIC AWARDS

AUGUST 25, 2013

Video of the Year: "Mirrors," Justin Timberlake

Artist to Watch: "What About Love,"
Austin Mahone

Best Song of the Summer: "Best Song Ever,"
One Direction

Best Video with a Social Message:
"Same Love," Macklemore & Ryan Lewis
featuring Mary Lambert

Best Female Video: "I Knew You Were Trouble,"
Taylor Swift

Best Hip-Hop Video: "Can't Hold Us,"
Macklemore & Ryan Lewis featuring Ray Dalton

Best Collaboration: "Just Give Me
a Reason," P!nk featuring Nate Ruess

Best Pop Video: "Come & Get It," Selena Gomez

Best Art Direction: "Q.U.E.E.N.," Janelle Monáe
featuring Erykah Badu

Best Cinematography: "Can't Hold Us,"
Macklemore & Ryan Lewis featuring Ray Dalton

Best Editing: "Mirrors," Justin Timberlake

Best Visual Effects: "Safe and Sound," Capital Cities

Justin Timberlake

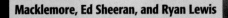

Macklemore, Ed Sheeran, and Ryan Lewis

TEEN CHOICE AWARDS

AUGUST 11, 2013

Choice Single by a Female Artist: "Heart Attack," Demi Lovato

Choice Single by a Male Artist: "Beauty and a Beat," Justin Bieber featuring Nicki Minaj

Choice Single by a Group: "Live While We're Young," One Direction

Choice Country Song: "We Are Never Ever Getting Back Together," Taylor Swift

Choice Rock Song: "Radioactive," Imagine Dragons

Choice R&B/Hip-Hop Song: "Can't Hold Us," Macklemore & Ryan Lewis featuring Ray Dalton

Choice Love Song: "Little Things," One Direction

Choice Breakup Song: "Come & Get It," Selena Gomez

Choice Breakout Artist: Ed Sheeran

Choice Breakout Group: Emblem3

Choice Female Country Artist: Taylor Swift

Choice Male Country Artist: Hunter Hayes

Choice Country Group: Lady Antebellum

Choice Female Artist: Demi Lovato

Choice Male Artist: Justin Bieber

Choice EDM Artist: David Guetta

Choice Music Group: One Direction

Choice R&B Artist: Bruno Mars

Choice Hip-Hop/Rap Artist: Macklemore & Ryan Lewis

Choice Rock Group: Paramore

Demi Lovato

Hayley Williams, of Paramore

PEOPLE'S CHOICE AWARDS

JANUARY 8, 2014

Favorite Male Artist: Justin Timberlake

Favorite Female Artist: Demi Lovato

Favorite Breakout Artist:
Ariana Grande

Favorite Pop Artist: Britney Spears

Favorite Country Artist: Taylor Swift

Favorite Country Music Icon:
Tim McGraw

Favorite Hip-Hop Artist:
Macklemore & Ryan Lewis

Favorite R&B Artist: Justin Timberlake

Favorite Band: One Direction

Favorite Alternative Band: Fall Out Boy

Favorite Song: "Roar," Katy Perry

Favorite Album: *The 20/20 Experience,*
Justin Timberlake

Favorite Music Video: "Roar," Katy Perry

Favorite Music Fan Following: Lovatics, Demi Lovato

Britney Spears

LL Cool J and Jennifer Hudson

GUESS WHAT? LL Cool J presented Jennifer Hudson with the Favorite Humanitarian Award at the People's Choice Awards. Hudson works with the Julian D. King Gift Foundation, which she founded with her sister Julia. The charity works to provide support and positive experiences to children.

MUSIC

PRESIDENTS

Peek into one of the 132 rooms of the White House. **Page 191**

Whose Birthday Are We Celebrating? BY TFK STAFF

Every February, the nation celebrates Presidents' Day. Or is it George Washington's Birthday? What about Abraham Lincoln's? Confused yet? Everyone agrees that the day is a holiday, but what should we call it? Some government offices call it Presidents' Day. Others say the holiday is officially Washington's Birthday.

THE HISTORY BEHIND PRESIDENTS' DAY

George Washington was elected the country's first president on April 30, 1789. Soon after, Americans began publicly celebrating his birthday.

Presidential historians say the actual date of George Washington's birth is February 11, 1732. A change in the calendar system 20 years later shifted all dates 11 days ahead, making Washington's birthday February 22. In 1879, Congress made Washington's Birthday an official federal holiday. It was the first federal holiday to celebrate an individual's birth date.

In 1968, Congress passed the Monday Holidays Act, which moved the holiday to the third Monday in February. The new law did not change the holiday's name. It was still called Washington's Birthday, even though some lawmakers wanted to call it Presidents' Day to include Abraham Lincoln. Lincoln's birthday is February 12.

THE GREAT PRESIDENTIAL DEBATE

Many people agree that the holiday should celebrate all past presidents. They feel Lincoln should be honored for his role in preserving the nation during the Civil War and helping free slaves. Others feel the holiday should only honor Washington, the country's first president. They say shifting the focus away from Washington would mean future generations of kids would not know about the Father of Our Country.

Laws have been introduced in Congress over the years to require use of the term "George Washington's Birthday," but none of those laws have passed. Meanwhile, many state governments and school districts now use the term "Presidents' Day." Many stores also use it to promote holiday sales.

What do you think? Should the holiday honor Washington, Washington and Lincoln, or all past presidents?

PRESIDENTS' DAY DILEMMA

In February 2013, TIME FOR KIDS took a poll to find out what its readers thought about which president or presidents the holiday should celebrate. Here are the results.

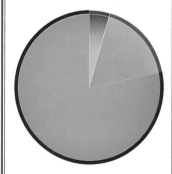

- George Washington, 4.6%
- George Washington and Abraham Lincoln, 17.3%
- All past presidents, 78.1%

Total votes: 4,119

FROM TIME FOR KIDS MAGAZINE

PATHWAYS TO POWER

Every president has his own story. Follow the tangled paths in the puzzle below, and uncover a little something about three U.S. leaders.

John Adams

William Howard Taft

James Monroe

CAPITOL

1. _____ was the first U.S. senator to go on to become president.

SUPREME COURT

2. _____ is the only president to have also served on the Supreme Court.

WHITE HOUSE

3. _____ was the first president to live in the White House.

Answers on page 277

What Does the **President** Do?

The president has the following powers and responsibilities:

★ Carry out the laws of the land

★ Appoint U.S. ambassadors, Supreme Court Justices, federal judges, and Cabinet secretaries (who then must be approved by the Senate)

★ Give the annual State of the Union address to Congress

★ Receive foreign ambassadors, thus recognizing their government

★ Propose treaties with other nations

★ Serve as Commander in Chief of the Armed Forces; send troops overseas (he needs congressional approval to declare war)

★ Approve or veto bills passed by Congress

★ Call both houses of Congress to meet in a special session

★ Grant pardons for federal crimes

President Obama delivers a speech.

WHO CAN BE PRESIDENT?

The president serves a term of four years, with a maximum of two terms. To be president, a person must meet these requirements. He or she must:

★ Be a native-born U.S. citizen

★ Be at least 35 years old

★ Have lived in the United States for at least 14 years

The White House

Can you imagine a house with 35 bathrooms? Well, you don't have to rely on your imagination. And you won't have to look further than Washington, D.C. The president's house features 132 rooms, including three kitchens, eight staircases, three elevators, a bowling alley, a movie theater . . . and 35 bathrooms. The rooms are spread over six levels. Presidents and their families have been living in the White House for more than 200 years.

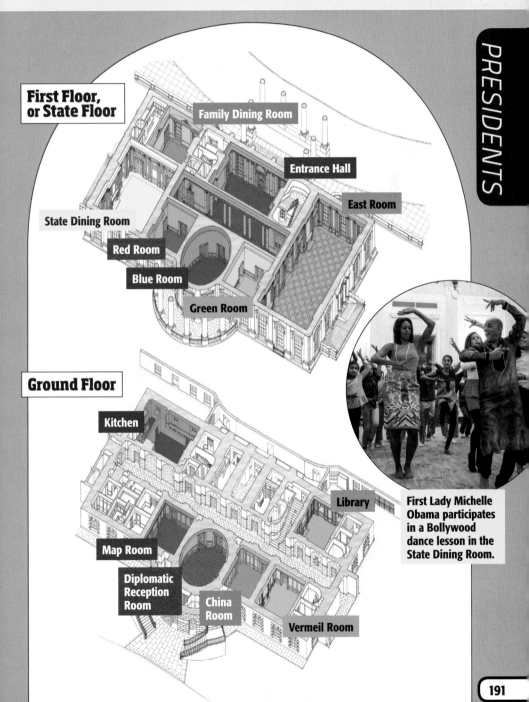

First Floor, or State Floor

Family Dining Room

Entrance Hall

East Room

State Dining Room

Red Room

Blue Room

Green Room

Ground Floor

Kitchen

Library

Map Room

Diplomatic Reception Room

China Room

Vermeil Room

First Lady Michelle Obama participates in a Bollywood dance lesson in the State Dining Room.

U.S. Presidents in Order

1. GEORGE WASHINGTON, served 1789–1797
Political Parties: None (first term), Federalist (second term)
Lived: February 22, 1732–December 14, 1799
Vice President: John Adams
First Lady: Martha Dandridge Custis

2. JOHN ADAMS, served 1797–1801
Political Party: Federalist
Lived: October 30, 1735–July 4, 1826
Vice President: Thomas Jefferson
First Lady: Abigail Smith

3. THOMAS JEFFERSON, served 1801–1809
Political Party: Democratic-Republican
Lived: April 13, 1743–July 4, 1826
Vice Presidents: Aaron Burr, George Clinton
First Lady: Martha Wayles Skelton

4. JAMES MADISON, served 1809–1817
Political Party: Democratic-Republican
Lived: March 16, 1751–June 28, 1836
Vice Presidents: George Clinton, Elbridge Gerry
First Lady: Dorothy "Dolley" Payne Todd

5. JAMES MONROE, served 1817–1825
Political Party: Democratic-Republican
Lived: April 28, 1758–July 4, 1831
Vice President: Daniel D. Tompkins
First Lady: Elizabeth "Eliza" Kortright

6. JOHN QUINCY ADAMS, served 1825–1829
Political Party: Democratic-Republican
Lived: July 11, 1767–February 23, 1848
Vice President: John C. Calhoun
First Lady: Louisa Catherine Johnson

7. ANDREW JACKSON, served 1829–1837
Political Party: Democratic
Lived: March 15, 1767–June 8, 1845
Vice Presidents: John C. Calhoun, Martin Van Buren
First Lady: Rachel Donelson Robards

8. MARTIN VAN BUREN, served 1837–1841
Political Party: Democratic
Lived: December 5, 1782–July 24, 1862
Vice President: Richard M. Johnson
First Lady: Hannah Hoes

⑤ COOL THINGS ABOUT MARTIN VAN BUREN

1. President Van Buren was given two tiger cubs as a gift from the sultan of Oman.

2. Van Buren was born six years after the Declaration of Independence was signed. He was the first natural-born American citizen to be president.

3. One of Van Buren's nicknames was "Little Magician."

4. Van Buren was the only president whose first language was not English. He grew up speaking Dutch in the Dutch community of Kinderhook, New York.

5. While in office, Van Buren ran for a second term. He was defeated. In 1848, Van Buren ran for president as a member of the antislavery Free Soil Party.

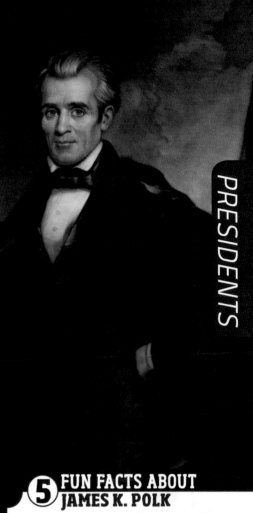

9. WILLIAM HENRY HARRISON, served 1841
Political Party: Whig
Lived: February 9, 1773–April 4, 1841
Vice President: John Tyler
First Lady: Anna Tuthill Symmes

10. JOHN TYLER, served 1841–1845
Political Party: Whig
Lived: March 29, 1790–January 18, 1862
Vice President: None
First Ladies: Letitia Christian (d. 1842),
Julia Gardiner

11. JAMES K. POLK, served 1845–1849
Political Party: Democratic
Lived: November 2, 1795–June 15, 1849
Vice President: George M. Dallas
First Lady: Sarah Childress

12. ZACHARY TAYLOR, served 1849–1850
Political Party: Whig
Lived: November 24, 1784–July 9, 1850
Vice President: Millard Fillmore
First Lady: Margaret Mackall Smith

13. MILLARD FILLMORE, served 1850–1853
Political Party: Whig
Lived: January 7, 1800–March 8, 1874
Vice President: None
First Lady: Abigail Powers

14. FRANKLIN PIERCE, served 1853–1857
Political Party: Democratic
Lived: November 23, 1804–October 8, 1869
Vice President: William R. King
First Lady: Jane Means Appleton

15. JAMES BUCHANAN, served 1857–1861
Political Party: Democratic
Lived: April 23, 1791–June 1, 1868
Vice President: John C. Breckinridge
First Lady: None

16. ABRAHAM LINCOLN, served 1861–1865
Political Party: Republican
Lived: February 12, 1809–April 15, 1865
Vice Presidents: Hannibal Hamlin, Andrew Johnson
First Lady: Mary Todd

PRESIDENTS

5 FUN FACTS ABOUT JAMES K. POLK

1. Polk was the first president to have his picture taken.

2. As a young man, Polk suffered from bladder stones, which are hardened mineral deposits that can form in the bladder. At 17, Polk had these bladder stones removed without anesthesia (drugs to keep him from feeling pain).

3. First Lady Sarah Childress Polk was very religious. She banned dancing and playing card games in the White House.

4. President Polk and First Lady Sarah Childress Polk hosted the first Thanksgiving dinner at the White House.

5. During Polk's presidency, the United States grew by 1.2 million square miles (3.1 million sq km).

17. ANDREW JOHNSON, served 1865–1869
Political Parties: Union, Democratic
Lived: December 29, 1808–July 31, 1875
Vice President: None
First Lady: Eliza McCardle

18. ULYSSES S. GRANT, served 1869–1877
Political Party: Republican
Lived: April 27, 1822–July 23, 1885
Vice Presidents: Schuyler Colfax, Henry Wilson
First Lady: Julia Boggs Dent

19. RUTHERFORD B. HAYES, served 1877–1881
Political Party: Republican
Lived: October 4, 1822–January 17, 1893
Vice President: William A. Wheeler
First Lady: Lucy Ware Webb

20. JAMES A. GARFIELD, served 1881
Political Party: Republican
Lived: November 19, 1831–September 19, 1881
Vice President: Chester A. Arthur
First Lady: Lucretia Rudolph

21. CHESTER A. ARTHUR, served 1881–1885
Political Party: Republican
Lived: October 5, 1829–November 18, 1886
Vice President: None
First Lady: Ellen Lewis Herndon

22. GROVER CLEVELAND, served 1885–1889
Political Party: Democratic
Lived: March 18, 1837–June 24, 1908
Vice President: Thomas A. Hendricks
First Lady: Frances Folsom

23. BENJAMIN HARRISON, served 1889–1893
Political Party: Republican
Lived: August 20, 1833–March 13, 1901
Vice President: Levi P. Morton
First Lady: Caroline Lavinia Scott (d. 1892)

24. GROVER CLEVELAND, served 1893–1897
Political Party: Democratic
Lived: March 18, 1837–June 24, 1908
Vice President: Adlai E. Stevenson
First Lady: Frances Folsom

⑤ NEAT FACTS ABOUT GROVER CLEVELAND

1. Cleveland's first name was actually Stephen. Many of the children in his family, including Grover, went by their middle names.

2. Cleveland was the only president to serve two nonconsecutive terms. That means his terms were not one after the other.

3. Cleveland is the only president to have been married in the White House.

4. As a young man, Cleveland briefly worked for the New York Institution for the Blind.

5. Cleveland's face appeared on the $1,000 bill, which is no longer in use.

25. WILLIAM MCKINLEY, served 1897–1901
Political Party: Republican
Lived: January 29, 1843–September 14, 1901
Vice Presidents: Garret A. Hobart, Theodore Roosevelt
First Lady: Ida Saxton

26. THEODORE ROOSEVELT, served 1901–1909
Political Party: Republican
Lived: October 27, 1858–January 6, 1919
Vice President: Charles W. Fairbanks
First Lady: Edith Kermit Carow

27. WILLIAM H. TAFT, served 1909–1913
Political Party: Republican
Lived: September 15, 1857–March 8, 1930
Vice President: James S. Sherman
First Lady: Helen Herron

28. WOODROW WILSON, served 1913–1921
Political Party: Democratic
Lived: December 28, 1856–February 3, 1924
Vice President: Thomas R. Marshall
First Ladies: Ellen Louise Axson (d. 1914), Edith Bolling Galt

29. WARREN G. HARDING, served 1921–1923
Political Party: Republican
Lived: November 2, 1865–August 2, 1923
Vice President: Calvin Coolidge
First Lady: Florence Kling

30. CALVIN COOLIDGE, served 1923–1929
Political Party: Republican
Lived: July 4, 1872–January 5, 1933
Vice President: Charles G. Dawes
First Lady: Grace Anna Goodhue

31. HERBERT C. HOOVER, served 1929–1933
Political Party: Republican
Lived: August 10, 1874–October 20, 1964
Vice President: Charles Curtis
First Lady: Lou Henry

32. FRANKLIN D. ROOSEVELT, served 1933–1945
Political Party: Democratic
Lived: January 30, 1882–April 12, 1945
Vice Presidents: John Garner, Henry Wallace, Harry S Truman
First Lady: Anna Eleanor Roosevelt

PRESIDENTS

⑤ WACKY DETAILS ABOUT THEODORE ROOSEVELT

1. Theodore Roosevelt was the first president to leave the United States while in office. He traveled to Central America to see the construction of the Panama Canal.

2. Theodore Roosevelt was known by his nickname "Teddy."

3. Before Teddy Roosevelt moved into the White House, it was known as the Executive Mansion. Starting in 1901, Roosevelt put "White House-Washington" on the official stationery, and the name stuck.

4. Teddy Roosevelt was often sick as a child. He had many asthma attacks.

5. While delivering a campaign speech in 1912, Teddy Roosevelt was shot in the chest. He had a steel eyeglass case in his pocket, as well as a copy of the long speech he was planning to give. The case and the wad of papers probably saved his life. Even with the bullet in his chest, he delivered a 90-minute speech.

33. HARRY S TRUMAN, served 1945–1953
Political Party: Democratic
Lived: May 8, 1884–December 26, 1972
Vice President: Alben W. Barkley
First Lady: Elizabeth "Bess" Virginia Wallace

34. DWIGHT D. EISENHOWER, served 1953–1961
Political Party: Republican
Lived: October 14, 1890–March 28, 1969
Vice President: Richard M. Nixon
First Lady: Mamie Geneva Doud

35. JOHN F. KENNEDY, served 1961–1963
Political Party: Democratic
Lived: May 29, 1917–November 22, 1963
Vice President: Lyndon B. Johnson
First Lady: Jacqueline Lee Bouvier

36. LYNDON B. JOHNSON, served 1963–1969
Political Party: Democratic
Lived: August 27, 1908–January 22, 1973
Vice President: Hubert H. Humphrey
First Lady: Claudia Alta "Lady Bird" Taylor

37. RICHARD NIXON, served 1969–1974
Political Party: Republican
Lived: January 9, 1913–April 22, 1994
Vice Presidents: Spiro T. Agnew, Gerald R. Ford
First Lady: Thelma Catherine "Pat" Ryan

38. GERALD R. FORD, served 1974–1977
Political Party: Republican
Lived: July 14, 1913–December 26, 2006
Vice President: Nelson A. Rockefeller
First Lady: Elizabeth "Betty" Anne Bloomer Warren

39. JIMMY CARTER, served 1977–1981
Political Party: Democratic
Born: October 1, 1924, in Georgia
Vice President: Walter F. Mondale
First Lady: Rosalynn Smith

40. RONALD REAGAN, served 1981–1989
Political Party: Republican
Lived: February 6, 1911–June 5, 2004
Vice President: George H.W. Bush
First Lady: Nancy Davis

⑤ FUN FACTS ABOUT DWIGHT EISENHOWER

1. Eisenhower was the only president to serve in both World War I and World War II.

2. In 1958, Eisenhower signed the act that created the National Aeronautic and Space Administration (NASA).

3. Eisenhower had six brothers. He was the third child in the family.

4. Eisenhower suffered a heart attack during his first term in office.

5. Known by his nickname "Ike," Eisenhower used the popular campaign slogan "I like Ike."

41. GEORGE H.W. BUSH, served 1989–1993
Political Party: Republican
Born: June 12, 1924, in Massachusetts
Vice President: J. Danforth Quayle
First Lady: Barbara Pierce

42. BILL CLINTON, served 1993–2001
Political Party: Democratic
Born: August 19, 1946, in Arkansas
Vice President: Albert Gore Jr.
First Lady: Hillary Rodham

43. GEORGE W. BUSH, served 2001–2009
Political Party: Republican
Born: July 6, 1946, in Connecticut
Vice President: Richard B. "Dick" Cheney
First Lady: Laura Welch

44. BARACK OBAMA, served 2009–
Political Party: Democratic
Born: August 4, 1961, in Hawaii
Vice President: Joe Biden
First Lady: Michelle Robinson

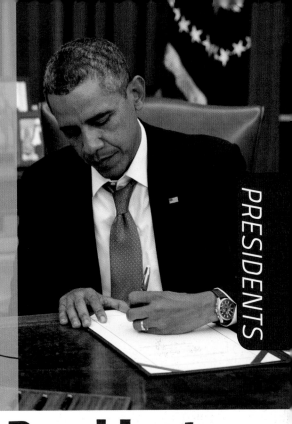

PRESIDENTS

TOP 5 Youngest **Presidents**

According to the Constitution, the president must be at least 35 years old. Theodore Roosevelt is the youngest person to have become president. He succeeded William McKinley, who was assassinated. Here are the youngest presidents and their ages when they took office.

1. Theodore Roosevelt
42 years, 322 days

2. John F. Kennedy
43 years, 236 days

3. Bill Clinton
46 years, 149 days

4. Ulysses S. Grant
46 years, 311 days

5. Barack Obama
47 years, 169 days

SCIENCE

Meet a soil scientist who studies ancient Mayan dirt. **Page 202**

TYPES OF SCIENTISTS

Do you like to look for fossils? Are you fascinated by butterflies? Have you ever wanted to prevent people from getting sick? No matter what your interests are, there is a possible career for you in science. Here are some neat scientific specialties that you may want to check out.

An **ASTRONOMER** examines stars, planets, comets, asteroids, galaxies, and other things in space.

A **COMPUTER SCIENTIST** knows a lot about computer systems and how computers work. He or she could create software, research new applications, or program computer systems.

CRIMINOLOGISTS study criminals and the causes of their behavior within a society.

An **EPIDEMIOLOGIST** is a scientist who examines diseases and how they spread.

ETHOLOGISTS study animal behavior.

The origins, history, surface, structure, and makeup of Earth are major subjects of study for a **GEOLOGIST**.

GENETICISTS focus on genes and the traits that living things get from their parents.

A scientist who learns all about glaciers and ice is a **GLACIOLOGIST**.

To become an **OCEANOGRAPHER**, you must study the ocean, including marine life, water currents, and the geology of the ground beneath the ocean.

HERPETOLOGISTS examine amphibians and reptiles.

IMMUNOLOGISTS focus on the immune systems of all living things. An organism's immune system protects it from diseases and infections.

A biologist who focuses on butterflies is called a **LEPIDOPTERIST**.

MALACOLOGISTS study mollusks (such as snails, oysters, and clams).

Someone who is dedicated to learning about weather and climate is a **METEOROLOGIST**.

MINERALOGISTS are experts in the chemical and physical makeup of minerals.

NEUROSCIENTISTS study the human nervous system and how it works.

PALEOBOTANISTS focus on the biology and evolution of prehistoric plants.

A scientist who studies the remains of organisms that lived long ago is a **PALEONTOLOGIST**.

A **ROBOTICIST** designs, builds, and operates robots.

A **VOLCANOLOGIST** is a type of geologist who studies volcanoes.

A **SEISMOLOGIST** is an expert on earthquakes.

The Scientific Method

The scientific method is a set of steps that all scientists follow to create and conduct experiments. Here are the basic steps.

☐ ASK A QUESTION.

Are you concerned about beach erosion? Do you wish you understood more about the weather? Do some research, and come up with a question you would like to answer. For example, is dish liquid more effective in warm water or cold?

☐ DO RESEARCH ON THE TOPIC.

Investigate your topic, and find out what similar experiments have been done. What you learn will help you design a better experiment.

☐ FORM A HYPOTHESIS.

A hypothesis is a prediction based on what you have observed and read about. Hypotheses are usually put into this format: "If _____, then _____ because _____." For example, "If I put a can of soda in the freezer, then it will explode because there is a lot of water in soda, and water expands when it freezes."

☐ TEST THE HYPOTHESIS WITH AN EXPERIMENT.

Come up with a list of the materials you will need, and gather them. Write down each step in the experiment, and follow them carefully. Record your observations in writing and in pictures, wherever possible. Change only one variable in your experiment.

☐ ANALYZE THE RESULTS.

What happened in your experiment? Think about the data you collected during your experiment. Put your findings into a graph or chart.

☐ DRAW A CONCLUSION.

Did the results of your experiment support your hypothesis? If not, come up with a new hypothesis, and try the experiment again.

☐ SHARE YOUR FINDINGS.

When professional scientists complete an experiment, they will often publish a paper or article about their work and what they've found. You can do the same. Tell your parents, teachers, and friends.

SINK OR FLOAT?

Use the scientific method to predict whether an object will sink or float in water. Here are some ideas for objects to test: raisin, penny, paper clip, button, cork, crayon, and sponge.

Remember: An object's density—how solid it is—determines whether the object will float or sink in water. When an object is denser than water, it will sink. When it is less dense, it will float.

ORANGE YOU CURIOUS?

Try the sink-or-float experiment with an orange. Use a whole orange first, then peel the orange and conduct the experiment again. (Be sure to place the orange carefully in the water both times. Don't just drop it in.)

Most likely, the unpeeled orange floated, and the peeled orange sank. That's because an orange rind has lots of tiny air pockets. Those pockets give the orange a low enough density to keep it afloat in the water.

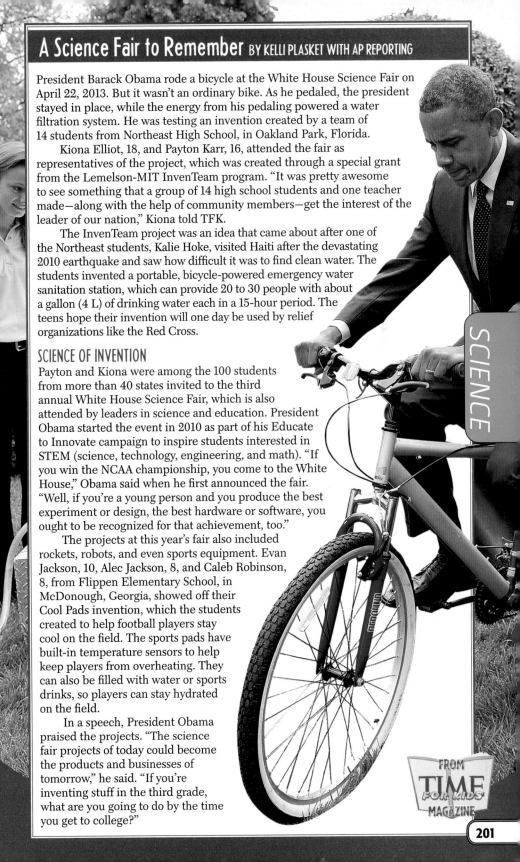

A Science Fair to Remember BY KELLI PLASKET WITH AP REPORTING

President Barack Obama rode a bicycle at the White House Science Fair on April 22, 2013. But it wasn't an ordinary bike. As he pedaled, the president stayed in place, while the energy from his pedaling powered a water filtration system. He was testing an invention created by a team of 14 students from Northeast High School, in Oakland Park, Florida.

Kiona Elliot, 18, and Payton Karr, 16, attended the fair as representatives of the project, which was created through a special grant from the Lemelson-MIT InvenTeam program. "It was pretty awesome to see something that a group of 14 high school students and one teacher made—along with the help of community members—get the interest of the leader of our nation," Kiona told TFK.

The InvenTeam project was an idea that came about after one of the Northeast students, Kalie Hoke, visited Haiti after the devastating 2010 earthquake and saw how difficult it was to find clean water. The students invented a portable, bicycle-powered emergency water sanitation station, which can provide 20 to 30 people with about a gallon (4 L) of drinking water each in a 15-hour period. The teens hope their invention will one day be used by relief organizations like the Red Cross.

SCIENCE OF INVENTION

Payton and Kiona were among the 100 students from more than 40 states invited to the third annual White House Science Fair, which is also attended by leaders in science and education. President Obama started the event in 2010 as part of his Educate to Innovate campaign to inspire students interested in STEM (science, technology, engineering, and math). "If you win the NCAA championship, you come to the White House," Obama said when he first announced the fair. "Well, if you're a young person and you produce the best experiment or design, the best hardware or software, you ought to be recognized for that achievement, too."

The projects at this year's fair also included rockets, robots, and even sports equipment. Evan Jackson, 10, Alec Jackson, 8, and Caleb Robinson, 8, from Flippen Elementary School, in McDonough, Georgia, showed off their Cool Pads invention, which the students created to help football players stay cool on the field. The sports pads have built-in temperature sensors to help keep players from overheating. They can also be filled with water or sports drinks, so players can stay hydrated on the field.

In a speech, President Obama praised the projects. "The science fair projects of today could become the products and businesses of tomorrow," he said. "If you're inventing stuff in the third grade, what are you going to do by the time you get to college?"

SCIENCE

Soil scientist Richard Terry, who is also a science professor at Brigham Young University, in Provo, Utah, talks to TFK about his work.

TFK: When and why did you decide to become a soil scientist?

RICHARD TERRY: I grew up on a farm in Idaho, but I did not want to become a farmer. Milking cows every morning before school and every afternoon after school was a good incentive for me to go to college and become a scientist. I enjoyed my science courses at the university, but once I saw the application of chemistry, math, and physics in soil science, I knew that was what I wanted to focus on in my career.

TFK: Why are soil scientists important? What do they help us learn?

TERRY: Soil scientists help us understand how soil particles like sand and silt and clay help to filter pollutants from our water. The bacteria and fungi that live in the soil help to decompose our wastes. Soil supports plants and delivers nutrients and water to plants so that we have food and fiber to help us live.

TFK: What are some tools that you use as a soil scientist?

TERRY: In the field, my students and I use shovels, trowels, and drilling devices to collect soil samples. In the laboratory, we use chemicals to extract nutrients that were deposited on the soil surface by ancient people.

TFK: Since 1997, you've been studying the soils of ancient Maya settlements in what is now Guatemala. What are some highlights of your findings?

TERRY: We started out looking for ancient waste piles left over from food processing and waste disposal by the Maya. The organic matter has decomposed and been lost from the soil. But phosphorus is a component of all food materials and becomes attached to soil particles, where it remains for thousands of years.

We then used these techniques to determine the locations of ancient kitchens and workshops. One of those workshops was used to make polished mirrors that the king of Aguateca wore when performing ceremonies. Archaeologists found carved stones in that workshop that were once part of the king's crown. We then started to examine the soils of large public plazas to find chemical residues of

Scientist Richard Terry takes soil samples at an ancient Maya site.

ancient marketplace activities. We are currently examining the organic matter, or the humus, of the soil to find the residues of ancient corn plants. This helps us to determine where corn was grown.

TFK: Why did you want to study the Maya? What do you find most interesting about their ancient civilization?

TERRY: I started out helping geographers and archaeologists who were interested in soil phosphorus as a sign of ancient activities. It was not long before other interesting questions about ancient human activities and soil science were asked by archaeologists, my students, and myself. The research just keeps coming. One thing that you learn as a scientist is that for each scientific question that we are able to answer, there will be 10 more questions that need to be answered. Scientists will always have more questions to answer.

The ancient Mayan city of Tikal had tall pyramid-like temples.

SCIENCE

THE MAYA

The Maya belonged to a civilization that lived in southern Mexico and northern Central America. They flourished from about 250 to 900 A.D. During this period, they grew crops, built huge stone structures, and had bustling cities filled with people. In the 1400s and 1500s, Spanish conquistadors, or conquerors, defeated the Maya and took control of the area.

The Maya are known for their advancements in art, architecture, mathematics, and astronomy. The Maya also created the first pre-Columbian society in the Americas to have a fully developed writing system. (Pre-Columbian refers to the cultures of North, South, and Central America before the arrival of Christopher Columbus in 1492.) Many Mayan ruins, such as Tulum, Chichén Itzá, and Tikal, can still be seen in Mexico and Guatemala. Today, nearly 42% of the Guatemalan population is of Mayan descent.

Why Do Paper Towels Soak Up Water So Fast?

Paper towels use capillary action to soak up water and other liquids. Capillary action is the natural upward movement of a liquid within a narrow space. Paper towels have tiny, narrow spaces between their fibers. A liquid quickly flows up and into those spaces when it comes in contact with the paper towel.

Why is a liquid like water able to defy gravity and flow upward? Although water likes to stick to itself, it also likes to stick to other substances. If the forces that make water cling to a paper towel are stronger than the forces within the water itself that make it stay together, then the water will "climb" up the paper towel.

GUESS WHAT? Capillary action also explains why a bath towel helps dry you off. The water from your body flows into the spaces between the fibers in the bath towel. The towel gets wet while your body gets dry!

How Does Salt Get into Peanuts That Are Still in Their Shells?

Here's how it's done:

1. The unshelled peanuts are put into a huge metal bin.

2. The bin is filled with salt water (brine).

3. A vacuum pump sucks the air out of the bin, including all the air that's inside the peanut shells. The air is pulled out of the shells because peanut shells are very porous. Porous means they have lots of tiny holes.

4. The shells then fill up with the salt water (through those same holes).

5. The salt water is drained from the bin.

6. The peanuts are heated and dried. The heat removes all the water, but leaves a light coating of salt on the inside of the shells.

GUESS WHAT? Eggshells are also very porous. Tiny holes in the shells allow air to flow in and out. Unborn chicks breathe this air before they hatch from the shells.

IN THE KITCHEN!

Why Do Ice Cubes Float?

All things are made up of molecules. A molecule is the smallest amount of something (like water, oxygen, or carbon dioxide) that has all of its characteristics. When water freezes, the spaces between its molecules expand. Because of that extra space, ice is less dense than water. That means it weighs less than water, and it rises to the top of the water.

It's a good thing ice floats. If ice sank in water, the surface of a lake would sink as soon as it froze in winter. Eventually, all the water in the lake would freeze and sink. The lake would then become a solid block of ice. That would kill the fish and other living creatures that live in the lake.

GUESS WHAT? Water expands by about 10% when it's frozen. So if you put 10 cups of water into a freezer, you'll take out about 11 cups of ice. That's why putting some liquids in the freezer is a bad idea: Their containers could explode!

Why Does Orange Juice Taste Weird After You've Brushed Your Teeth?

Scientists aren't exactly sure why. But they think the bad taste may have something to do with one of the ingredients in toothpaste: sodium lauryl sulfate. That's the ingredient that makes toothpaste foamy.

Sodium lauryl sulfate temporarily alters the taste buds in your mouth. It makes the buds less sensitive to sweet tastes and more sensitive to bitter ones. So if you take a sip of orange juice after brushing your teeth, two things will happen:

1. You'll be less likely to taste the natural sugar (fructose) in the juice.

2. You'll be more likely to notice the juice's bitter citric acid.

But don't worry! Your taste buds will return to normal after about an hour.

SCIENTISTS IN THE NEWS

A Secret Stash of Ancient Seawater

An asteroid (or perhaps a comet) crashed into Earth about 35 million years ago. It landed in what is now the Chesapeake Bay on the East Coast of the United States. The asteroid, which was at least 0.6 mile (1 km) wide, created huge sprays of water that reached 30 miles (48 km) into the air. It also triggered gigantic tsunamis that spread for hundreds of miles.

The asteroid hollowed out a crater at the bottom of the ocean that was more than 50 miles (80 km) wide. Over centuries, the crater was covered up with hundreds of feet of sand, silt, and clay. Scientists only discovered its existence in the early 1990s. They decided to drill down under the crater to learn more about what happens to Earth when it is hit with a large asteroid or comet.

One of those scientists was Ward Sanford, a **hydrologist** with the U.S. Geological Survey. Using special equipment, he and his team drilled more than 1 mile (1.6 km) into the sediment under the crater. They found something amazing: tiny pockets of ancient seawater. The water had been trapped there for more than 100 million years—even before the asteroid hit. And when the scientists tested the water, they discovered something else: It was twice as salty as today's seawater. Sanford and his team are now doing further tests on the water to learn more about the evolution of Earth's oceans.

A **HYDROLOGIST** studies the location, movement, and quality of water on Earth and on other planets.

GUESS WHAT? Asteroids are made of metals and rocky materials. Comets are made of rocks, dust, and ice.

Mosquitoes Like Smelly Socks!

Scientists are getting a better understanding of exactly what it is that attracts mosquitoes to humans. They've known for a long time that mosquitoes track down humans by the smell of carbon dioxide—the gas that people exhale when they breathe. But once the mosquitoes get close to a human, how do they choose which fleshy place to land on—and bite?

Entomologist Anandasankar Ray has discovered that mosquitoes recognize both carbon dioxide and skin odors with the same special nerve cells. The cells are located in sensing pads that stick out from the insects' head.

An **ENTOMOLOGIST** is a scientist who studies insects.

This finding helps explain why mosquitoes are attracted to stinky socks, dirty or worn clothes, and used bedding even when no one is nearby exhaling carbon dioxide. Ray and other scientists are now trying to identify which body odors attract the insects and which ones don't. They hope to use that knowledge to develop more effective mosquito repellents.

A Sweet Discovery

Archaeologist Dorothy Washburn has discovered traces of chocolate inside bowls dug up from the ancient ruins of a Pueblo village in southeastern Utah. The bowls were buried in the 8th century. That's more than 1,200 years ago! Those may be the oldest traces of chocolate ever found in North America.

Chocolate is made from the dried seeds of the cacao tree. The trees grow only where it's hot and humid, such as in the tropical forests of Central and South America. The chocolate found in the North American Pueblo village must have been brought there from cacao trees thousands of miles away. That means that people throughout the Americas traded goods with one another much earlier than archaeologists previously believed.

To learn more about the lives and cultures of prehistoric people, an **ARCHAEOLOGIST** analyzes human-made objects and other artifacts left behind.

Undersea Mystery Solved!

In the mid-1990s, scuba divers discovered something very unusual off the coast of Japan. Carved in the sand on the ocean floor, some 80 feet (24 m) below sea level, were a series of elaborately designed geometric patterns. Each pattern formed a circle about 7 feet (2 m) in diameter.

What had made these mystery circles? That question was finally answered in 2012. A team of scientists took underwater cameras down to the ocean floor. They discovered that the circles are created by tiny puffer fish less than 5 inches (12 cm) long. The male puffer fish uses one of its fins to sculpt the circle in the sand to attract a female mate. He even decorates the circles with tiny pieces of shell and coral! The female then lays her eggs at the center of the circle. The ridges in the circle protect the eggs from being swept away by ocean currents.

Sea Studies

MARINE BIOLOGY is the study of the organisms that live in our seas and oceans. Scientists in this watery field observe and analyze the behavior and interactions of these creatures. Some marine biologists are experts on whales. Others know all there is to know about kelp. Still others focus on the field called marine biotechnology. These scientists use their knowledge of marine organisms to create new things. For example, some researchers are working on developing materials that are not toxic to sea life but that can keep mussels and barnacles from attaching to the bottoms of ships. This could be used by the military or shipping industry. Animals and plants that live in water may have chemicals in them that can be used to help sick people. Some marine biologists look to the sea to come up with new medicines and foods.

Marine biologists study algae on the seafloor in Hawaii.

THE WORLD'S FIRST
VENOMOUS
CRUSTACEAN

In 2013, scientists announced the discovery of the first known venomous crustacean: a tiny creature called *Speleonectes tulumensis*. White, wiggly, and only about 1 inch (25 mm) long, *S. tulumensis* lives in the water inside underground caves in several areas of the world, including Central America and western Australia.

Scientists have known about *S. tulumensis* for about 30 years. But only recently did they discover how this small, blind crustacean uses venom to kill and eat shrimp, fish, and other prey. First, it bites its prey with its needlelike fangs. The fangs release a toxin similar to rattlesnake venom, which then paralyzes the prey. The toxin also causes the prey's insides to turn into a liquid mush. *S. tulumensis* then sucks up those insides—as if it were drinking a milkshake!

There are more than 70,000 species of crustacean in the world. Scientists are now actively searching for other venomous ones.

SCIENCE

GUESS WHAT? Crustaceans are animals with hard outer shells, or crusts. Most, like crabs and lobsters, live in water. But some, like wood lice, live on land.

MYSTERY PERSON

I was a chemist who was born in Sweden in 1833. I was especially interested in explosives. In 1867, I invented dynamite. It was used to create canals, blast tunnels, and make railroads. Before I died, I asked that most of my money be used for annual international awards. The prizes are named after me.

WHO AM I?

Answer on page 277

Meet a pair of space-traveling twins. **Page 216**

A Chat with Sally Ride BY TFK KID REPORTER LAUREN DAWN

Have you ever dreamed of blasting off into space? That was always Sally Ride's dream. It turned into a reality on June 18, 1983, when she became the first American woman to travel into space.

After making two unforgettable space trips, Ride dedicated her time to getting kids excited about science, technology, engineering, and math. Together, these subjects are known as STEM.

TFK: When did you first become interested in science?

SALLY RIDE: I have been interested in science for as long as I can remember. I loved science even when I was in second grade and third grade. It was my favorite subject in school. I also loved sports and was outside all the time. When I was inside, my main interests in school were science and math.

TFK: When did you become interested in being an astronaut?

RIDE: Partly because of my interest in science and partly because of the time that I grew up, I was always fascinated by the space program. I grew up in the early days of the space program. It was big news all the time. I can still remember our teachers in fourth and fifth grade wheeling these big old black-and-white TV sets into the classroom so that we could watch some of the early space launches.

The whole class was just fascinated. I admired astronauts even from that time. If you asked me when I was 12 whether I wanted to be an astronaut, I'm sure I would have said yes. But I didn't even think about that as a possible career until I was just finishing [graduate school]. NASA put out an announcement that they were accepting applications for astronauts, and this was the first time they had done that in over 10 years. It was the first time they were bringing women into the astronaut program. As soon as I saw that, I knew that's what I wanted to do. So I applied. It was always a dream of mine starting in elementary and middle school, but I didn't think that dream would become a reality until I was almost out of graduate school.

TFK: What did it feel like to blast off into space for the first time?

RIDE: There is no amusement park ride on earth that even comes close. You strap into the space shuttle, and believe me, you have to be strapped in. When the rockets ignite and the shuttle starts moving, there is so much noise and vibration and so much going on. There are just tons and tons of rocket fuel exploding underneath you. You get this kick, and you're off the launchpad. It's hard to take it all in. For several seconds, I was overwhelmed by the power of the launch.

TFK: What do you think is your most important accomplishment?

Sally Ride in space, in 1983

RIDE: The accomplishment that I will be remembered for is being the first American woman to go into space. Looking back on it, that's really important to me. I went into the astronaut program not to be the first woman but just to get a chance to go into space. I realized how important it was for a woman to break that barrier and open the door for other women to join the astronaut corps, and be able to do the same exciting things that the men had been doing. I am proud and honored to be picked to be the first one. I am most proud of training for and completing that first mission.

TFK: What can young girls do to prepare for a career in science?

RIDE: To prepare for a career in science, it is important to understand what scientists do. Just having a good background in science is a very important thing these days. Look around on the Web, and talk to your teachers. Find examples of women who are alive today and part of this exciting work. What girls will find is that there are a wide variety of types of people that became interested in science for very different reasons. They also have other interests and lead normal lives. It is a very rewarding career that allows you to have a real impact on your community, on other people's lives, or on things that we know about our planet or the universe.

TFK: The U.S. was recently ranked 29th in science and 35th in math compared with other countries. What do you think is the reason for this?

RIDE: I think the main reason is that we as a country have not put a focus on math and science education like we used to. When I was growing up, it was one of the most important things to the country. It was really important on a national level that we give students a strong education in math and science. We encouraged them to become scientists and engineers. Back when I was growing up, it was really cool to be a scientist, and that hasn't been the case in the last many years in this country. Nationally, we haven't put the emphasis on it, and we are seeing the results. Because other countries are placing an emphasis on it and are really working hard to make sure that their students are well prepared in math and science, they are jumping ahead of us in the international ranking.

Sally Ride in 1978

FROM TIME FOR KIDS MAGAZINE

HUGE HURRICANE SPOTTED ON SATURN

In 2013, the Cassini spacecraft took photographs of a strange hexagon-shaped hurricane on Saturn's north pole. The six-sided storm is huge. It is 20,000 miles (32,000 km) wide—twice the width of Earth. And its "eye"—the relatively quiet region at the center of the hurricane—is 50 times larger than the average hurricane eye seen on Earth. The storm is also very strong. Its winds reach speeds of 200 miles (322 km) per hour.

This monstrous hurricane was photographed in the 1980s by earlier spacecraft. That means that the hurricane is at least three decades old. But scientists believe the storm may be hundreds of years old. Why Saturn's hurricane has lasted that long is a mystery. Hurricanes on Earth last only about a week.

Scientists have added color to this view of Saturn's north pole. It shows the humongous hexagon-shaped storm.

GUESS WHAT? NASA scientists sent the Cassini spacecraft to Saturn in 1997. It reached Saturn in 2004, and has been orbiting—and photographing—the planet ever since.

The eye of Saturn's massive hurricane

DRINKABLE WATER ON MARS?

Scientists have known for many years that Mars once had water. Its surface has dried-out lakes and riverbeds, and ice has been found in the planet's soil.

But scientists didn't know what that water was like. They didn't know if it would have been able to support forms of life, like some of the tiny, primitive ones once found on Earth.

In 2012, a NASA **space rover** called Curiosity landed on Mars. It drilled into clay rocks in a dry and dusty area that was once a lake. Experiments conducted on those rocks suggested that water had been in the lake when the rocks were formed billions of years ago. The experiments also found evidence that the water had been low in salt. In fact, scientists believe that the quality of the water might even have been okay for humans to drink!

A space rover is a spacecraft that is built to move across the surface of a celestial body, like the moon or Mars. Rovers take photographs, and some carry equipment that enables them to conduct experiments on soil and rocks.

CURIOSITY'S COOL FINDS

The Curiosity rover discovered that the rocks on Mars contained some of the key chemical ingredients for life, including carbon, hydrogen, oxygen, nitrogen, phosphorus, and sulfur. That finding suggests that primitive one-celled organisms might have existed in the lake when it had water more than 3.5 billion years ago. That's about the same time that tiny forms of life were evolving on Earth.

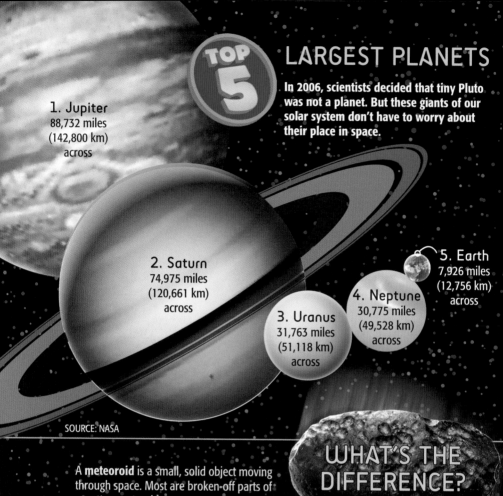

LARGEST PLANETS

TOP 5

In 2006, scientists decided that tiny Pluto was not a planet. But these giants of our solar system don't have to worry about their place in space.

1. Jupiter
88,732 miles
(142,800 km)
across

2. Saturn
74,975 miles
(120,661 km)
across

3. Uranus
31,763 miles
(51,118 km)
across

4. Neptune
30,775 miles
(49,528 km)
across

5. Earth
7,926 miles
(12,756 km)
across

SOURCE: NASA

WHAT'S THE DIFFERENCE?

A **meteoroid** is a small, solid object moving through space. Most are broken-off parts of comets or asteroids.

A **meteor** is a meteoroid that enters the Earth's atmosphere. Meteors tend to burn and glow brightly as they fall toward Earth. For that reason, they are sometimes called shooting stars. Most meteors are very small (much smaller than a pebble) and burn up completely before reaching Earth.

A **meteorite** is the part of the meteor that actually lands on Earth.

EXPLODING METEOR OVER RUSSIA

On the morning of February 15, 2013, a meteor entered the Earth's atmosphere over the city of Chelyabinsk in southwestern Russia. It sped across the sky at 33,000 miles (53,108 km) per hour.

At about 14 miles (23 km) above Earth, the meteor exploded, creating a fireball that was 30 times as bright as the sun. The meteor explosion set off a shock wave of air that blew out windows and damaged buildings in an area 55 miles (88 km) wide. Many people were knocked off their feet. About 1,500 people were injured, most by flying glass.

Fortunately, the biggest piece of the meteor landed in Lake Chebarkul, far from any people. It slammed through 2 feet (61 cm) of ice, creating a hole 20 feet (6 m) wide. When scientists recovered the meteorite from the bottom of the lake several months later, they found it was only about 5 feet (1.5 m) across. Most of the rock had burned up as it flew across the sky. Scientists believe that the meteor had probably been 65 feet (20 m) wide before it entered the Earth's atmosphere.

A dashboard camera captured a photo of the meteor.

A piece of the meteor left a large hole in the ice on Lake Chebarkul.

SPACE

The Tunguska River region after the 1908 meteorite strike

SHOCK AND AWE

Large meteors rarely hit Earth. The last big one was in 1908. It landed in Russia, in an uninhabited forest near the Podkamennaya Tunguska River in central Siberia. Nobody was seriously injured, but the meteorite's shock waves stripped the leaves and branches from trees—and knocked the trees down—for hundreds of miles.

Twins in Space BY JEFFREY KLUGER FOR TIME

No one ever pretends outer space is a welcoming place. The human body seems to fight the very idea of being there. No sooner do astronauts arrive in space than up to 40% of them begin throwing up. Most of them adjust soon enough, but they may continue to feel dizzy and tired. There's also back pain, increased blood pressure, and long-term health risks—all a result of trying to adjust to zero gravity.

But how much can you blame exclusively on space? NASA now has a way to begin investigating the mystery, in the form of Scott and Mark Kelly, identical twins who just happen to be astronauts.

OH, BROTHER!

Mark Kelly has completed four shuttle missions and spent a total of 54 days in space. Scott Kelly has completed two shuttle flights, including a six-month stay aboard the International Space Station (ISS). Mark has since retired from NASA, but Scott is still flying. Scott is set for a full year aboard the ISS, beginning in March 2015. And that has provided NASA with an unprecedented opportunity to run a nifty experiment.

Twins can be extremely valuable to scientists trying to understand the human body. Because identical twins are a perfect genetic match, most differences in how they age and the illnesses they do or do not develop can be linked to environmental factors or life experiences. NASA will run comparison tests on the two men, both during and after the yearlong mission.

Scott Kelly aboard the International Space Station

NASA will use the results of the study to try to reduce the risks for future astronauts. Long-term plans to explore distant places like Mars and Europa (Jupiter's moon) will require astronauts to spend long stretches in space, in some cases even years at a time. In preparing to explore deep space, making sure we can survive the trip is a vital first step.

Twin astronauts Scott Kelly (left) and Mark Kelly (right) work together.

FROM TIME FOR KIDS MAGAZINE

SLEEPING IN SPACE

After a busy day in the International Space Station, astronauts want—and need—a good night's sleep. But sleeping in space is a bit more complicated than lying down on a soft bed and turning off the lights. Here are three problems and some solutions.

1. Everything in space is weightless. To keep from floating around the ISS and bumping into things while they're asleep, the astronauts hook their sleeping bags to a wall. Each sleeping bag is in a separate sleep pod. It doesn't matter if the sleeping bag is vertical or horizontal within the sleep pod. That's because there is no up or down in gravity-free space. Astronauts also don't need a pillow or mattress. Without gravity, the space around them always feels soft.

2. The ISS is very noisy. Its pressurized cabins contain many fans and air filters to keep the air fresh for the astronauts to breathe. But those fans and filters—and other machines within the space station—make a constant humming sound. Many astronauts wear earplugs to shut out those sounds while they sleep.

3. The sun rises and sets every 90 minutes at the ISS. That's how long it takes for the space station to orbit the Earth. Such a short day-night cycle can make it difficult to fall asleep. Astronauts often wear black sleep masks to keep each new sunrise from waking them up.

Astronauts are encouraged to sleep 8 hours during every 24-hour cycle while in the space station. But getting a good night's sleep in such a strange environment can be difficult. Astronauts tend to sleep 30 to 60 minutes less each "night" in the space station than they do in their own beds at home.

GUESS WHAT? In 2007, astronaut Sunita Williams became the first person to run a complete marathon in space. Strapped to a treadmill, Williams ran 26.2 miles (42.2 km) in 4 hours and 23 minutes.

SPACE

Japanese astronaut Koichi Wakata sleeps aboard the ISS.

SPORTS

Check out the awesome athletes from this year's X Games. **Page 234**

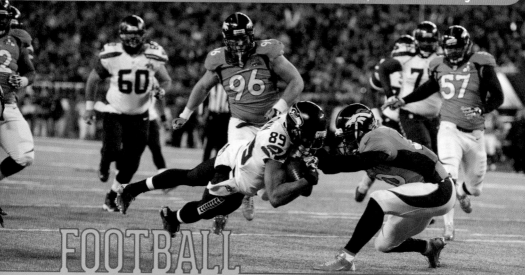

FOOTBALL

2013-2014 NFL AWARD WINNERS

Most Valuable Player:
Peyton Manning, Denver Broncos

Offensive Player of the Year:
Peyton Manning, Denver Broncos

Defensive Player of the Year:
Luke Kuechly, Carolina Panthers

Offensive Rookie of the Year:
Eddie Lacy, Green Bay Packers

Defensive Rookie of the Year:
Sheldon Richardson, New York Jets

Coach of the Year:
Ron Rivera, Carolina Panthers

Comeback Player of the Year:
Philip Rivers, San Diego Chargers

Walter Payton Man of the Year:
Charles Tillman, Chicago Bears

SUPER BOWL
February 2, 2014

Super Bowl XLVIII was supposed to be a tough matchup between the Denver Broncos' unstoppable offense and the Seattle Seahawks' great defense. It wasn't. In fact, it took only 12 seconds for it to become obvious that this Super Bowl was going to be nothing like what was expected. On the first play, the ball was snapped over Broncos quarterback Peyton Manning's head. It flew into the end zone, and Seattle had a safety and two points. They just kept on scoring.

When it was all over, the Seahawks had won their first Super Bowl, crushing the Broncos 43–8. Seattle linebacker Malcolm Smith returned a pass interception 69 yards for a touchdown and was named the game's MVP.

GUESS WHAT? It was the first Super Bowl to be played outdoors in a cold-weather city (East Rutherford, New Jersey), but at 49°F (9.4°C), it wasn't the coldest. The temperature at kickoff for Super Bowl VI in 1972 in New Orleans, Louisiana, was 39°C (3.9°C).

COLLEGE FOOTBALL CHAMPIONS!

The Bowl Championship Series (BCS) National Championship Game pitted the Tigers of Auburn University in Alabama against the Seminoles of Florida State University (FSU)—two teams that had scored lots of points all season. FSU scored first, with a field goal, but Auburn came right back, with a touchdown in the first quarter and two more in the second, extending their lead to 18 points.

FSU slowly caught up, including returning an Auburn kickoff 100 yards for a touchdown. Auburn scored a touchdown with just over a minute left in the game to put them ahead, 31–27. But Florida State scored a touchdown with 13 seconds left on the clock. FSU won 34–31. At one point in the game, they were behind by 18 points. This was the largest deficit ever overcome to win the BCS championship.

OTHER 2014 BCS GAMES

Rose Bowl (Pasadena, California)
January 1, 2014
Michigan State Spartans 24
Stanford Cardinal 20

Fiesta Bowl (Glendale, Arizona)
January 1, 2014
University of Central Florida (UCF) Knights 52
Baylor Bears 42

Sugar Bowl (New Orleans, Louisiana)
January 2, 2014
Oklahoma Sooners 45
Alabama Crimson Tide 31

Orange Bowl (Miami, Florida)
January 3, 2014
Clemson Tigers 40
Ohio State Buckeyes 35

THE HEISMAN TROPHY

Every year, the Heisman Trophy, named after legendary coach John Heisman, is given to the outstanding player in college football "whose performance best exhibits the pursuit of excellence with integrity." The winner is chosen by a panel of sportswriters from around the country. The 2013 Heisman went to FSU quarterback Jameis Winston.

In one of the World Series' most memorable moments, Jacoby Ellsbury escaped a rundown between second and third base.

BASEBALL

2013 MLB LEAGUE LEADERS

Ⓐ AMERICAN LEAGUE   Ⓝ NATIONAL LEAGUE

BATTING

Runs Batted In
Ⓐ **Chris Davis,**
Baltimore Orioles, 138
Ⓝ **Paul Goldschmidt,**
Arizona Diamondbacks, 125

Home Runs
Ⓐ **Chris Davis,**
Baltimore Orioles, 53
Ⓝ **Pedro Alvarez,**
Pittsburgh Pirates, 36
Ⓝ **Paul Goldschmidt,**
Arizona Diamondbacks, 36

Batting Average
Ⓐ **Miguel Cabrera,**
Detroit Tigers, .348
Ⓝ **Michael Cuddyer,**
Colorado Rockies, .331

PITCHING

Earned Run Average
Ⓐ **Anibal Sanchez,**
Detroit Tigers, 2.57
Ⓝ **Clayton Kershaw,**
Los Angeles Dodgers, 1.83

Strikeouts
Ⓐ **Yu Darvish,**
Texas Rangers, 277
Ⓝ **Clayton Kershaw,**
Los Angeles Dodgers, 232

Wins
Ⓐ **Max Scherzer,**
Detroit Tigers, 21
Ⓝ **Adam Wainwright,**
Saint Louis Cardinals, 19
Ⓝ **Jordan Zimmermann,**
Washington Nationals, 19

LITTLE LEAGUE WORLD SERIES

The 2013 Little League Baseball World Series Championship game was held August 25, 2013, in South Williamsport, Pennsylvania. The team from Tokyo, Japan, defeated the U.S. West Region team from Chula Vista, California, with a final score of 6–4. This was Tokyo's second consecutive win at the series and ninth championship overall.

2013 MLB AWARD WINNERS

Most Valuable Player
- (A) **Miguel Cabrera,** Detroit Tigers
- (N) **Andrew McCutchen,** Pittsburgh Pirates

Cy Young Award (Best Pitcher)
- (A) **Max Scherzer,** Detroit Tigers
- (N) **Clayton Kershaw,** Los Angeles Dodgers

Rookie of the Year
- (A) **Wil Myers,** Tampa Bay Rays
- (N) **Jose Fernandez,** Miami Marlins

Manager of the Year
- (A) **Terry Francona,** Cleveland Indians
- (N) **Clint Hurdle,** Pittsburgh Pirates

WORLD SERIES
October 23–31, 2013

The Boston Red Sox defeated the St. Louis Cardinals in six games to win the World Series. It was a great start for Boston's new manager, John Farrell, who was hired in 2013. It was also a big turnaround from 2012, when Boston finished last in their division.

MYSTERY PERSON

On April 15, 1947, I stepped up to the plate for the Brooklyn Dodgers and became the first African American to play modern Major League Baseball. I spent years fighting for civil rights. In 1962, I was elected to the Baseball Hall of Fame.

WHO AM I?

Answer on page 277

2012–2013 NBA REGULAR SEASON LEADERS

Rajon Rondo, Boston Celtics, averaged 11.1 assists per game.

Greivis Vásquez, New Orleans Hornets, had the most total assists, with 704.

Dwight Howard, Los Angeles Lakers, averaged 12.4 rebounds per game.

Omer Asik, Houston Rockets, had the most total rebounds, with 956.

Carmelo Anthony, New York Knicks, averaged 28.7 points per game.

Kevin Durant, Oklahoma City Thunder, had the most total points, with 2,280.

LeBron James, Miami Heat, was named the season MVP.

NBA FINALS
June 6–20, 2013

The Miami Heat won back-to-back NBA championships when they defeated the San Antonio Spurs, after seven hard-fought games. The Heat was almost eliminated in Game 6. The team was behind by 10 points at the end of the third quarter. But, led by forward LeBron James, the Heat scored 20 points at the start of the fourth quarter. Then the Spurs went on their own point-scoring run. With just 28 seconds remaining, the Spurs were ahead 94–89. Some fans started to leave. But the Heat tied the score as time ran out and won the game in overtime. In Game 7, James scored 37 points and Miami won the championship.

LeBron James

BASKETBALL

2012-2013 WNBA REGULAR SEASON LEADERS

Angel McCoughtry, Atlanta Dream, averaged 21.5 points per game. She also had the most total points, with 711.

Danielle Robinson, San Antonio Stars, averaged 6.7 assists per game. **Diana Taurasi,** Phoenix Mercury, tied with **Lindsay Whalen,** Minnesota Lynx, for most total assists, with 197.

Sylvia Fowles, Chicago Sky, averaged 11.5 rebounds per game. She also had the most total rebounds, with 369.

WNBA FINALS
October 10, 2013

The Minnesota Lynx swept the Atlanta Dream in three games in the WNBA Finals, winning the first two games by more than 20 points. Minnesota forward Maya Moore led her team in scoring in two of the games and was named series MVP. Moore has also won three consecutive Georgia State High School championships, two NCAA championships at the University of Connecticut, and an Olympic gold medal in London in 2012. Moore was the first pick in the 2011 WNBA draft and won the WNBA championship in her rookie season.

Angel McCoughtry

NCAA DIVISION 1 CHAMPIONSHIPS

On April 8, 2013, the University of Louisville Cardinals defeated the University of Michigan Wolverines 82–76 to win the NCAA Division 1 Men's championship.

On April 9, 2013, the University of Connecticut Huskies held off the University of Louisville Cardinals 93–60 to win the NCAA Division 1 Women's championship.

Brent Seabrook (7) and Brad Marchand (63) in Game 4 of the Stanley Cup Finals

HOCKEY

2013 NHL AWARD WINNERS

AWARD	RECIPIENT	WINNER (TEAM)
Conn Smythe Trophy	Stanley Cup playoffs MVP	**Patrick Kane** (Chicago Blackhawks)
Hart Memorial Trophy	Most valuable player	**Alex Ovechkin** (Washington Capitals)
Ted Lindsay Award	Best player as voted by fellow NHL players	**Sidney Crosby** (Pittsburgh Penguins)
Vezina Trophy	Best goaltender	**Sergei Bobrovsky** (Columbus Blue Jackets)
James Norris Memorial Trophy	Best defenseman	**P.K. Subban** (Montreal Canadiens)
Calder Memorial Trophy	Best rookie	**Jonathan Huberdeau** (Florida Panthers)
Art Ross Trophy	Top point scorer	**Martin St. Louis** (Tampa Bay Lightning)
Frank J. Selke Trophy	Best defensive forward	**Jonathan Toews** (Chicago Blackhawks)
Jack Adams Award	Best coach	**Paul MacLean** (Ottawa Senators)

The U.S. National Junior Ice Hockey team celebrates its big win.

JUNIORS FOR THE WIN!

The World Junior Hockey Championships in January 2013 got a lot of extra attention because the NHL was not playing. In the semifinals, the United States beat Canada by a score of 5–1 and moved on to face the defending champion, Sweden, in the gold medal game. The United States took home the gold medal, winning by a score of 3–1. Team USA included players from Pennsylvania, California, Florida, Illinois, Michigan, Ohio, Texas, and Wisconsin. The game is growing in popularity, even in warm regions of the country.

STANLEY CUP
June 12–26, 2013

The NHL season was almost canceled because the league and its players could not agree on a basic contract. But after months of heated talks, the season that was supposed to start in October 2012 finally started on January 19, 2013. It was cut back from the usual 82 games to just 48.

In a short season, the teams that start strong have an advantage. From their first game, it was clear the Chicago Blackhawks were that team. The Blackhawks set an NHL record, going 24 games without a loss. Ray Emery became the first goaltender to start the season with 10 straight wins. Then he won two more and set a record for the longest winning streak for a goalie.

The Blackhawks finished the regular season with the most points. They met the Boston Bruins in the Stanley Cup finals and wrapped up the series in Game 6 when Blackhawks center Dave Bolland scored the winning goal with less than 18 seconds left in the game.

CONFEDERATIONS CUP

The year before the World Cup (which is held every four years), soccer's governing body, FIFA, sponsors the Confederations Cup. The FIFA champions from Europe, South America, North and Central America, Africa, Asia, and Oceania—plus the last World Cup winner and the World Cup host team—played in the June 2013 tournament. World Cup 2014 host Brazil came out on top, defeating Spain 3–0.

MAJOR LEAGUE SOCCER

The 2013 Major League Soccer (MLS) season ended on December 7, when Sporting Kansas City met Real Salt Lake. After regulation play and an overtime period, the game was still tied 1–1. Then came the longest shootout in the history of MLS playoffs. It took 10 rounds to decide a winner. Sporting Kansas City defender Aurélien Collin scored both his team's only goal and the winning shootout goal.

GUESS WHAT? Aurélien Collin (78) was named the MLS Cup MVP.

NATIONAL WOMEN'S SOCCER LEAGUE

In April 2013, the National Women's Soccer League (NWSL) made its debut with eight professional teams. The NWSL's first season ran through August, with each team playing 22 regular season games. The Portland Thorns defeated the Western New York Flash, 2–0, to win the first NWSL championship.

GUESS WHAT? In the 2013 European (UEFA) Women's Championship, held in July in Sweden, defending champion Germany defeated Norway 1–0 in the final.

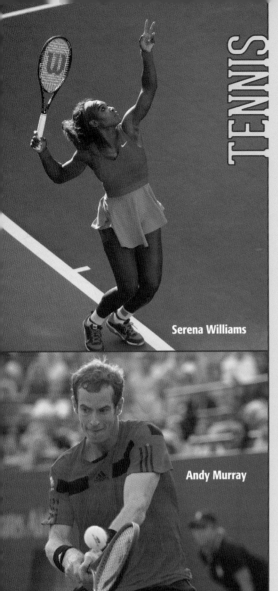

TENNIS

Serena Williams

Andy Murray

GUESS WHAT?
Playing in front of an ecstatic hometown crowd, Andy Murray became the first man from Britain to win the Wimbledon men's singles title in 77 years.

INTERNATIONAL TEAM TENNIS
The **Czech Republic** defeated Serbia, three matches to two, to win the 2013 Davis Cup (Men's International Team Tennis). And **Italy** bested Russia, winning four straight matches, to take home the Fed Cup championship (Women's International Team Tennis).

TENNIS CHAMPIONSHIPS

In tennis, the four Grand Slam tournaments (also called Majors) are the Australian Open in January, the French Open in May/June, Wimbledon in June/July, and the U.S. Open in August/September. The Australian and U.S. Opens are played on hard courts. The French Open is played on clay, and Wimbledon is played on grass. These competitions offer the most prize money and attract the best players.

2013 TOURNAMENT WINNERS

AUSTRALIAN OPEN
Men's Singles: **Novak Djokovic**
Women's Singles: **Victoria Azarenka**
Men's Doubles: **Bob Bryan and Mike Bryan**
Women's Doubles: **Sara Errani and Roberta Vinci**
Mixed Doubles: **Jarmila Gajdosova and Matthew Ebden**

FRENCH OPEN
Men's Singles: **Rafael Nadal**
Women's Singles: **Serena Williams**
Men's Doubles: **Bob Bryan and Mike Bryan**
Women's Doubles: **Ekaterina Makarova and Elena Vesnina**
Mixed Doubles: **Frantisek Cermak and Lucie Hradecka**

WIMBLEDON
Men's Singles: **Andy Murray**
Women's Singles: **Marion Bartoli**
Men's Doubles: **Bob Bryan and Mike Bryan**
Women's Doubles: **Su-Wei Hsieh and Shuai Peng**
Mixed Doubles: **Daniel Nestor and Kristina Mladenovic**

U.S. OPEN
Men's Singles: **Rafael Nadal**
Women's Singles: **Serena Williams**
Men's Doubles: **Leander Paes and Radek Stepanek**
Women's Doubles: **Andrea Hlavackova and Lucie Hradecka**
Mixed Doubles: **Andrea Hlavackova and Max Mirnyi**

AUTO RACING

INDIANAPOLIS 500

The 97th Indy 500 set a record for most lead changes, with 68. Near the end of the race, it was obvious that Tony Kanaan was going to win. That's because, with three laps to go, a car crashed and race officials put up a yellow caution flag. The yellow flag means drivers must maintain their positions until the track is deemed safe. Three laps later, Kanaan crossed the finish line first, with the caution flag still out. This was Kanaan's 11th Indy 500. Kanaan's average speed was 187.433 miles (301.644 km) per hour, a new Indy 500 record.

GUESS WHAT? During the 2013 Indy 500, 15 different drivers took the lead. That's a record! There were five lead changes in the last 30 laps.

Brazilian racer Tony Kanaan leads the pack.

NASCAR'S SPRINT CUP

The Sprint Cup Series is the top racing series of the National Association for Stock Car Auto Racing (NASCAR). It consists of 36 races. The first 26 make up the regular season. Since 2007, the 12 drivers with the most points compete in the last 10 races of the Chase. The driver with the most points after those 10 races is awarded the Sprint Cup, NASCAR's greatest prize.

2013 FINAL STANDINGS OF THE TOP THREE DRIVERS

1. **Jimmie Johnson**   2,419

2. **Matt Kenseth**   2,400

3. **Kevin Harvick**   2,385

In 2014, NASCAR announced some major rule changes, making the final Chase race winner-takes-all. Under the new rules, the Chase will begin with the 16 drivers with the most wins. After every three races, four drivers will be cut until four drivers compete in the final race. The winner in that race will take the title.

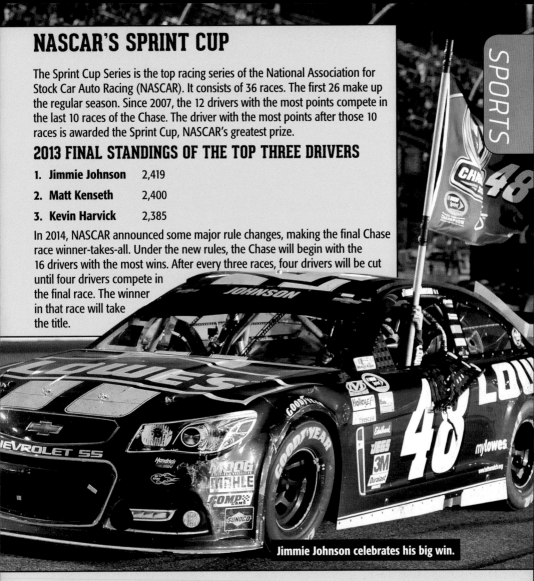

Jimmie Johnson celebrates his big win.

2013 CHASE CHAMPIONS

RACE	LOCATION	WINNER
GEICO 400	Chicagoland Speedway	**Matt Kenseth**
Sylvania 300	New Hampshire Motor Speedway	**Matt Kenseth**
AAA 400	Dover International Speedway	**Jimmie Johnson**
Hollywood Casino 400	Kansas Speedway	**Kevin Harvick**
Bank of America 500	Charlotte Motor Speedway	**Brad Keselowski**
Camping World RV Sales 500	Talladega Superspeedway	**Jamie McMurray**
Goody's Headache Relief Shot 500	Martinsville Speedway	**Jeff Gordon**
AAA Texas 500	Texas Motor Speedway	**Jimmie Johnson**
AdvoCare 500	Phoenix International Raceway	**Kevin Harvick**
Ford EcoBoost 400	Homestead-Miami Speedway	**Denny Hamlin**

GOLF

2013 MAJORS

MEN

Masters:
Adam Scott

U.S. Open:
Justin Rose

British Open:
Phil Mickelson

PGA Championship:
Jason Dufner

U.S. Amateur
Championship:
Matt Fitzpatrick

WOMEN

Kraft Nabisco
Championship:
Inbee Park

U.S. Women's Open:
Inbee Park

Women's British Open:
Stacy Lewis

LPGA Championship:
Inbee Park

U.S. Amateur
Championship:
Emma Talley

Inbee Park

GUESS WHAT? There are three types of golf clubs: woods, irons, and putters. Each type of club is used for a different purpose. Woods are used for driving the ball long distances, usually off the tee. Putters are used for the shortest shots, when golfers need to roll the ball along the green and into the hole. Irons are used for everything in between.

CYCLING

TOUR DE FRANCE

The Tour de France is a grueling bike race that takes place every summer. In 2013, the race celebrated its 100th anniversary. Unlike previous years, the entire event took place in France. The race began in Porto-Vecchio and ended 23 days later in Paris. Cyclists covered 2,115 miles (3,404 km). Here are the top five finishers.

2013 TOP FINISHERS

NAME	COUNTRY	RACE TIME
1. Chris Froome	U.K.	83:56:40
2. Nairo Quintana	Colombia	84:01:00
3. Joaquim Rodríguez	Spain	84:01:44
4. Alberto Contador	Spain	84:03:07
5. Roman Kreuziger	Czech Republic	84:04:07

DOGSLEDDING

2013 IDITAROD

The Iditarod is an annual dogsled race covering 998 miles (1,606 km) across the mountain ranges, frozen rivers, and icy forests of Alaska, from Anchorage to Nome. It's been called the last great race on Earth. On March 2, 2013, Mitch Seavey, led by his pack of 10 huskies, rode into Nome after nine days, seven hours, 39 minutes, and 56 seconds. At 53, Mitch is the oldest champion in Iditarod history. This win marked back-to-back victories for the Seavey family, as last year's winner was Mitch's son Dallas.

Mitch Seavey races to the finish line with his lead dog, Tanner, at the head of the pack.

Oxbow takes the lead in the Preakness Stakes.

HORSE RACING

TRIPLE CROWN

The three most famous horse races in the United States are the Kentucky Derby, at Churchill Downs, in Louisville, Kentucky; the Preakness Stakes, at Pimlico Race Course, in Baltimore, Maryland; and the Belmont Stakes, at Belmont Park, in Elmont, New York. These three races are for 3-year-old horses only and take place within a five-week period from early May to early June. Together, they make up the Triple Crown of Thoroughbred Racing, or Triple Crown for short.

2013 RACE RESULTS

Kentucky Derby
1. Orb
2. Golden Soul
3. Revolutionary

Preakness Stakes
1. Oxbow
2. Itsmyluckyday
3. Mylute

Belmont Stakes
1. Palace Malice
2. Oxbow
3. Orb

Sam Mikulak

GYMNASTICS

2013 U.S. NATIONAL CHAMPIONSHIPS

Simone Biles and Sam Mikulak took top honors at the P&G Gymnastics Championships, in Hartford, Connecticut, from August 15 to 18.

EVENT	GOLD MEDALIST	EVENT	GOLD MEDALIST
Men's All-Around	Sam Mikulak	Women's All-Around	Simone Biles
Men's Floor Exercise	Steven Legendre	Women's Vault	McKayla Maroney
Men's Pommel Horse	Alex Naddour	Women's Uneven Bars	Kyla Ross
Men's Still Rings	Brandon Wynn	Women's Balance Beam	Kyla Ross
Men's Vault	Eddie Penev* Sean Senters*	Women's Floor Exercise	McKayla Maroney
Men's Parallel Bars	Sam Mikulak		
Men's Horizontal Bars	Sam Mikulak		

*Indicates a tie

Kyla Ross

Aliya Mustafina

2013 WORLD CHAMPIONSHIPS

The Artistic Gymnastics World Championships were held in Antwerp, Belgium, from September 30 to October 6.

EVENT	GOLD MEDALIST	COUNTRY
Men's Individual All-Around	Kohei Uchimura	Japan
Men's Floor Exercise	Kenzo Shirai	Japan
Men's Pommel Horse	Kohei Kameyama	Japan
Men's Rings	Arthur Nabarrete Zanetti	Brazil
Men's Vault	Hak Seon Yang	Korea
Men's Parallel Bars	Kohei Uchimura* Chaopan Lin*	Japan China
Men's Horizontal Bars	Epke Zonderland	Netherlands
Women's Individual All-Around	Simone Biles	United States
Women's Vault	McKayla Maroney	United States
Women's Uneven Bars	Huidan Huang	China
Women's Balance Beam	Aliya Mustafina	Russia
Women's Floor Exercise	Simone Biles	United States

*Indicates a tie

COLLEGE GYMNASTICS

On April 20, 2013, the University of Florida won the NCAA Women's Gymnastics Championships. On the men's side, the University of Michigan took the title for the fifth time.

233

Bucky Lasek

X GAMES

2013 SUMMER X GAMES
August 1–4, Los Angeles, California

MOTO X

Moto X Freestyle: **Taka Higashino**
Speed & Style: **Nate Adams**
Men's Moto X Racing: **Justin Brayton**
Women's Moto X Racing: **Vicki Golden**
Moto X Adaptive: **Chris Ridgway**
Men's Enduro: **Tadeusz Błazusiak**
Women's Enduro: **Laia Sanz**
Moto X Step Up: **Ronnie Renner**
Moto X Best Whip: **Josh Hansen**

RALLYCROSS

RallyCross Lites: **Joni Wiman**
RallyCross Super Car: **Toomas Heikkinen**

SKATEBOARD

Street League Skateboarding Select Series:
Ryan Decenzo
Skateboard Big Air: **Elliot Sloan**
Skateboard Vert: **Bucky Lasek**
Red Bull Phenom Skateboard Street:
Tyson Bowerbank
Women's Skateboard Street: **Leticia Bufoni**
Street League Skateboarding: **Nyjah Huston**

BMX

GoPro BMX Big Air: **Morgan Wade**
BMX Street: **Chad Kerley**
Red Bull Phenom BMX Street: **Felix Prangenberg**

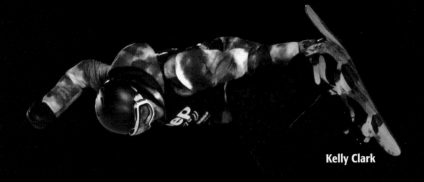

Kelly Clark

2014 WINTER X GAMES
January 23–26, Aspen, Colorado

SKI

Big Air: **Henrik Harlaut**
Women's Slopestyle: **Kaya Turski**
Men's Slopestyle: **Nick Goepper**
Women's SuperPipe: **Maddie Bowman**
Men's SuperPipe: **David Wise**

SNOWMOBILE

Freestyle: **Colten Moore**
Long Jump: **Levi LaVallee**
SnoCross: **Tucker Hibbert**
SnoCross Adaptive: **Mike Schultz**

SNOWBOARD

Big Air: **Max Parrot**
Women's Snowboarder X: **Lindsey Jacobellis**
Men's Snowboarder X: **Nate Holland**
Women's Slopestyle: **Silje Norendal**
Men's Slopestyle: **Max Parrot**
Women's SuperPipe: **Kelly Clark**
Men's SuperPipe: **Danny Davis**

SNOWBOARDER SWITCH-UP

One of these snowboarders is not like the others.
Circle the one that stands out from the rest.

Answer on page 277

Patrick Chan

FIGURE SKATING

2013 WORLD CHAMPIONSHIPS

Here are the winners from the World Figure Skating Championships, held March 11 to 17, in London, Ontario, Canada.

CATEGORY	WINNER(S)	COUNTRY
Men	**Patrick Chan**	Canada
Women	**Kim Yu-Na**	South Korea
Pairs	**Maxim Trankov and Tatiana Volosozhar**	Russia
Ice Dance	**Meryl Davis and Charlie White**	United States

GUESS WHAT? In 2014, Patrick Chan won his seventh straight Canadian figure skating title.

2014 U.S. CHAMPIONSHIPS

Here are the winners from the U.S. Figure Skating Championships, held January 5 to 12, in Boston, Massachusetts.

CATEGORY	WINNER(S)
Men	**Jeremy Abbott**
Women	**Gracie Gold**
Pairs	**Marissa Castelli and Simon Shnapir**
Ice Dance	**Meryl Davis and Charlie White**

Charlie White and Meryl Davis

GUESS WHAT? In addition to being an excellent skater, Gracie Gold is a talented juggler.

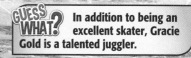

2013 WORLD TOUR

The Association of Surfing Professionals (ASP) gives out titles every year based on the points surfers receive in competitions on the ASP World Tour. In 2013, Australian surfer Mick Fanning was the men's champion. Hawaiian Carissa Moore won the women's championship for the second time in three years. Peruvian Piccolo Clemente was the men's longboard champion, while Hawaiian Kelia Moniz reclaimed her title of women's longboard champ.

SURFING

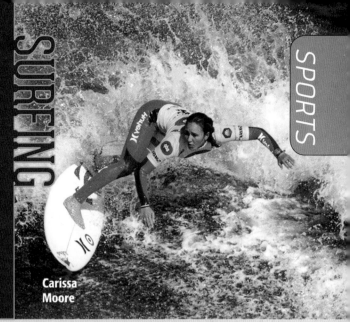

Carissa Moore

TIME FOR KIDS GAME

COURT CUTOUTS

Oh, no! Someone snipped some pieces out of this championship showdown. Can you put the game back together again? Match the tiles below with their correct spot on the court.

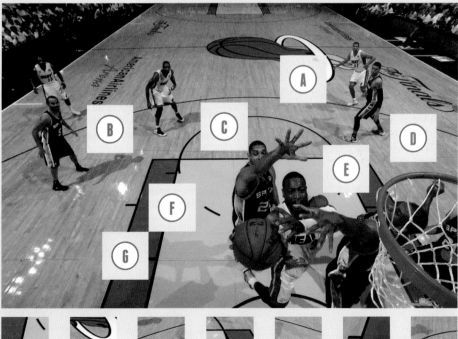

1   2   3   4   5   6   7

Answer on page 277

UNITED STATES

This cave salamander is the official amphibian of which state? **Page 262**

Huge Snowball Fight BY REBECCA NELSON WITH ADDITIONAL AP REPORTING

Seattle, Washington, may be nicknamed "Rain City," but it was snow that made the news in 2013. On January 12, Seattle residents set the Guinness World Record for the largest snowball fight. More than 5,800 people showed up to toss snowballs at one another at the Seattle Center, a park, arts, and entertainment campus that includes the city's famous Space Needle.

It didn't snow in Seattle on that day, but there was snow in a small corner of the city—enough to make a lot of kids' dreams come true. Trucks hauled 34 loads of snow from Snoqualmie Pass, an hour away in Washington's Cascade mountain range, to the Seattle Center. It took 162,000 pounds (73,482 kg) of the white stuff to build the winter wonderland.

The goal? To break the Guinness World Record for biggest snowball fight. The event, dubbed "Snow Day," was also a fundraiser for the Boys and Girls Clubs of King County. Seattle businessman Neil Bergquist took three months to organize the playful battle. He wanted to raise money for kids "by remembering what it was like to feel like a kid."

Although Seattle residents aren't used to snow, they succeeded in getting enough people to come out and play. About 6,000 tickets were sold online, and participants were given bar-coded wristbands when they arrived. The wristbands were scanned as event-goers entered and left the location, so Guinness had a head count at all times. There were 130 judges for the official minute-and-a-half snowball fight. Anyone not throwing snowballs was not counted in the total, Bergquist said Monday.

To raise money for the Boys and Girls Clubs, companies paid for space to build their own snow forts. Some highlights included a snow slide and even a few snow toilets. A Guinness official confirmed the count of 5,834 people. Seattle beat the previous world record of about 5,400 at a 2010 snowball fight in South Korea.

"We had a lot of fun, set a Guinness record, raised some money for kids, and everyone had a chance to act like a kid for a day," Bergquist said.

FROM TIME FOR KIDS MAGAZINE

HIGHEST POINT

LONGEST BRIDGE SPAN

UNITED STATES

MOUNT MCKINLEY, ALASKA
20,322 feet (6,194 m)

GOING TO THE EXTREME

Here are a few of the standout record-holders across the United States.

VERRAZANO-NARROWS BRIDGE, NEW YORK
4,260 feet (1,298 m)

DEEPEST LAKE

LOWEST POINT

DEATH VALLEY, CALIFORNIA
282 feet (86 m) below sea level

CRATER LAKE, OREGON
1,943 feet (592 m)

TOP 10

MOST POPULAR U.S. BABY NAMES

In 2012, parents in the United States picked these names more than any others. To see how popular a name is now and was in the past, go to *ssa.gov/oact/babynames*.

BOY NAMES

1. Jacob
2. Mason
3. Ethan
4. Noah
5. William
6. Liam
7. Jayden
8. Michael
9. Alexander
10. Aiden

GIRL NAMES

1. Sophia
2. Emma
3. Isabella
4. Olivia
5. Ava
6. Emily
7. Abigail
8. Mia
9. Madison
10. Elizabeth

BABY NAMES BY STATE

Liam's in the lead in Iowa, but William's winning in Alabama. Sophia reigns supreme, but Emmas are everywhere! Which names took top honors in your home state?

BOY NAMES

GIRL NAMES

ALL-AMERICAN GIRL

This patriotic picture has gotten all jumbled. Can you spot 10 things that have changed? Circle the changes and check off a number at the bottom for each difference you find.

Answers on page 277

TASTE THE DIFFERENCE

Every year, people in the United States eat approximately 7 billion hot dogs between Memorial Day and Labor Day. That means 818 hot dogs are eaten every second in the summertime!

U.S. diners use more yellow mustard than diners in any other country. The National Mustard Museum in Wisconsin has a collection of more than 5,500 types of mustard.

Tomato-based salsa now outsells ketchup in the United States, two to one.

241

STATE BREAKDOWN Check out each individual state for information about its population, motto (or mottoes), state symbols, and more.

ALABAMA

CAPITAL: Montgomery

LARGEST CITY: Birmingham

POSTAL CODE: AL

LAND AREA:
50,750 square miles
(131,443 sq km)

POPULATION (2013):
4,833,722

ENTERED UNION (RANK):
December 14, 1819 (22)

MOTTO: *Audemus jura nostra defendere.* (We dare maintain our rights.)

TREE: Southern longleaf pine

FLOWER: Camellia

BIRD: Yellowhammer

NICKNAMES: Yellowhammer State, Cotton State, Heart of Dixie

FAMOUS ALABAMIAN: Hank Williams, country singer and songwriter

GUESS WHAT? Helen Keller, the famous deaf and blind author and activist, grew up in Tuscumbia, Alabama. Her childhood home, Ivy Green, is open for visitors.

ALASKA

CAPITAL: Juneau

LARGEST CITY: Anchorage

POSTAL CODE: AK

LAND AREA:
570,374 square miles
(1,477,267 sq km)

POPULATION (2013):
735,132

ENTERED UNION (RANK):
January 3, 1959 (49)

MOTTO: North to the future

TREE: Sitka spruce

FLOWER: Forget-me-not

BIRD: Willow ptarmigan

NICKNAMES: The Last Frontier, Land of the Midnight Sun

FAMOUS ALASKAN: Jewel, singer and songwriter

GUESS WHAT? In 1927, Alaska's state flag was designed by Benny Benson, who was only 13 years old at the time.

ARIZONA

CAPITAL: Phoenix

LARGEST CITY: Phoenix

POSTAL CODE: AZ

LAND AREA:
113,642 square miles
(296,400 sq km)

POPULATION (2013):
6,626,624

ENTERED UNION (RANK):
February 14, 1912 (48)

MOTTO: *Ditat deus.*
(God enriches.)

TREE: Palo verde

FLOWER: Saguaro cactus blossom

BIRD: Cactus wren

NICKNAME: Grand Canyon State

FAMOUS ARIZONAN:
Emma Stone, actress

Phoenix

GUESS WHAT? Arizona was the first state to have official state neckwear. It is the bolo tie, which is a cord worn around the neck and fastened with a decorative clasp.

ARKANSAS

ARKANSAS

CAPITAL: Little Rock

LARGEST CITY: Little Rock

POSTAL CODE: AR

LAND AREA:
52,075 square miles
(134,874 sq km)

POPULATION (2013):
2,959,373

ENTERED UNION (RANK):
June 15, 1836 (25)

MOTTO: *Regnat populus.*
(The people rule.)

TREE: Pine

FLOWER: Apple blossom

BIRD: Mockingbird

NICKNAME: Natural State

FAMOUS ARKANSAN:
Maya Angelou, author and poet

Little Rock

GUESS WHAT? Stuttgart, Arkansas, is home to the World's Championship Duck Calling Contest.

CALIFORNIA

CALIFORNIA REPUBLIC

CAPITAL: Sacramento

LARGEST CITY: Los Angeles

POSTAL CODE: CA

LAND AREA:
155,973 square miles
(403,970 sq km)

POPULATION (2013):
38,332,521

ENTERED UNION (RANK):
September 9, 1850 (31)

MOTTO: *Eureka!* (I have found it!)

TREE: California redwood

FLOWER: Golden poppy

BIRD: California valley quail

NICKNAME: Golden State

FAMOUS CALIFORNIAN:
Katy Perry, pop singer

Sacramento ✪

Los Angeles

GUESS WHAT? The La Brea Tar Pits is one of the most famous fossil sites in the world. More than 3 million fossils, including mammoths, saber-toothed cats, and giant ground sloths, have been found there. These animals were preserved in sticky tar for 40,000 years.

COLORADO

CAPITAL: Denver

LARGEST CITY: Denver

POSTAL CODE: CO

LAND AREA:
103,730 square miles
(268,660 sq km)

POPULATION (2013):
5,268,367

ENTERED UNION (RANK):
August 1, 1876 (38)

MOTTO: *Nil sine numine* (Nothing without the deity)

TREE: Colorado blue spruce

FLOWER: Rocky Mountain columbine

BIRD: Lark bunting

NICKNAME: Centennial State

FAMOUS COLORADAN: Roy Halladay, baseball player

✪ Denver

GUESS WHAT? A mesa is a flat-topped mountain. Grand Mesa, in Colorado, is the largest mesa in the world.

CONNECTICUT

CAPITAL: Hartford

LARGEST CITY: Bridgeport

POSTAL CODE: CT

LAND AREA:
5,018 square miles
(12,997 sq km)

POPULATION (2013):
3,596,080

ENTERED UNION (RANK):
January 9, 1788 (5)

MOTTO: *Qui transtulit sustinet.* (He who transplanted still sustains.)

TREE: White oak

FLOWER: Mountain laurel

BIRD: American robin

NICKNAMES: Constitution State, Nutmeg State

FAMOUS CONNECTICUTER: P.T. Barnum, circus founder

Hartford

Bridgeport

The praying mantis is the state insect of Connecticut.

DELAWARE

CAPITAL: Dover

LARGEST CITY: Wilmington

POSTAL CODE: DE

LAND AREA:
1,955 square miles
(5,063 sq km)

POPULATION (2013):
925,749

ENTERED UNION (RANK):
December 7, 1787 (1)

MOTTO: Liberty and independence

TREE: American holly

FLOWER: Peach blossom

BIRD: Blue hen chicken

NICKNAMES: Diamond State, First State, Small Wonder

FAMOUS DELAWAREAN: Henry Heimlich, doctor and inventor of the Heimlich maneuver

Wilmington

Dover

In 2002, the horseshoe crab became the state marine animal of Delaware.

UNITED STATES

FLORIDA

CAPITAL: Tallahassee

LARGEST CITY: Jacksonville

POSTAL CODE: FL

LAND AREA:
53,927 square miles
(139,670 sq km)

POPULATION (2013):
19,552,860

ENTERED UNION (RANK):
March 3, 1845 (27)

MOTTO: In God we trust.

TREE: Sabal palm
(cabbage palmetto)

FLOWER: Orange
blossom

BIRD: Mockingbird

NICKNAME: Sunshine State

FAMOUS FLORIDIAN:
Bella Thorne, actress

Jacksonville

Tallahassee

GUESS WHAT? The process for making artificial ice was developed in sunny Florida. Dr. John Gorrie of Apalachicola patented the technique in 1851.

GEORGIA

CAPITAL: Atlanta

LARGEST CITY: Atlanta

POSTAL CODE: GA

LAND AREA:
57,919 square miles
(150,010 sq km)

POPULATION (2013):
9,992,167

ENTERED UNION (RANK):
January 2, 1788 (4)

MOTTO: Wisdom, justice, and moderation

TREE: Live oak

FLOWER: Cherokee rose

BIRD: Brown thrasher

NICKNAMES: Peach State, Empire State of the South

FAMOUS GEORGIAN:
Dwight Howard, basketball player

Atlanta

GUESS WHAT? Since 1990, Georgia has had an official state historical drama: *The Reach of Song.* The play is about life in the Georgia mountains between World War I and World War II. The story is often performed using music, dance, poetry, and folktales.

HAWAII

CAPITAL: Honolulu (on the island of Oahu)

LARGEST CITY: Honolulu

POSTAL CODE: HI

LAND AREA:
6,423 square miles
(16,636 sq km)

POPULATION (2013):
1,404,054

ENTERED UNION (RANK):
August 21, 1959 (50)

MOTTO: *Ua mau ke ea o ka aina i ka pono.* (The life of the land is perpetuated in righteousness.)

TREE: Kuku'i (candlenut)

FLOWER:
Yellow hibiscus

BIRD: Nene
(Hawaiian goose)

NICKNAME: Aloha State

FAMOUS HAWAIIAN:
Bethany Hamilton, surfer

Honolulu

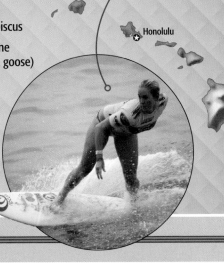

GUESS WHAT? Hawaii is the only U.S. state that grows coffee.

IDAHO

CAPITAL: Boise

LARGEST CITY: Boise

POSTAL CODE: ID

LAND AREA:
82,751 square miles
(214,325 sq km)

POPULATION (2013):
1,612,136

ENTERED UNION (RANK):
July 3, 1890 (43)

MOTTO: *Esto perpetua.* (Let it be perpetual.)

TREE: Western white pine

FLOWER: Syringa

BIRD: Mountain bluebird

NICKNAME: Gem State

FAMOUS IDAHOAN:
Gutzon Borglum, Mount Rushmore sculptor

Boise

GUESS WHAT? The Balanced Rock, in central Idaho, is more than 48 feet (15 m) tall and weighs about 40 tons (36 metric tons). This large rock sits on top of a much smaller rock, which is only about 3 feet (1 m) by 17 inches (43 cm).

ILLINOIS

ILLINOIS

CAPITAL: Springfield

LARGEST CITY: Chicago

POSTAL CODE: IL

LAND AREA:
55,593 square miles
(143,986 sq km)

POPULATION (2013):
12,882,135

ENTERED UNION (RANK):
December 3, 1818 (21)

MOTTO: State sovereignty, national union

TREE: White oak

FLOWER: Purple violet

BIRD: Cardinal

NICKNAMES: Prairie State, Land of Lincoln

FAMOUS ILLINOISAN:
Michelle Obama, First Lady

Chicago

Springfield

GUESS WHAT? The Adler Planetarium, in Chicago, opened in 1930, was the first planetarium to be built in the United States. In fact, it was the first planetarium in the Western Hemisphere.

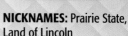

INDIANA

CAPITAL: Indianapolis

LARGEST CITY: Indianapolis

POSTAL CODE: IN

LAND AREA:
35,870 square miles
(92,903 sq km)

POPULATION (2013):
6,570,902

ENTERED UNION (RANK):
December 11, 1816 (19)

MOTTO: The crossroads of America

TREE: Tulip tree (yellow poplar)

FLOWER: Peony

BIRD: Cardinal

NICKNAMES: Hoosier State, Crossroads of America

FAMOUS INDIANAN, OR HOOSIER: Michael Jackson, pop singer

Indianapolis

GUESS WHAT? One of Indiana's most historic sites is the Levi Coffin House, which was an important stop on the Underground Railroad. More than 2,000 escaped slaves stayed in this home on their way to Canada.

IOWA

IOWA

CAPITAL: Des Moines

LARGEST CITY: Des Moines

POSTAL CODE: IA

LAND AREA:
55,875 square miles
(144,716 sq km)

POPULATION (2013):
3,090,416

ENTERED UNION (RANK):
December 28, 1846 (29)

MOTTO: Our liberties we
prize, and our rights
we will maintain.

TREE: Oak

FLOWER: Wild prairie rose

BIRD: Eastern goldfinch
(American goldfinch)

NICKNAME: Hawkeye State

FAMOUS IOWAN: Shawn
Johnson, gymnast

Des Moines

GUESS WHAT? The Effigy Mounds, in northeast Iowa, are prehistoric
Native American burial mounds. The mounds are
shaped like birds, mammals, and reptiles.

KANSAS

KANSAS

CAPITAL: Topeka

LARGEST CITY: Wichita

POSTAL CODE: KS

LAND AREA:
81,823 square miles
(211,922 sq km)

POPULATION (2013):
2,893,957

ENTERED UNION (RANK):
January 29, 1861 (34)

MOTTO: *Ad astra per
aspera* (To the stars through
difficulties)

TREE: Cottonwood

FLOWER: Sunflower

BIRD: Western
meadowlark

NICKNAMES: Sunflower
State, Jayhawk State,
Wheat State

FAMOUS KANSAN:
Janelle Monae, R&B and
soul musician

Topeka

● Wichita

GUESS WHAT? About 90% of Kansas is flat.
The state is mostly farmland.

KENTUCKY

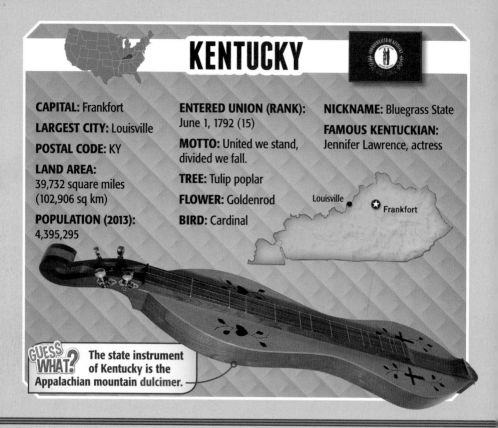

CAPITAL: Frankfort

LARGEST CITY: Louisville

POSTAL CODE: KY

LAND AREA:
39,732 square miles
(102,906 sq km)

POPULATION (2013):
4,395,295

ENTERED UNION (RANK):
June 1, 1792 (15)

MOTTO: United we stand, divided we fall.

TREE: Tulip poplar

FLOWER: Goldenrod

BIRD: Cardinal

NICKNAME: Bluegrass State

FAMOUS KENTUCKIAN:
Jennifer Lawrence, actress

Louisville • ⭐ Frankfort

GUESS WHAT? The state instrument of Kentucky is the Appalachian mountain dulcimer.

LOUISIANA

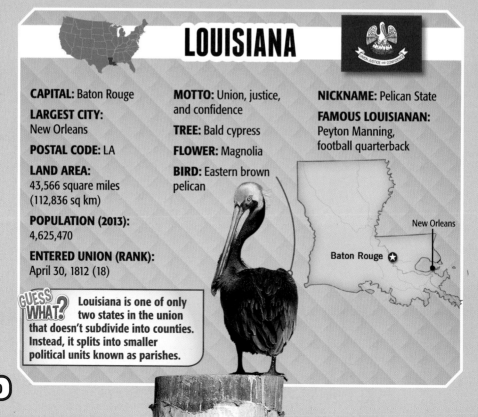

CAPITAL: Baton Rouge

LARGEST CITY:
New Orleans

POSTAL CODE: LA

LAND AREA:
43,566 square miles
(112,836 sq km)

POPULATION (2013):
4,625,470

ENTERED UNION (RANK):
April 30, 1812 (18)

MOTTO: Union, justice, and confidence

TREE: Bald cypress

FLOWER: Magnolia

BIRD: Eastern brown pelican

NICKNAME: Pelican State

FAMOUS LOUISIANAN:
Peyton Manning, football quarterback

New Orleans

Baton Rouge ⭐

GUESS WHAT? Louisiana is one of only two states in the union that doesn't subdivide into counties. Instead, it splits into smaller political units known as parishes.

MAINE

CAPITAL: Augusta

LARGEST CITY: Portland

POSTAL CODE: ME

LAND AREA:
30,865 square miles
(79,940 sq km)

POPULATION (2013):
1,328,302

ENTERED UNION (RANK):
March 15, 1820 (23)

MOTTO: *Dirigo.* (I lead.)

TREE: White pine

FLOWER: White pine cone and tassel

BIRD: Black-capped chickadee

NICKNAME: Pine Tree State

FAMOUS MAINER:
Henry Wadsworth Longfellow, author and poet

Augusta

Portland

GUESS WHAT? Ninety percent of the lobsters caught in the United States are found off the coast of Maine.

MARYLAND

CAPITAL: Annapolis

LARGEST CITY: Baltimore

POSTAL CODE: MD

LAND AREA:
9,775 square miles
(25,317 sq km)

POPULATION (2013):
5,928,814

ENTERED UNION (RANK):
April 28, 1788 (7)

MOTTO: *Fatti maschii, parole femine* (Manly deeds, womanly words)

TREE: White oak

FLOWER: Black-eyed Susan

BIRD: Baltimore oriole

NICKNAMES: Free State, Old Line State

FAMOUS MARYLANDER:
Michael Phelps, swimmer and Olympic gold medalist

Baltimore

Annapolis

GUESS WHAT? The state sport in Maryland is jousting. Once enjoyed by medieval knights, jousting involves two contestants, mounted on horses, charging each other and attempting to dismount each other with a lance.

MASSACHUSETTS

CAPITAL: Boston

LARGEST CITY: Boston

POSTAL CODE: MA

LAND AREA:
7,838 square miles
(20,300 sq km)

POPULATION (2013):
6,692,824

ENTERED UNION (RANK):
February 6, 1788 (6)

MOTTO: *Ense petit placidam sub libertate quietem.* (By the sword we seek peace, but peace only under liberty.)

TREE: American elm

FLOWER: Mayflower

BIRD: Black-capped chickadee

NICKNAMES: Bay State, Old Colony State, Baked Bean State

FAMOUS BAY STATER:
Benjamin Franklin, inventor, statesman, U.S. Founding Father

Boston ★

GUESS WHAT? The official Massachusetts state heroine is Deborah Sampson, who dressed up as a man in order to fight during the Revolutionary War. Her secret came out after she was wounded in battle.

MICHIGAN

CAPITAL: Lansing

LARGEST CITY: Detroit

POSTAL CODE: MI

LAND AREA:
56,809 square miles
(147,135 sq km)

POPULATION (2013):
9,895,622

ENTERED UNION (RANK):
January 26, 1837 (26)

MOTTO: *Si quaeris peninsulam amoenam circumspice.* (If you seek a pleasant peninsula, look about you.)

TREE: White pine

FLOWER: Apple blossom

BIRD: American robin

NICKNAMES: Wolverine State, Great Lakes State

FAMOUS MICHIGANDER, OR MICHIGANIAN: Taylor Lautner, actor

GUESS WHAT? Motown Records, famous for producing such artists as Stevie Wonder, the Supremes, Marvin Gaye, and the Jackson 5, was originally headquartered in Detroit.

Lansing ★

Detroit ●

MINNESOTA

CAPITAL: Saint Paul

LARGEST CITY: Minneapolis

POSTAL CODE: MN

LAND AREA:
79,617 square miles
(206,208 sq km)

POPULATION (2013):
5,420,380

ENTERED UNION (RANK):
May 11, 1858 (32)

MOTTO: *L'Etoile du nord*
(Star of the north)

TREE: Red (or Norway) pine

FLOWER: Pink-and-white
lady's-slipper

BIRD: Common loon

NICKNAMES: North Star
State, Gopher State, Land
of 10,000 Lakes

FAMOUS MINNESOTAN:
Bob Dylan, singer and
songwriter

GUESS WHAT? In 2002, *Grace*, by Eric Enstrom, was chosen as Minnesota's state photograph. The photo was taken in Bovey, Minnesota.

Minneapolis ★

St. Paul

MISSISSIPPI

CAPITAL: Jackson

LARGEST CITY: Jackson

POSTAL CODE: MS

LAND AREA:
46,914 square miles
(121,507 sq km)

POPULATION (2013):
2,991,207

ENTERED UNION (RANK):
December 10, 1817 (20)

MOTTO: *Virtute et armis*
(By valor and arms)

TREE: Magnolia

FLOWER: Magnolia

BIRD: Mockingbird

NICKNAME: Magnolia State

FAMOUS MISSISSIPPIAN:
Jim Henson, *Muppets* creator

GUESS WHAT? Every June, the Elvis Festival is held, in Tupelo, Mississippi, to honor hometown singing legend Elvis Presley.

● Jackson

MISSOURI

CAPITAL: Jefferson City

LARGEST CITY: Kansas City

POSTAL CODE: MO

LAND AREA:
68,898 square miles
(178,446 sq km)

POPULATION (2013):
6,044,171

ENTERED UNION (RANK):
August 10, 1821 (24)

MOTTO: *Salus populi suprema lex esto.* (The welfare of the people shall be the supreme law.)

TREE: Flowering dogwood

FLOWER: Hawthorn

BIRD: Bluebird

NICKNAME: Show Me State

FAMOUS MISSOURIAN:
Mark Twain, author of *The Adventures of Tom Sawyer* and *Adventures of Huckleberry Finn*

Kansas City

Jefferson City

GUESS WHAT? Missouri's state rock is mozarkite. This neat rock comes in many colors, including red, pink, purple, green, gray, and brown.

MONTANA

MONTANA

CAPITAL: Helena

LARGEST CITY: Billings

POSTAL CODE: MT

LAND AREA:
145,556 square miles
(376,990 sq km)

POPULATION (2013):
1,015,165

ENTERED UNION (RANK):
November 8, 1889 (41)

MOTTO: *Oro y plata* (Gold and silver)

TREE: Ponderosa pine

FLOWER: Bitterroot

BIRD: Western meadowlark

NICKNAME: Treasure State

FAMOUS MONTANAN:
Phil Jackson, basketball coach

Helena

Billings

GUESS WHAT? On January 15, 1972, the temperature of Loma, Montana, hit a low of –54°F (–48°C) and a high of 49°F (9°C). The temperature changed 103° in one day—that's the biggest temperature change in a single day ever in the United States!

NEBRASKA

CAPITAL: Lincoln

LARGEST CITY: Omaha

POSTAL CODE: NE

LAND AREA:
76,878 square miles
(199,114 sq km)

POPULATION (2013):
1,868,516

ENTERED UNION (RANK):
March 1, 1867 (37)

MOTTO: Equality before the law

TREE: Eastern cottonwood

FLOWER: Goldenrod

BIRD: Western meadowlark

NICKNAMES: Cornhusker State, Beef State

FAMOUS NEBRASKAN: Standing Bear, Native American civil rights advocate

Omaha •

Lincoln ⭐

GUESS WHAT? Carhenge, in Alliance, Nebraska, is a replica of Stonehenge, the prehistoric rock formation in England. Instead of being built from stone like Stonehenge, Carhenge is formed by 38 different cars. This wacky sculpture was built in 1987.

NEVADA

CAPITAL: Carson City

LARGEST CITY: Las Vegas

POSTAL CODE: NV

LAND AREA:
109,806 square miles
(284,397 sq km)

POPULATION (2013):
2,790,136

ENTERED UNION (RANK):
October 31, 1864 (36)

MOTTO: All for our country

TREE: Single-leaf piñon pine

FLOWER: Sagebrush

BIRD: Mountain bluebird

NICKNAMES: Sagebrush State, Silver State, Battle Born State

FAMOUS NEVADAN: Adam Hicks, actor and singer

⭐ Carson City

Las Vegas —

GUESS WHAT? To build the Hoover Dam, which is 726 feet (221 m) tall, circus acrobats were employed as high scalers. While hanging from ropes attached to canyon walls, they drilled with jackhammers and packed dynamite into the rock.

NEW HAMPSHIRE

CAPITAL: Concord

LARGEST CITY: Manchester

POSTAL CODE: NH

LAND AREA:
8,969 square miles
(23,230 sq km)

POPULATION (2013):
1,323,459

ENTERED UNION (RANK):
June 21, 1788 (9)

MOTTO: Live free or die.

TREE: White birch (canoe birch or paper birch)

FLOWER: Purple lilac

BIRD: Purple finch

NICKNAME: Granite State

FAMOUS NEW HAMPSHIRITE: Bode Miller, skier and Olympic medalist

Concord

Manchester

GUESS WHAT? New Hampshire is home to the first free public library in the country: The Dublin Juvenile Library was opened in 1822. Eleven years later, the Peterborough Town Library was founded. It was the first library supported by public taxation.

NEW JERSEY

CAPITAL: Trenton

LARGEST CITY: Newark

POSTAL CODE: NJ

LAND AREA:
7,419 square miles
(19,215 sq km)

POPULATION (2013):
8,899,339

ENTERED UNION (RANK):
December 18, 1787 (3)

MOTTO: Liberty and prosperity

TREE: Red oak

FLOWER: Common meadow violet

BIRD: Eastern goldfinch (American goldfinch)

NICKNAME: Garden State

FAMOUS NEW JERSEYITE: Ashley Tisdale, actress

Newark

Trenton

GUESS WHAT? In 1870, a boardwalk was built along the beach in Atlantic City, New Jersey. This was the first boardwalk in the world.

NEW MEXICO

CAPITAL: Santa Fe

LARGEST CITY: Albuquerque

POSTAL CODE: NM

LAND AREA: 121,365 square miles (314,335 sq km)

POPULATION (2013): 2,085,287

ENTERED UNION (RANK): January 6, 1912 (47)

MOTTO: *Crescit eundo.* (It grows as it goes.)

TREE: Piñon pine

FLOWER: Yucca

BIRD: Roadrunner

NICKNAMES: Land of Enchantment, Cactus State

FAMOUS NEW MEXICAN: Willow Shields, actress

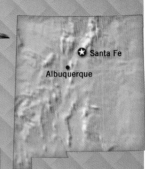

GUESS WHAT? Vexillology is the study of flags. In 2001, the North American Vexillological Association conducted a poll to find the best-designed flag in North America. New Mexico's flag won!

NEW YORK

CAPITAL: Albany

LARGEST CITY: New York City

POSTAL CODE: NY

LAND AREA: 47,224 square miles (122,310 sq km)

POPULATION (2013): 19,651,127

ENTERED UNION (RANK): July 26, 1788 (11)

MOTTO: *Excelsior* (Ever upward)

TREE: Sugar maple

FLOWER: Rose

BIRD: Bluebird

NICKNAME: Empire State

FAMOUS NEW YORKER: Jennifer Lopez, actress and pop singer

GUESS WHAT? The subway system in New York City has about 660 miles (1,062 km) of track in use.

NORTH CAROLINA

CAPITAL: Raleigh

LARGEST CITY: Charlotte

POSTAL CODE: NC

LAND AREA:
48,708 square miles
(126,154 sq km)

POPULATION (2013):
9,848,060

ENTERED UNION (RANK):
November 21, 1789 (12)

MOTTO: *Esse quam videri*
(To be rather than to seem)

TREE: Pine

FLOWER: Flowering dogwood

BIRD: Cardinal

NICKNAME: Tar Heel State

FAMOUS NORTH CAROLINIAN: Dale Earnhardt Jr., race-car driver

GUESS WHAT? The first miniature golf course in the United States was in North Carolina.

NORTH DAKOTA

CAPITAL: Bismarck

LARGEST CITY: Fargo

POSTAL CODE: ND

LAND AREA:
68,994 square miles
(178,694 sq km)

POPULATION (2013):
723,393

ENTERED UNION (RANK):
November 2, 1889 (39)

MOTTO: Liberty and union, now and forever, one and inseparable

TREE: American elm

FLOWER: Wild prairie rose

BIRD: Western meadowlark

NICKNAMES: Sioux State, Flickertail State, Peace Garden State, Rough Rider State

FAMOUS NORTH DAKOTAN: Kellan Lutz, actor

GUESS WHAT? The world's largest intact triceratops skull can be viewed at the Dakota Dinosaur Museum in Dickinson, North Dakota. The skull weighs about 1,500 pounds (680 kg).

OHIO

CAPITAL: Columbus

LARGEST CITY: Columbus

POSTAL CODE: OH

LAND AREA:
40,953 square miles
(106,068 sq km)

POPULATION (2013):
11,570,808

ENTERED UNION (RANK):
March 1, 1803 (17)

MOTTO: With God, all things are possible.

TREE: Buckeye

FLOWER: Scarlet carnation

BIRD: Cardinal

NICKNAME: Buckeye State

FAMOUS OHIOAN: LeBron James, basketball player

Columbus

GUESS WHAT? The Rock and Roll Hall of Fame is located in Cleveland, Ohio. The artists and bands added to the hall of fame in 2014 include: Peter Gabriel, Daryl Hall and John Oates, Nirvana, Cat Stevens, and Kiss.

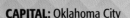

OKLAHOMA

CAPITAL: Oklahoma City

LARGEST CITY:
Oklahoma City

POSTAL CODE: OK

LAND AREA:
68,679 square miles
(177,879 sq km)

POPULATION (2013):
3,850,568

ENTERED UNION (RANK):
November 16, 1907 (46)

MOTTO: *Labor omnia vincit.* (Labor conquers all things.)

TREE: Eastern redbud

FLOWER: Mistletoe

BIRD: Scissor-tailed flycatcher

NICKNAME: Sooner State

FAMOUS OKLAHOMAN: Carrie Underwood, singer

Oklahoma City

GUESS WHAT? The state reptile of Oklahoma is the collared lizard, or mountain boomer. These colorful lizards are incredible sprinters. They can move as fast as 16 miles (26 km) per hour for short distances.

OREGON

CAPITAL: Salem

LARGEST CITY: Portland

POSTAL CODE: OR

LAND AREA:
96,003 square miles
(248,648 sq km)

POPULATION (2013):
3,930,065

ENTERED UNION (RANK):
February 14, 1859 (33)

MOTTO: *Alis volat propriis.*
(She flies with her own wings.)

TREE: Douglas fir

FLOWER: Oregon grape

BIRD: Western meadowlark

NICKNAME: Beaver State

FAMOUS OREGONIAN:
Ahmad Rashad, football player and sports commentator

GUESS WHAT? Every year, the town of Cannon Beach, Oregon, holds an enormous sand castle contest. Contestants are given about 12 hours—from one high tide to the next—to build sculptures of anything they want: traditional castles, cars, animals . . . you name it!

PENNSYLVANIA

CAPITAL: Harrisburg

LARGEST CITY: Philadelphia

POSTAL CODE: PA

LAND AREA:
44,820 square miles
(116,084 sq km)

POPULATION (2013):
12,773,801

ENTERED UNION (RANK):
December 12, 1787 (2)

MOTTO: Virtue, liberty, and independence

TREE: Hemlock

FLOWER: Mountain laurel

BIRD: Ruffed grouse

NICKNAME: Keystone State

FAMOUS PENNSYLVANIAN:
Betsy Ross, seamstress who sewed the first American flag

GUESS WHAT? Lakemont Park, in Altoona, Pennsylvania, is home to the world's oldest operating wooden roller coaster. The coaster, named "Leap-the-Dips," was built in 1902.

RHODE ISLAND

CAPITAL: Providence

LARGEST CITY: Providence

POSTAL CODE: RI

LAND AREA:
1,045 square miles
(2,707 sq km)

POPULATION (2013):
1,051,511

ENTERED UNION (RANK):
May 29, 1790 (13)

MOTTO: Hope

TREE: Red maple

FLOWER: Violet

BIRD: Rhode Island red (chicken)

NICKNAME: Ocean State

FAMOUS RHODE ISLANDER: Billy Gilman, country singer

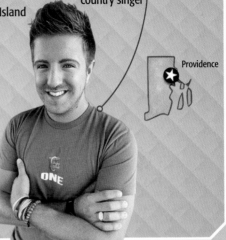

Providence

GUESS WHAT? When the first census in Rhode Island was taken, in 1708, only 7,181 people lived there. By 1771, there were 40,414 people in the state.

SOUTH CAROLINA

CAPITAL: Columbia

LARGEST CITY: Columbia

POSTAL CODE: SC

LAND AREA:
30,111 square miles
(77,987 sq km)

POPULATION (2013):
4,774,839

ENTERED UNION (RANK):
May 23, 1788 (8)

MOTTOES: *Animis opibusque parati* (Prepared in mind and resources); *Dum spiro spero.* (While I breathe, I hope.)

TREE: Palmetto

FLOWER: Yellow jessamine

BIRD: Carolina wren

NICKNAME: Palmetto State

FAMOUS SOUTH CAROLINIAN: Aziz Ansari, actor and comedian

Columbia

GUESS WHAT? During the Revolutionary War, American troops used logs from palmetto trees to bolster Fort Sullivan (now called Fort Moultrie), on Sullivan Island, South Carolina. The fort remained standing after a 16-hour battle with British forces. Now, the palmetto tree represents the colonists' victory over the English and appears on the state flag and the state seal.

SOUTH DAKOTA

CAPITAL: Pierre

LARGEST CITY: Sioux Falls

POSTAL CODE: SD

LAND AREA:
75,898 square miles
(196,575 sq km)

POPULATION (2013):
844,877

ENTERED UNION (RANK):
November 2, 1889 (40)

MOTTO: Under God the people rule.

TREE: Black Hills spruce

FLOWER: Pasqueflower

BIRD: Ring-necked pheasant

NICKNAMES: Mount Rushmore State, Coyote State

FAMOUS SOUTH DAKOTAN: Sitting Bull, Sioux chief

GUESS WHAT? **Badlands National Park, in southwestern** South Dakota, was once home to ancient horses, rhinoceroses, and saber-toothed cats. Scientists there have unearthed the remains of ancient camels that were about the size of dogs.

TENNESSEE

CAPITAL: Nashville

LARGEST CITY: Memphis

POSTAL CODE: TN

LAND AREA:
41,220 square miles
(106,760 sq km)

POPULATION (2013):
6,495,978

ENTERED UNION (RANK):
June 1, 1796 (16)

MOTTO: Agriculture and commerce

TREE: Tulip poplar

FLOWER: Iris

BIRD: Mockingbird

NICKNAME: Volunteer State

FAMOUS TENNESSEAN: Dolly Parton, musician and actress

GUESS WHAT? **The Tennessee cave salamander was picked to be the state** amphibian in 1995. These creatures have three red gills on the outside of the body. Gills are the organs that make it possible for fish and some amphibians to pull oxygen from water. Gills allow these creatures to breathe air underwater.

TEXAS

CAPITAL: Austin

LARGEST CITY: Houston

POSTAL CODE: TX

LAND AREA:
261,914 square miles
(678,357 sq km)

POPULATION (2013):
26,448,193

ENTERED UNION (RANK):
December 29, 1845 (28)

MOTTO: Friendship

TREE: Pecan

FLOWER: Texas
bluebonnet

BIRD:
Mockingbird

NICKNAME: Lone Star State

FAMOUS TEXAN:
Selena Gomez, actress
and pop singer

Austin ⭐   Houston

GUESS WHAT? Bracken Cave, near San Antonio, Texas, is home to the largest bat colony in the world. Every summer, more than 20 million Mexican free-tailed bats live there.

UTAH

CAPITAL: Salt Lake City

LARGEST CITY:
Salt Lake City

POSTAL CODE: UT

LAND AREA:
82,168 square miles
(212,815 sq km)

POPULATION (2013):
2,900,872

ENTERED UNION (RANK):
January 4, 1896 (45)

MOTTO: Industry

TREE: Blue spruce

FLOWER: Sego lily

BIRD: California gull

NICKNAME: Beehive State

FAMOUS UTAHN: Philo
Farnsworth, inventor of
the television

Salt Lake City ⭐

GUESS WHAT? The Sundance Film Festival—one of the most respected film festivals in the world—is held in Park City, Utah, every winter. Each year, 200 films are chosen from more than 9,000 submissions, and more than 50,000 people make their way to the snowy city to participate in the festivities.

VERMONT

CAPITAL: Montpelier

LARGEST CITY: Burlington

POSTAL CODE: VT

LAND AREA:
9,249 square miles
(23,956 sq km)

POPULATION (2013):
626,630

ENTERED UNION (RANK):
March 4, 1791 (14)

MOTTO: Freedom and unity

TREE: Sugar maple

FLOWER: Red clover

BIRD: Hermit thrush

NICKNAME: Green Mountain State

FAMOUS VERMONTER:
John Deere, founder of the tractor company John Deere & Company

Burlington

Montpelier

GUESS WHAT? Vermont is the only state in New England that does not border the Atlantic Ocean.

VIRGINIA

CAPITAL: Richmond

LARGEST CITY:
Virginia Beach

POSTAL CODE: VA

LAND AREA:
39,598 square miles
(102,559 sq km)

POPULATION (2013):
8,260,405

ENTERED UNION (RANK):
June 25, 1788 (10)

MOTTO: *Sic semper tyrannis*
(Thus always to tyrants)

TREE: Flowering dogwood

FLOWER: American dogwood

BIRD: Cardinal

NICKNAMES: The Old Dominion, Mother of Presidents

FAMOUS VIRGINIAN:
Gabby Douglas, gymnast

Richmond

Virginia Beach

GUESS WHAT? Virginia has had three capital cities: Jamestown, Williamsburg, and Richmond.

WASHINGTON

CAPITAL: Olympia

LARGEST CITY: Seattle

POSTAL CODE: WA

LAND AREA:
66,582 square miles
(172,447 sq km)

POPULATION (2013):
6,971,406

ENTERED UNION (RANK):
November 11, 1889 (42)

MOTTO: *Al-ki* (an Indian word meaning "by and by" or "hope for the future")

TREE: Western hemlock

FLOWER: Coast rhododendron

BIRD: Willow goldfinch

NICKNAME: Evergreen State

FAMOUS WASHINGTONIAN:
Bill Gates, co-founder of Microsoft

Seattle

Olympia

GUESS WHAT? Washington grows more apples than any other state in the union.

WEST VIRGINIA

CAPITAL: Charleston

LARGEST CITY: Charleston

POSTAL CODE: WV

LAND AREA:
24,087 square miles
(62,385 sq km)

POPULATION (2013):
1,854,304

ENTERED UNION (RANK):
June 20, 1863 (35)

MOTTO: *Montani semper liberi.* (Mountaineers are always free.)

TREE: Sugar maple

FLOWER: Rhododendron

BIRD: Cardinal

NICKNAME: Mountain State

FAMOUS WEST VIRGINIAN:
Brad Paisley, country musician

Charleston

GUESS WHAT? In 1984, Mary Lou Retton, from Fairmont, West Virginia, became the first U.S. woman to win a gold medal in gymnastics at the Olympics.

WISCONSIN

CAPITAL: Madison

LARGEST CITY: Milwaukee

POSTAL CODE: WI

LAND AREA:
54,314 square miles
(140,673 sq km)

POPULATION (2013):
5,742,713

ENTERED UNION (RANK):
May 29, 1848 (30)

MOTTO: Forward

TREE: Sugar maple

FLOWER: Wood violet

BIRD: American robin

NICKNAMES: Badger State, Dairy State

FAMOUS WISCONSINITE:
Georgia O'Keeffe, artist

GUESS WHAT? The state dance of Wisconsin is the polka, which reflects the strong Czech, Polish, and German heritage found in the state.

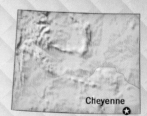

Milwaukee

Madison

WYOMING

CAPITAL: Cheyenne

LARGEST CITY: Cheyenne

POSTAL CODE: WY

LAND AREA:
97,105 square miles
(251,502 sq km)

POPULATION (2013):
582,658

ENTERED UNION (RANK):
July 10, 1890 (44)

MOTTO: Equal rights

TREE: Plains cottonwood

FLOWER: Indian paintbrush

BIRD: Meadowlark

NICKNAMES: Big Wyoming, Equality State, Cowboy State

FAMOUS WYOMINGITE:
Travis Rice, snowboarder

Cheyenne

GUESS WHAT? Wyoming is known as the Equality State because it was the first state in the union to extend the right to vote to women.

WASHINGTON, D.C.
THE NATION'S CAPITAL

The District of Columbia, which covers the same area as the city of Washington, is the capital of the United States. The seat of the U.S. government was transferred from Philadelphia, Pennsylvania, to Washington, D.C., on December 1, 1800.

LAND AREA: 68.25 square miles (177 sq km)

POPULATION (2013): 646,449

MOTTO: *Justitia omnibus* (Justice for all)

TREE: Scarlet oak

FLOWER: American beauty rose

BIRD: Wood thrush

FAMOUS WASHINGTONIAN:
John Philip Sousa, composer

The Lincoln Memorial, in Washington, D.C., pays tribute to the 16th president of the United States. Lincoln was president during the Civil War.

UNITED STATES

U.S. TERRITORIES

In addition to the 50 states and the District of Columbia, the United States government administers some tiny, mostly uninhabited islands around the world, including Kingman Reef, Palmyra Atoll, and Howland Island. The major U.S. territories are Puerto Rico, American Samoa, Guam, the U.S. Virgin Islands, and the Northern Mariana Islands.

PUERTO RICO is in the Caribbean Sea, about 1,000 miles (1,609 km) southeast of Miami, Florida. A U.S. possession since 1898, it consists of the island of Puerto Rico plus the adjacent islets of Vieques, Culebra, and Mona. Its capital is San Juan. Puerto Rico has an estimated population of 3,615,086.

AMERICAN SAMOA, a group of islands in the South Pacific Ocean, is situated about halfway between Hawaii and New Zealand. It has a land area of 76 square miles (199 sq km) and a population of 54,719.

GUAM, in the North Pacific Ocean, was given to the United States by Spain in 1898. It has a land area of 209 square miles (541 sq km) and a population of approximately 160,378.

U.S. VIRGIN ISLANDS, which include Saint Croix, Saint Thomas, Saint John, and many other islands, are located in the Caribbean Sea, east of Puerto Rico. Together, they have a land area of 136 square miles (351 sq km) and a population of 104,737.

THE NORTHERN MARIANA ISLANDS, located in the North Pacific Ocean, have been administered by the United States since the end of World War II. They have a land area of 179 square miles (464 sq km) and a population of 51,170.

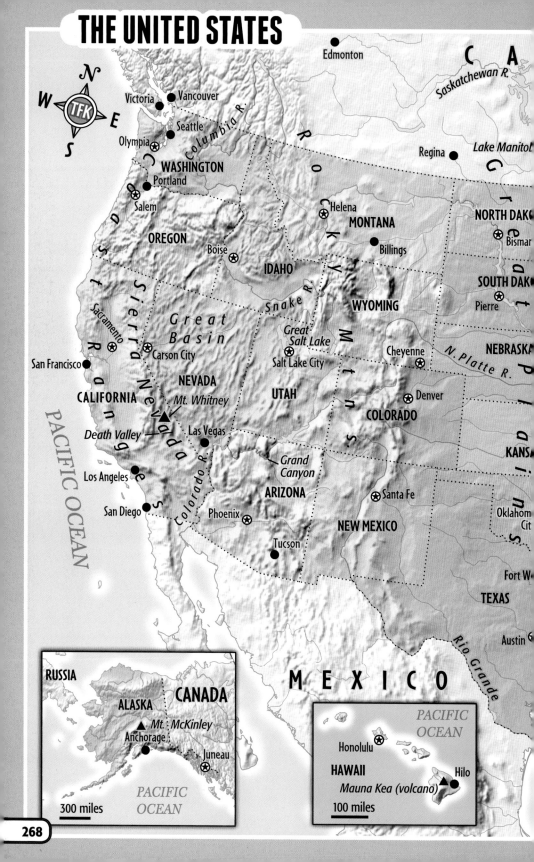

THE UNITED STATES

N
W — TFK — E
S

Edmonton

C A
Saskatchewan R.

Victoria Vancouver

Seattle

Olympia
WASHINGTON
Portland

Columbia R.

Regina Lake Manito[

Salem

OREGON

Helena
MONTANA

Billings

NORTH DAK

Bismar

Boise

IDAHO

Sierra

Snake R.

WYOMING

SOUTH DAK

Pierre

Great
Basin

Great
Salt Lake

Cheyenne

N. Platte R.

NEBRASKA

Sacramento

Carson City

Salt Lake City

Nevada

San Francisco

NEVADA

UTAH

Denver

CALIFORNIA

Mt. Whitney

COLORADO

Death Valley

Las Vegas

KANS

Grand
Canyon

Colorado R.

Range

Los Angeles

ARIZONA

Santa Fe

San Diego

Phoenix

NEW MEXICO

Oklahom
Cit

PACIFIC OCEAN

Tucson

Fort W

Rocky

Mtns

Great

Plains

TEXAS

Rio Grande

Austin

RUSSIA

CANADA

ALASKA Mt. McKinley

Anchorage

Juneau

PACIFIC
OCEAN

300 miles

PACIFIC
OCEAN

Honolulu

HAWAII Hilo

Mauna Kea (volcano)

100 miles

A D A

nipeg

James Bay

Lake of the Woods

Lake Nipigon

NESOTA

Lake Superior

MICHIGAN

Lake Huron

Lake Michigan

St. Paul
eapolis

WISCONSIN

Milwaukee

Madison

Detroit

Lansing

Toronto

Lake Ontario

Lake Erie

St. Lawrence R.

Montreal

Ottawa ✪

Montpelier

VERMONT

MAINE

Augusta ✪

Concord

NEW HAMPSHIRE

Albany ✪

Boston ✪

MASSACHUSETTS

NEW YORK

Niagara Falls

Hartford ✪

Providence

RHODE ISLAND

CONNECTICUT

IOWA

Des Moines

Chicago

ILLINOIS

INDIANA

Indianapolis ✪

Columbus ✪

OHIO

PENNSYLVANIA

Harrisburg ✪

Trenton

Philadelphia

New York City

NEW JERSEY

Dover ✪

DELAWARE

Springfield ✪

St. Louis

Ohio R.

WEST VIRGINIA

Charleston ✪

Annapolis

Washington, D.C.

MARYLAND

Kansas City

Jefferson City ✪

MISSOURI

Frankfort ✪

KENTUCKY

Richmond ✪

VIRGINIA

ARKANSAS

Little Rock ✪

Mississippi R.

Memphis

Nashville ✪

TENNESSEE

Raleigh ✪

NORTH CAROLINA

Cape Hatteras

Appalachian Mtns.

Columbia ✪

SOUTH CAROLINA

MISSISSIPPI

Jackson ✪

ALABAMA

Atlanta ✪

GEORGIA

Charleston

Savannah

LOUISIANA

Montgomery ✪

Mobile

on Baton Rouge ✪

New Orleans

Tallahassee ✪

FLORIDA

ATLANTIC OCEAN

Gulf of Mexico

BAHAMAS

Miami

Key West

0 | 500 miles

0 | 750 kilometers

Havana ✪

CUBA

269

WHAT'S NEXT?

In the future, doctors will be able to print out new organs. **Page 273**

SPECIAL DELIVERY!

One day soon, we may not rely as much on pilots and truck drivers to move goods around the country. Amazon would like to use drones, which are small pilotless aircraft, to deliver its packages all around the country. The head of the company announced, in late 2013, that it had already begun testing a drone-delivery program.

The minute a customer clicks the send button on an order, the delivery process would be set in motion. The package would be put into a yellow bucket and loaded onto a small aircraft called an octocopter. The octocopter would then fly it to the customer's home or place of business. As long as the item is in stock, the customer would have his or her package within half an hour.

As of early 2014, the federal government prohibits the use of drones in this way. But as engineers at Amazon perfect the aircraft and the delivery system, other people will be working with the Federal Aviation Administration to come up with new rules for unmanned aircraft.

NO **CHARGER** NECESSARY

People today have lots of gadgets: cell phones, tablets, music players, video game players, laptops, and more. All of these devices need to be charged in order to function. So, some companies have begun researching ways to make it easier for people on the go to charge all of their electronics. One company is hard at work creating a solid material that will have wireless charging technology hidden inside. In the future, you may be able to charge your phone just by placing it on what looks like an ordinary kitchen counter or tabletop. This material could be used to make lamps, bookshelves, or even building exteriors.

MESSAGES FROM MARS

Humans have been trying to visit Mars since the 1960s. While no manned spacecraft or astronaut has landed on the Red Planet, scientists have learned quite a bit about its past. Its average current temperature is −81°F (−63°C), but it used to be a warm place. Until about 3.7 billion years ago, there were rivers and oceans on the planet. Scientists don't yet know why the atmosphere changed. In hopes of answering some questions about Mars, NASA launched a spacecraft in November 2013.

Called MAVEN, this craft has a wingspan of 37.5 feet (11.4 m). It weighs 1,991 pounds (903 kg). After a 10-month journey, MAVEN will reach Mars's upper atmosphere and begin collecting information to help us understand why there is so little air on Mars. Curiosity, the rover that is currently exploring the surface of Mars, has been sending data back to Earth since 2012. Space fans hope information from MAVEN and Curiosity will soon be able to shed some light on the secrets of the planet's past.

GUESS WHAT? While orbiting Mars, MAVEN will fly as fast as 3,278 miles (5,275 km) per hour and as slow as 93 miles (150 km) per hour.

BIONIC BODIES

Doctors and scientists have been working hard to develop new devices to help people who have lost limbs or who have organs that are failing. Here are a few of the advances that you'll hear about in the years to come. Some of them already exist, but as scientists perfect the devices, more and more people will benefit from them.

KIDNEYS ON THE WAY

Your kidneys are a pair of bean-shaped organs. They do very important work in the body. As blood passes through them, the kidneys filter out extra water and waste products to get rid of the stuff your body does not need. When a person's kidneys stop working well, he or she may need to use a special machine that cleans the blood. This is called kidney dialysis. It is expensive and time-consuming. But a group of researchers have come up with a device that can be implanted into the body to do the work of the kidneys. Clinical trials of this new artificial kidney are supposed to begin in 2017.

GUESS WHAT? Kidneys are always working. Every 30 minutes, a person's kidneys filter all of the blood in his or her body.

Approximately 430,000 people in the United States are on kidney dialysis.

FAKE BLOOD

Blood transfusions (the transfer of blood from one person to another) have saved countless lives. But what happens when there is a shortage of donated blood? Or an injured person is not near a hospital? The search for a practical blood substitute to carry oxygen throughout the body has had ups and downs over the years. But some researchers have recently been working on some promising blood substitutes. Maybe one day soon, hospitals will be able to stock up on artificial blood rather than relying on donations. Military medics, emergency workers, and doctors in remote places could carry artificial blood and save more lives. Some scientists believe that once a substitute oxygen-carrying substance has been found, it may also be used to carry medicine throughout the body.

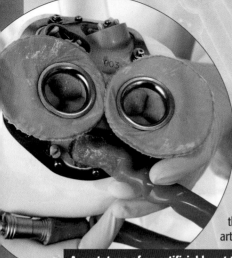

ARTIFICIAL HEARTS

Biomedicial engineers have developed devices that can help people whose hearts are failing. Today's artificial hearts are temporary but can be used while a patient waits for a heart transplant. Now scientists are testing out devices that could be used for much longer amounts of time, even permanently. Instead of pumping like an actual heart, one new machine would push blood through the body in a steady flow. A person with that type of artificial heart would have no heartbeat!

A prototype of an artificial heart that could be permanently implanted

ELECTRONIC EYES

Scientists have discovered a way to insert tiny microchips into people's eyes. These itty-bitty devices can detect light and then pass information along to the nerves that transmit information to a person's brain. This will allow a person to see more clearly.

NEED A NEW KIDNEY?
JUST PRINT IT

Scientists, engineers, and entrepreneurs are coming up with lots of incredible ways to use 3D printers. But some of the most mind-boggling and exciting news about 3D printing is coming out of the biomedical field. Bioprinters, or printers that have been modified to use biological materials, can now be used to print out certain kinds of cells that can grow into organs or tissues to help patients. Bioengineers are already testing out ears, heart valves, skin, and even bones and joints made by bioprinters. Printed bones, livers, and kidneys may not be usable yet, but there is no doubt that bioprinting is changing what will be possible in the hospital operating rooms of the future.

GUESS WHAT? Many researchers working on printable organs are actually using modified versions of regular desktop printers—like the ones you use at home or at school. Instead of using ink, these machines have been tweaked so they can use cells or human tissue.

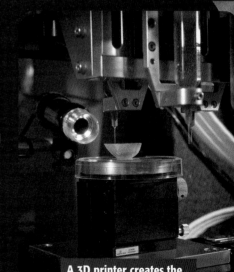

A 3D printer creates the structure of a kidney.

THE **PASSWORD**
BECOMES A THING OF THE PAST?

When you choose an online password, it is important to use a combination of letters, numbers, and symbols (when possible). That makes it difficult for someone else to access your information. But some of the most popular passwords today are: *password, qwerty, 123456, 12345678,* and *abc123.* There are computer scientists, researchers, and engineers who work hard to come up with ways to keep people's private information safe. And one way to do that is to get rid of the password entirely.

Some computers and mobile devices already have fingerprint scanners in them. Some high-security facilities rely on eye scans to identify people. That's because the colored part of the eye, called the iris, has a pattern unique to each person. The use of characteristics of the human body to identify individuals is called biometrics.

Soon, your e-mail may open only when a program recognizes your voice or scans your written signature. And websites may require you to plug in or scan an object, as well as match the fingerprint or iris image on file. One Spanish company is developing a system that can identify and verify people based on how they smell. Each person can have his or her own, personal stinky password!

COMING SOON
TO A THEATER NEAR YOU!

Fans of the Hunger Games series have a lot to look forward to, but the final two installments of that series aren't the only films coming out soon. Stay tuned for these movies!

Alexander and the Terrible, Horrible, No Good, Very Bad Day
Alice in Wonderland 2
The Amazing Spider-Man 3
Angry Birds
Annie
Avengers: Age of Ultron
B.O.O.: Bureau of Otherworldly Operations
The Boxtrolls
The Croods 2
Despicable Me 3
Finding Dory
The Giver
The Good Dinosaur
Guardians of the Galaxy
Hotel Transylvania 2
How to Train Your Dragon 3
The Hunger Games: Mockingjay, Part 1
The Hunger Games: Mockingjay, Part 2
Ice Age 5
Kung Fu Panda 3
Night at the Museum 3
Paddington

Jennifer Lawrence, star of the Hunger Games series

WHAT'S NEXT?

SPORTS FORECAST

Soccer fans, get ready! The next FIFA World Cup will kick off in Russia in the summer of 2018.

In 2016, the Summer Olympics will be held in Rio de Janeiro, Brazil. Two years later, Pyeongchang, South Korea, will host the Winter Games. And, in 2020, the Summer Olympics will be in Tokyo, Japan.

ANSWERS

Page 29:

ODD OCTOPUS

The underside of one arm has no suckers.

Page 35:

CRITTERS ACROSS . . . AND DOWN

Page 36:

MYSTERY PERSON: Maurice Sendak

Page 41:

MASTERPIECE MATCHUP

1. Fresco, 2. Collage, 3. Portrait,
4. Watercolor, 5. Still life, 6. Relief

Page 53:

MYSTERY PERSON: Washington Irving

Page 63:

PICK THE RIGHT PUMPKIN

Page 65:

MYSTERY PERSON: Charles Dickens

Page 111:

JUMBLED GEOGRAPHY

1. India, 2. China, 3. Egypt, 4. Germany,
5. Greece, 6. France, 7. Madagascar,
8. Canada, 9. Chile, 10.Russia, 11. Italy

Page 121:

HIDDEN HABITATS

F	K	E	O	R	H	F	C	E	T	M	G
R	A	B	B	I	T	O	T	C	A	O	V
O	Y	W	T	M	J	S	A	A	T	N	I
G	Z	O	D	E	E	B	N	C	E	K	B
D	E	S	E	R	T	U	R	T	L	E	E
A	B	E	O	K	U	E	A	U	R	Y	Z
R	R	F	H	V	N	G	F	S	V	M	E
E	A	A	L	O	D	A	O	C	E	A	N
C	T	E	I	M	R	Q	X	B	H	K	O
A	N	G	R	A	S	S	L	A	N	D	

Page 141:

MYSTERY PERSON: Thurgood Marshall

Page 149:

MYSTERY PERSON: Queen Isabella I of Spain

Page 152:
MYSTERY PERSON: General Douglas MacArthur

Page 161:
RIDDLE ME THIS
1. Phone, 2. Refrigerator, 3. Bicycle, 4. Zipper

MYSTERY PERSON: Dr. Patricia Bath

Page 173:
MUDDLED MAPS
1. Indian Ocean, 2. South America, 3. Longitude, 4. North Pole, 5. Pacific Ocean, 6. Equator, 7. Europe, 8. Latitude, 9. Australia
Riddle Answer: Ice Caps

Page 181:
MYSTERY PERSON: Mandy Moore

Page 189:
PATHWAYS TO POWER
1. James Monroe, 2. William Howard Taft, 3. John Adams

Page 209:
MYSTERY PERSON: Alfred Nobel

Page 221:
MYSTERY PERSON: Jackie Robinson

Page 235:
SNOWBOARDER SWITCH-UP

The strings on one snowboarder's sweatshirt are extra long.

Page 237:
COURT CUTOUTS
1. F, 2. A, 3. B, 4. E, 5. D, 6. G, 7. C

Page 241:
ALL-AMERICAN GIRL

(Obama). 189: Library of Congress, Prints and Photographs Division (Adams, Taft, and Monroe); Andrea Izzotti/Shutterstock.com (Capitol building); Orhan Cam/Shutterstock.com (Supreme Court building); Mesut Dogan/Shutterstock.com (White House). 190: Official White House Photo by Pete Souza (Obama); Lorelyn Medina/Shutterstock.com (girl at podium). 191: Library of Congress, Prints and Photographs Division (White House floor plans); Official White House Photo by Chuck Kennedy (Obama). 192–195: Library of Congress, Prints and Photographs Division (all). 196: U.S. Navy photo courtesy Eisenhower Presidential Library & Museum (Eisenhower). 197: Official White House Photo by Pete Souza (Obama); Library of Congress, Prints and Photographs Division (Grant, Kennedy, and Roosevelt); U.S. Navy photo by Mass Communication Specialist 1st Class Chad J. McNeeley (Clinton); Official White House Photo by Pete Souza (Obama); spirit of america/Shutterstock.com (presidential seal).

SCIENCE: 198: Courtesy of Oregon State University (oceanographer); My Nguyen/Shutterstock.com (Mayan city); Courtesy of the Oak Ridge National Laboratory, U.S. Dept. of Energy (geneticist); Courtesy of Kenneth Dewey of UNL (herpetologist). 199: USGS (seismologist). 200: YasnaTen/Shutterstock.com (clipboard); bikeriderlondon/Shutterstock.com (kids). 201: Jewel Samad/AFP/Getty Images (Obama). 202–203: My Nguyen/Shutterstock.com (Mayan city). 202: Mark A. Philbrick/BYU, Courtesy of Richard Terry (Terry). 203: tandemich/Shutterstock.com (Mayan calendar). 204–205: artjazz/Shutterstock.com (ice in water). 204: ©iStockPhoto/AVAVA (woman cleaning); jeehyun/Shuttertock.com (peanuts). 205: mylisa/Shutterstock.com (orange juice). 206: Nicolle Rager-Fuller/National Science Foundation (asteroid in Chesapeake Bay). 207: mrfiza/Shutterstock.com (mosquito); ©President and Fellows of Harvard College, Peabody Museum of Archaeology and Ethnology, PM# 33-44-10/3040 (digital file# 99030084) (ancient bowl). 208: Courtesy of Yoji Okata (puffer fish close-up and crop circle); Dr. Jean Kenyon, NOAA/NMFS/PISC/CRED (marine biologists). 209: Wes C. Skiles/National Geographic Creative (*Speleonectes tulumensis*); Alexandra Lande/Shutterstock.com (crab); Photos.com (Nobel).

SPACE: 210–211: Vladimir Arndt/Shutterstock.com (background). 210–211: NASA (all). 212: NASA/JPL-Caltech/SSI (background, hurricane); NASA/JPL-Caltech/SSI/Hampton University (north pole). 213: NASA/JPL-Caltech/MSSS (Curiosity). 214: A-R-T/Shutterstock.com (background); fluidworkshop/Shutterstock.com (Jupiter, Saturn, Uranus, Neptune, and Earth). 215: AP Photo/Chelyabinsk.ru, Yekaterina Pustynnikova (meteor across sky); AP Photo/AP Video (dashboard camera image); *The Asahi Shimbun* via Getty Images (Lake Chebarkul); Sovfoto/UIG via Getty Images (forest). 216–217: NASA (all).

SPORTS: 218: Harry How/Getty Images (Lasek); John Biever/Sports Illustrated (Super Bowl). Robert Beck/Sports Illustrated (BCS championship); Bill Frakes/Sports Illustrated (Winston). 220–221: Al Tielemans/Sports Illustrated (World Series). 220: David E. Klutho/Sports Illustrated (Davis); Rick Yeatts/Getty Images (Darvish). 221: Robert Beck/Sports Illustrated (Little League); Neil Leifer/Sports Illustrated/Getty Images (Robinson). 222: John W. McDonough/Sports Illustrated (all). 223: AP Photo/Todd Kirkland (McCoughtry); David E. Klutho/Sports Illustrated (Men's NCAA Division 1 Championships); Cal Sport Media via AP Photo (Women's NCAA Division 1 Championships). 224–225: David E. Klutho/Sports Illustrated (Stanley Cup). 225: Yuri Kuzmin/AFP/Getty Images (Junior Hockey Championship). 226: Laurence Griffiths/Getty Images (Confederations Cup); Ed Zurga/Getty Images (Collin); Brett Carlsen/Getty Images (National Women's Soccer League). 227: Erick W. Rasco/Sports Illustrated (all). 228: Chris Graythen/Getty Images (Indianapolis 500). 229: AP Photo/Autostock, Nigel Kinrade (Johnson car). 230: AP Photo/Frank Franklin II (Park); Bryn Lennon/Getty Images (Tour de France). 231: AP Photo/*The Anchorage Press, The Alaska Dispatch* (Iditarod); Bill Frakes/Sports Illustrated (horse racing). 232: AP Photo/Elise Amendola (Mikulak); AP Photo/Elise Amendola (Ross). 233: John Thys/AFP/Getty Images (Mustafina). 234: Harry How/Getty Images (Lasek); Harry How/Getty Images (Kerley). 235: RJ Sangosti/*The Denver Post* via Getty Images (Clark); Johnny-ka/Shutterstock.com (snowboarders). 236: Dave Sandford/Getty

Images (Chan); AP Photo/Elise Amendola (White and Davis). 237: Damien Poullenot/ASP via Getty Images (Carissa Moore); John W. McDonough/Sports Illustrated (basketball game).

UNITED STATES: 238: Stephen Alvarez/National Geographic/Getty Images (Tennessee cave salamander); Courtesy Seattle Snow Day (snowball fight). 239: Galyna Andrushko/Shutterstock.com (Mount McKinley); holbox/Shutterstock.com (Death Valley); iofoto/Shutterstock.com (Verrazano-Narrows Bridge); JR Trice/Shutterstock.com (Crater Lake). 240: Kate Pru/Shutterstock.com (map); Vietrov Dmytro/Shutterstock.com (baby). 241: Art Phaneuf-LostArts/Shutterstock.com (girl); Luba V Nel/Shutterstock.com (ring in game); BGSmith/Shutterstock.com (prairie dogs in game); javi merino/Shutterstock.com (hot dog); PILart/Shutterstock.com (mustard and ketchup splatter). 242: Library of Congress, Prints and Photographs Division (Keller); Le Do/Shutterstock.com (forget-me-not). 243: Olga K/Shutterstock.com (bolo tie); Courtesy of Stuttgart Chamber of Commerce (World Championship Duck Calling Contest). 244: s_bukley/Shutterstock.com (Perry); ©iStock/creighton359 (lark bunting). 245: Rashid Valitov/Shutterstock.com (praying mantis); Wasu Watcharadachaphong/Shutterstock.com (horseshoe crab). 246: s_bukley/Shutterstock.com (Thorne); SeanPavonePhoto/Shutterstock.com (Cherokee rose). 247: Brian A. Witkin/Shutterstock.com (Hamilton); Charles Knowles/Shutterstock.com (Balanced Rock). 248: Official White House Photo by Chuck Kennedy (Michelle Obama); vig64/Shutterstock.com (peony). 249: Peter Read Miller/Sports Illustrated (Johnson); Aija Lehtonen/Shutterstock.com (Monáe). 250: Anita Patterson Peppers/Shutterstock.com (Appalachian mountain dulcimer); Kenneth Rush/Shutterstock.com (eastern brown pelican). 251: Library of Congress, Prints and Photographs Division (Longfellow); txking/Shutterstock.com (jousting). 252: Library of Congress, Prints and Photographs Division (Samson); Jstone/Shutterstock.com (Lautner). 253: Photo by Eric Enstrom (*Grace*); MaxyM/Shutterstock.com (magnolia). 254: Missouri Office of Secretary of State, Publications Division (mozarkite); John W. McDonough/Sports Illustrated (Jackson). 255: Chad Bontrager/Shutterstock.com (Carhenge); Joe Seer/Shutterstock.com (Hicks). 256: Nancy Bauer/Shutterstock.com (purple finch); s_bukley/Shutterstock.com (Tisdale). 257: Erni/Shutterstock.com (roadrunner); Steve Byland/Shutterstock.com (bluebird). 258: Le Do/Shutterstock.com (flowering dogwood); David Herraez Calzada/Shutterstock.com (triceratops skull). 259: John W. McDonough/Sports Illustrated (James); Joe Farah/Shutterstock.com (collared lizard). 260: George Vetter/Cannon-Beach Net (sand castle contest); Photo by Bhakta Dano ("Leap-the-Dips"). 261: AP Photo/Ed Rode (Gilman); ©lumachina_99-Fotolia.com (Fort Sullivan). 262: Library of Congress, Prints and Photographs Division (Sitting Bull); Stephen Alvarez/National Geographic/Getty Images (Tennessee cave salamander). 263: ©Minden Pictures/SuperStock (Bracken Cave); fredlyfish4/123RF.com (sego lily). 264: Double Brow Imagery/Shutterstock.com (hermit thrush); Al Tielemans/Sports Illustrated (Douglas). 265: @erics/Shutterstock.com (apples); Randy Miramontez/Shutterstock.com (Paisley). 266: Library of Congress, Prints and Photographs Division (O'Keeffe); Tom Reichner/Shutterstock.com (Indian paintbrush). 267: Adam Parent (Lincoln Memorial); SeanPavonePhoto (Puerto Rico). 268–269: Map by Joe Lemonnier and Joe Lertola (map).

WHAT'S NEXT: 270: Wake Forest Institute for Regenerative Medicine (printing organ); AP Photo/Amazon (Amazon Prime Air); baitong333/Shutterstock.com (box left); bannosuke/Shutterstock.com (box right); bloomua/Shutterstock.com (tablet on table). 271: NASA/Goddard (Mars MAVEN). 272–273: Shutterstock.com (background). 272: Picsfive/Shutterstock.com (dialysis). 273: AP Photo/Jacques Brinon (artificial heart); Wake Forest Institute for Regenerative Medicine (3D printer). 274: Andrea Danti/Shutterstock.com (eye scan); Antonio Guillem/Shutterstock.com (phone); DWaschnig/Shutterstock.com (woman). 275: Featureflash/Shutterstock.com (Lawrence); James Steidl/Shutterstock.com (movie theater); cartoons/Shutterstock.com (soccer ball).

BACK COVER: Eric Isselee/Shutterstock.com (background); Atlas Robot image courtesy of Boston Dynamics Atlas Robot (robot); s_bukley/Shutterstock.com (Perry); SeanPavonePhoto/Shutterstock.com (Taipei 101).

INDEX